Averting Extinction

TIM W. CLARK

Averting Extinction

RECONSTRUCTING ENDANGERED SPECIES RECOVERY

Yale University Press
New Haven and London

Set in Sabon Roman type.
Printed in the United States of America.

Drawing of black-footed ferrets in Chapter 1 by Edson Fichter.

Library of Congress Cataloging-in-Publication Data

Clark, Tim W.
    Averting extinction : reconstructing endangered species recovery / Tim W. Clark.
        p. cm.
    Includes bibliographical references and index.
    ISBN 0-300-06847-6 (cloth : alk. paper)

    1. Black-footed ferret — Wyoming. 2. Wildlife conservation — Government Policy — United States. 3. Endangered species — Government policy — United States. I. Title.
    QL737.C25A94   1997
    333.95′976629 — dc21   96-37273

A catalogue record for this book is available from the British Library.

The paper in this book meets the guidelines for permanence and durability of the Committee on Production Guidelines for Book Longevity of the Council on Library Resources.

10   9   8   7   6   5   4   3   2   1

Contents

Acknowledgments

A great many people assisted or supported me in searches for ferrets in the 1970s and 1980s, during my involvement in the ferret project in Meeteetse, and in writing this book. Without the combined aid of these many people, my involvement in endangered species conservation in general and in the ferret project in particular would have been impossible. I want to thank them and also make it clear that the contents of this volume are solely my responsibility.

I have a tremendous intellectual debt to acknowledge to four people in particular. Garry Brewer, professor (and former dean) of the University of Michigan's School of Natural Resources and Environment, generously shared ideas, papers, and time with me. It was he who formally introduced me to the interdisciplinary, problem-solving concepts of the policy sciences. Garry and I have since written a paper on the role of policy sciences in endangered species recovery. Ronald Brunner, professor of political science at the University of Colorado and former director of the Center for Public Policy Research, has also been instrumental in shaping my thinking through our numerous discussions and visits, my reading of his works, and his direct and clear answers to my inquiries. Both his theoretical and his applied insights have been invaluable. We recently wrote a paper on practical approaches to ecosystem management. Ronald Westrum, professor of sociology and interdisciplinary technology at

Eastern Michigan University, supplied me with much literature on organizational design and behavior. Many discussions with him, as well as two joint papers on improving organization and management of endangered species conservation programs, have greatly enhanced my knowledge of organizational systems. Stephen Kellert of Yale University's School of Forestry and Environmental Studies, like the other three men, has been a friend and colleague for many years. Our mutual exploration of wildlife policy in the United States, teaching graduate classes at Yale with him, and coauthoring several papers on conservation policy and endangered species have been highly educational for me. I have enormous respect for these four individuals and gratitude for their help and friendship.

My professional life as a conservation biologist, university professor, and member of the nongovernmental conservation community has been sustained by the assistance of many people. In the context of the ferret project, these people include colleagues in the field and classroom. Thomas Campbell III, Louise Richardson Forrest, Steven Forrest, and Denise Casey all worked many hard years in the field at Meeteetse studying ferrets. We shared countless cold, snowy days and nights on the windswept prairies together. Their commitment to quality work, integrity, and conservation was outstanding. Lucille and John Hogg, ranchers near Meeteetse who hosted us, were open and friendly and came to be very dear friends who supported us in the field studies. To the many temporary assistants who helped in the field work, numerous other Meeteetse area residents, and my coworkers in the state and federal agencies, I sincerely acknowledge your direct assistance and hard work.

Support for my work on ferrets has come from a wide variety of sources. The Meeteetse field studies were undertaken while I was president of Biota Research and Consulting, Inc., of Jackson, Wyoming, and an adjunct faculty member in the Department of Biological Sciences at Idaho State University in Pocatello. The expenses for logistics, travel, and equipment in the Meeteetse ferret studies were covered by many generous individuals and organizations. This, combined with years' worth of volunteered time that my colleagues and I offered, resulted in an astounding level of new knowledge about ferrets. Chief among the supporters were Jon Jensen and Wildlife Preservation Trust International, Archie Carr III and the New York Zoological Society's Wildlife Conservation Society, and the World Wildlife Fund-U.S. Other supporting organizations included the National Geographic Society, the Charles A. Lindbergh Fund, the National Wildlife Federation, Defenders of Wildlife, Sigma Xi, the Casper (Wyoming) Audubon Club, the Nature Conservancy, the National Academy of Sciences, the Murie Audubon Society of Wyoming, the Humane Society of the United States, the Chicago Zoological Society, the

New-Lands Foundation, the Fanwood Foundation, the Lost Arrow Foundation, Newman's Own, Catherine Patrick, Nu Lambda Trust, and the Eppley Foundation for Research. My affiliation with Idaho State University since 1975 has been much appreciated. My other teaching, research, and service affiliations in the last decade with Yale University, the University of Michigan, Montana State University, and the Northern Rockies Conservation Cooperative were also helpful.

Denise Casey's skilled editing, first-hand knowledge of the ferret conservation effort, and patience significantly improved the readability of the book. I sincerely appreciate the many constructive comments on earlier drafts of the manuscript both from people involved in the ferret program and from other readers with key perspectives: Ron Brunner, Steven Forrest, Jerome Jackson, Pam Lichtman, Brian Miller, Catherine Patrick, Richard Reading, Murray Rutherford, and Peter Wilshusen. Three anonymous reviewers selected by Yale University Press also offered very useful ideas for improving the manuscript. My thanks go to Astrid Varga and Dean Biggins for providing data for the epilogue and to Christina Cromley for library research.

Finally, to all those people too numerous to name individually but who helped directly and indirectly over the years, my most sincere thanks. Saving endangered species must be a cooperative task, and I have been most fortunate both personally and professionally to be part of a special community of dedicated people.

Abbreviations

BFAT   Black-Footed Ferret Advisory Team
BLM   Bureau of Land Management
CBSG   Captive Breeding Specialist Group
ESA   Endangered Species Act
FWS   Fish and Wildlife Service
GPO   Government Printing Office
ISU   Idaho State University
IUCN   International Union for the Conservation of Nature and Natural Resources
NGO   nongovernmental organization
NMFS   National Marine Fisheries Service
WGF   Wyoming Game and Fish Department

Averting Extinction

Introduction

In the past three decades, pitifully few endangered species have actually been restored to viable populations. Given the divisive conflicts over species restoration, it seems safe to say that we need more successful approaches to the problem. This book uses the story of efforts in the 1980s to save the black-footed ferret (*Mustela nigripes*) — once thought extinct but rediscovered in Wyoming in 1981 — to build a case for some new approaches to conserving and restoring species. I hope that these ideas will be discussed, improved upon, and widely used in the service of threatened species conservation into the twenty-first century. Some countries, in some situations, are already making practical use of them.

The new approach I advocate shifts the focus in conservation from science to practical problem solving in the public policy process. Of the myriad problems cited by critics of current efforts to conserve endangered species, few are biological. Nearly all relate to human systems and the dynamic patterns of interaction among people, worldviews, interests, values, organizational structures and cultures, processes of decision making, and many other aspects of human society. These human components undeniably constitute the contexts and conditions of species losses. Yet in past approaches to conservation that focused narrowly on science or particular organizations, they have rarely been acknowledged or identified, let alone explored, understood, or resolved. A policy-oriented view, on the other hand, locates the loss of biodiversity within this larger context and thus opens up new avenues, new methods, and new hope for species recovery. Past approaches have attempted to account for extinctions by giving lip service to "human dimensions," "biopolitics," or "socioeconomic considerations." The policy-oriented view goes beyond this: it is adaptive and promotes open-ended learning on individual, organizational, and political scales.

To build the rationale for reforming species conservation, this book journeys first through an actual conservation program to see how *real* policy is made in the field. I have chosen to examine in some detail certain aspects of the first few years of the Wyoming black-footed ferret case. I do not attempt a definitive description of the ferret conservation effort: it is not necessary for describing the policy orientation as a basis for practical improvements.

The ferret story is important in and of itself. The black-footed ferret has often been touted as the most critically endangered mammal in the United States. It is a distinctively marked, mink-sized, mammalian carnivore of the Great Plains and intermountain basins. It preys on prairie dogs and lives in their burrows. The ferret was almost extirpated in the late nineteenth and early twentieth centuries as farmers and ranchers, with the help of the federal government, transformed native western landscapes into livestock pastures and crop fields. The ferret was just one incidental casualty in this transformation. By 1980, many people feared that the ferret was extinct, but in late 1981, a small population was discovered in northwestern Wyoming near Meeteetse. This chance event provided a rare opportunity — perhaps the last ever — for recovery of America's only ferret. In 1985 a catastrophic disease struck the small ferret population, and most remaining animals were taken into captivity. Captive breeding was initiated, and reintroductions to the wild from the captive population began in 1991.

The ferret case gives insight into the process of making real endangered species policy, and it illustrates why new thinking and new practices are needed. This account concentrates on the first five years of intense labor by many dedicated people and organizations to restore the species from a single small population. It discusses how government officials and others went about organizing and conducting their affairs under the U.S. Endangered Species Act (ESA) to meet this life-or-extinction task. It is a story rich in lessons at several levels and thus serves as a foundation for the guidelines outlined in the last section of the book.

United States policy on endangered species, including the ferret and hundreds of other plants and animals, is codified in the 1973 Endangered Species Act (ESA, as amended, U.S. Congress 1983, Bean 1991a). This sweeping piece of environmental legislation sets as a national goal the prevention of any further extinctions and the restoration of species currently threatened with extinction. When the act was originally passed, it was highly popular: after all, no one advocated killing off entire species of plants and animals, and no one anticipated the intense conflicts with "development" interests. Even today, there is widespread popular, scientific, legislative, and judicial support for the ESA. But the simple, straightforward goal of saving species cloaks a convoluted process. The ferret case is a good illustration of how the ESA is actually implemented, how federal and state officials and others tackle the complex work of restoring species, and how problems come about in nearly all recovery programs. In short, the ferret rescue effort is a measure of how well the ESA really works.

After the serendipitous discovery of a small remnant population of black-footed ferrets near Meeteetse, Wyoming, in 1981, one might expect a well-led and smoothly coordinated effort to have been quickly organized to save a species that was recognized nationally and internationally as America's most endangered mammal. Many universities, conservation organizations, state and federal agencies, and local people were willing and able to help. Collectively, they commanded substantial resources, not only in terms of money: national and international expertise in population genetics and management of small populations, experienced field researchers, tested breeding facilities, and support staffs at several major zoos were also part of the assets available from the very beginning. All that was needed for the ferret to be restored swiftly, professionally, and efficiently was a means to bring this talent together in a productive, well-organized program.

Under the ESA, the task of organizing recovery efforts is the responsibility of the federal government acting through the U.S. Fish and Wildlife Service (FWS) and the U.S. National Marine Fisheries Service (NMFS). Federal officials had numerous options open to them at the inception of the ferret program, one of which was to function like administrators of a large hospital, pulling together a world-class professional team, supporting the necessary work with adequate funding, equipment, and facilities, and relying on the team's judgment to bring about the patient's recovery. But this model was not selected.

Observations on the Ferret Recovery Program

The ferret program was organized and operated very differently. Section 6 of the ESA requires that states be involved to the "maximum extent practicable." Early in 1982, the federal government turned the main responsibility for ferret restoration over to the State of Wyoming, specifically the Wyoming Game and Fish Department (WGF). Almost immediately, problems emerged that have persisted over the years. Many authors, some participants and some observers, have written about and helped define the problems in this program.

Through a formal resolution, the American Society of Mammalogists (1986:786) urged "the U.S. Fish and Wildlife Service, the Wyoming Fish and Game Department [*sic*], other state wildlife departments, and numerous interested conservation groups [to make] broader recovery efforts" than those exhibited by the current program.

After four years of observing government behavior in the ferret program, including several missed opportunities and the near total loss of the wild population in 1985, Chuck Carr (1986:7), of the New York Zoological Society's Wildlife Conservation International, concluded that the program "has failed the ferret" and "that the U.S. Endangered Species Act may no longer be the safety net for American wildlife that Congress intended it to be." Carr lamented the FWS's lack of leadership and limited ability to direct or carry out the tasks needed to restore ferrets in a timely manner or to hold WGF accountable to both the spirit and the intent of the ESA.

David Zimmerman (1986:6), then an investigative reporter for the New York Daily News and the author of a book on endangered birds, asked: "Does the ferret disaster [in 1985] . . . reveal shortcomings in the act, or in the actions of the U.S. Fish and Wildlife Service and other enforcement agencies?" This is a fundamental question that leads to another: was the ferret program flawed in some basic way?

Robert May (1986:14), an ecologist then at Princeton University, commented that "if such a mess can be made of efforts to save an attractive creature such as the black-footed ferret in a country as well organized and prosperous as the United States, prospects for conservation in other parts of the world are indeed bleak."

Steve Forrest (1987:1), hired by the U.S. Fish and Wildlife Service to help draft a new ferret recovery plan, concluded that WGF chronically demonstrated "reluctance to participate in open and collaborative discussions of problem-solving on ferret recovery. I do not believe recovery can succeed in this kind of management environment." Forrest recognized that the pace and direction of the ferret restoration effort was determined by WGF, and he questioned the wisdom of permitting a state to dominate a program that he felt should be national in scope.

Ken Alvarez (1993:343), a biologist with the Florida Park Service working on the Florida panther, followed the ferret program carefully and concluded that it was "a bureaucratic misadventure . . . [illustrating] anew the folly that ensues when a conservative institution finds itself in uncharted waters. . . .

[WGF] held every advantage in the way of expert advice, excellent field research teams and captive breeding facilities at its disposal, but the agency could not see past its traditional blinders." His insider's view of state agency behavior went to the heart of the matter by focusing on agency conservatism, culture, and ideology as the ultimate causes of the problems in the ferret program.

The Greater Yellowstone Coalition (1990:27), a regional conservation organization made up of more than seventy-five separate organizations, concluded that "the WG&F is interested in doing whatever is necessary to ensure that ferrets will be returned to the wild in Wyoming first, whether or not Wyoming is the best place to introduce them. . . . There may be sites in Montana which are better suited for [ferret] introduction, but the jealousy of the WG&F prevents them from considering such an alternative." The coalition concluded that state-level concerns had wrongly taken precedence over national recovery issues and that this significantly retarded ferret restoration (see also Ekey 1992).

Lynn Maguire (1991:123), a professor at Duke University's School of Forestry and Environmental Studies and an authority on decision analysis in endangered species management, noted that "in implementing both the California condor and the black-footed ferret recovery plans, concerns about captive husbandry and removing animals from the wild delayed captive breeding until the stability of the wild populations had declined to the point where continued inaction would have been clearly disastrous."

The Sierra Club Legal Defense Fund (1991:1) asked FWS officials to look into allegations that WGF was mismanaging its captive breeding facility, where nearly all ferrets were housed after 1987. The FWS complied and issued a report, to which Douglas Honnold of the Sierra Club Legal Defense Fund replied:

> I have just read the official report of the U.S. Fish and Wildlife Service concerning the management of the captive black-footed ferret population by the Wyoming Game and Fish Department at the Sybille facility. To put it bluntly, the report is appalling. The report fails to investigate in any fashion the critical issues — have there been any unnecessary deaths in the captive black-footed ferret population at Sybille [the WGF breeding facility] this year, and if so, what caused the excessive mortality? Instead, the [FWS] reporters investigated whether the Wyoming Game and Fish Department met all of the technical requirements of its federal permits. Any member of the public would be shocked and dismayed to read the report, which is clearly designed to exonerate and support the Wyoming Game and Fish Department rather than conduct an independent, searching, in-depth review of the management of the Sybille facility.

This letter questioned whether there was any accountability in the ferret program and whether the required system of checks and balances between federal and state interests — a keystone of democratic process — was really in place. It also asked who was in charge of implementing national ESA policy in the ferret case and concluded that, in practice, it was the state and not the FWS, as called for by the ESA. If true, this had serious implications for future implementation of ESA policy everywhere.

Richard Reading and Brian Miller (1994:95), two long-time ferret researchers, concluded that "despite the glowing stories of success in newspapers, newsletters, and popular magazines, ferrets remain far from recovered and the ferret recovery program suffers from a host of professional and organizational inadequacies. As the program expands to new areas and incorporates new figures, there is an excellent opportunity to develop a national focus and avoid the deep-seated problems of past efforts by reorganizing the program's structure. Without reorganization, the same problems could easily recur as the ferret program moves into new states." They identified organizational and operational weaknesses as the heart of the numerous difficulties in the ferret program (see also Reading 1992). Furthermore, they noted that organizational dimensions must be understood and altered to avoid perpetuating the problems that plagued the Wyoming program.

Miller, Reading, and Forrest (Miller et al. 1996:208) identify the FWS as the national agent responsible for maintaining professional restoration programs. "It is our contention," they write, "that Region 6 [of the FWS] failed to make ferret recovery a national program. It may have been easiest for Region 6 to acquiesce to Wyoming's agenda in the short term, but that strategy has probably impaired recovery over the long run. People, or agencies, in a position to improve conservation should not simply throw money at a problem, but invest time and attention as well" (citations in original omitted).

These represent just a few observations about the ferret restoration effort in the 1980s and early 1990s. Because they come from participants and close observers, they cannot be easily dismissed. Collectively, they suggest that from its inception the ferret program suffered from weaknesses having something to do with federal and state interrelationships in implementing ESA policy, with the nature of the agencies involved and their operating procedures (their perspectives and strategies), and with the kinds of decisions that were made and the way they were made.

Despite the apparently deeply rooted problems, however, some individuals recognized the limitations of the formal program and tried to work around them in various ways. The program's accomplishments to date are more a reflection of these collective contributions than anything else. Reintroductions into the wild of animals bred in captivity began six years after the original wild population collapsed from disease — an accomplishment that brought high praise, even awards, from some quarters.

Observations on ESA Implementation

The ferret program is just one among many restoration programs. Currently, more than nine hundred species are formally listed under the ESA as threatened or endangered. Over three thousand more wait on a list of candidates for such status (General Accounting Office 1992); Cohn (1993) noted that thirty-four species went extinct during the 1980s while on the waiting list. Is the ferret program representative of the overall national effort to recover species? The following reviews of the national endangered species program provide a useful backdrop for this account of the ferret program as well as for the search for a new prototype for endangered species policy implementation.

William Reffalt (1991:80) of The Wilderness Society concluded that of the 495 species listed in 1988, "only about 16 (3.2 percent) are recovering. Another 18 listed species (3.6 percent) may already be extinct. For most species, it is almost impossible to make a positive determination that absolutely no more of their kind live on this planet." He concluded that this is "a record that fails to demonstrate attainment of the basic promises of the act" (p. 79). The General Accounting Office (1992) added that of sixteen species removed from the list, five were recovered, seven went extinct, and four were reclassified because of misinformation.

Steven Yaffee (1982), a natural resource policy analyst, noted that the ESA, like all policies, is redefined in the course of implementation. Various organizations bring to the work their own ideologies, goals, and histories that predate ESA enactment and that may be hostile to the policy. Among the internal and external forces that shape ESA implementation are scientific and bureaucratic conservatism, resource constraints, conflicting organizational and professional roles and goals within and between agencies, uneven popularity and "sponsorship" of endangered species, conflicting interest groups, and the media.

Two federal audits of ESA implementation have been conducted. Concerned about possible deficiencies, the General Accounting Office (1988) reviewed the FWS endangered species program and found that the federal government did not maintain centralized information needed to determine how well the overall program was operating. Required recovery plans had not been developed and approved for many species. In the sixteen species recovery plans that the GAO investigated in depth, nearly half of the tasks listed had not been undertaken, even though the plans had been approved, on average, more than four years earlier. FWS officials attributed these shortcomings to a shortage of funds. Although noting that some progress had been made, the GAO concluded that much more needed to be done. More recently, "the inspector general of the Interior Department has lambasted his federal colleagues at the U.S. Fish and Wildlife Service, charging that they may be sending species to extinction" (Holden 1990:620). Various recommendations were generated to improve FWS performance on the basis of these two studies.

A detailed analysis of the ESA led Richard Tobin (1990:257), a political scientist, to conclude that "depending on one's hopes and expectations, efforts to protect endangered species in the United States are either a modest success or a massive failure." He remarked that the ESA program "can point to few successes, at least when measured against its statutory goal" (p. 257), and that it "can claim victory in a few skirmishes, but it is losing the larger and more important battle (p. 258)."

A legal analysis of ESA implementation in actual political settings was made by Oliver Houck (1993). He noted that the Departments of Interior and Commerce, which are primarily responsible for ESA implementation, "have interpreted each major stage of the ESA in a fashion of their choosing, albeit a fashion that Congress did not have in mind. The result is, in effect, an endangered species permit system in which the permitting is done largely at the Departments' discretion" (p. 279). His conclusion was that "the Endangered Species Act is not what it seems — either in the media or in the United States Code. It has, in effect, been substantially amended through regulations and practice, transforming it from an act of specific requirements into a more discretionary permit system" (p. 358).

Stephen Kellert (1996:202), a long-time student of the human dimensions of wildlife management, observed "significant shortcomings in traditional approaches to wildlife management and administration" with regard to endangered species protection. Government agencies are restricted by "strong historic allegiances and traditional ideologies and limited by an inability or unwillingness to consider all relevant wildlife values in formulating and implementing policy" (p. 202). He found such specific "institutional problems as inappropriate reward structures, conflicting administrative goals, limited competencies, inconsistent agendas, rigid leadership patterns, fragmented decision making, poor communication procedures, and inadequate accountability" (p. 203).

Reed Noss (1991), a conservation biologist, concluded that "clearly, the ESA is not accomplishing all that it proposed to do. . . . The ever-growing list of endangered species, the continual population declines of most listed species, the disruption of ecological processes around the globe — all demonstrate the inadequacies of the ESA at both species and ecosystem levels of organization" (pp. 228, 229).

The statistics and assessments show clearly that there are problems in ESA implementation. The causes are probably many and varied, but one major cause may lie embedded in the way government agencies go about their work. As Aaron Wildavsky (1979) put it, sometimes failures or barriers are unwittingly built into organizational designs and policy implementation efforts. The 1973 ESA, as amended, is a policy structure with a labyrinth of phases, planning steps, interrelated functions, and layers of overlapping jurisdictions with multiple agencies and interests. The act was not intended to inhibit the design and implementation of useful solutions to endangered species crises. Rather, it was meant to encourage different levels of government and the public to work together toward a common goal. But the controversy between federalism and states' rights has been a major variable in the complex calculus of endangered species policy (e.g., Ernst 1991, Miller et al. 1996).

For the most part, the separation of federal and state powers serves the nation well, but many resource management agencies at both levels are too ready to define the public interest in their own narrow terms (Light and Wodraska 1990). This "hardening of the institutional arteries" (p. 479) is a subtle yet serious problem, especially for recovery programs, because they usually involve several federal agencies (representing national interests), state agencies (representing local interests), as well as private organizations. Federal and state agencies are not ranged in an administrative hierarchy. Each agency possesses its own autonomous legal authority, political constituency, and bureaucracy. Each organizational participant is apt to have different objectives, or at least different priorities. Steven Bissell (1994:324) reviewed the situation:

> Under the Tenth Amendment to the U.S. Constitution, the states have traditionally assumed most of the authority to manage wildlife resources. However, court decisions since the turn of the century have gradually given more and more power to the federal government. With NEPA [National Environmental Policy Act] and the ESA the federal government has exerted increasing presence in on-the-ground management. There is widespread concern among the states that the emerging issues of biodiversity, ecosystem management, and landscape planning are being used by the federal government to further erode state control of wildlife policy. The history of intergovernmental cooperation in wildlife policy has not been smooth, and there are indications that there will be more problems in the future. The degree to which state and federal agencies can learn to work cooperatively in the formulation of policy on these management issues will largely determine the effectiveness of the policies.

Robert Keiter and Pat Holscher (1990) examined some fundamental questions about federal/state relations in the public domain in the case of the reintroduction of endangered wolves into Yellowstone National Park. They described how differences are being reconciled under the ESA and concluded that "federalism controversies are appropriately resolved in a political — rather than a judicial — forum" (p. 48).

As part of this strong undercurrent of federal/state contests, another political factor has been significant in endangered species policy making. Over the life of the ferret program, Wyoming produced a secretary of the interior, James Watt, under President Ronald Reagan, and a director of the U.S. Fish and Wildlife Service, John Turner, under President George Bush. Both showed a keen interest in supporting state interests. In addition, John Ernst (1991:108) noted that "while not changing the Endangered Species Act, the three members of Wyoming's congressional delegation have been successful in frustrating its implementation in general." These members of Congress have supported state interests in land management issues, but there is no public record of their influencing the black-footed ferret program.

The "New Federalism" dominated federal policy implementation during the Reagan and Bush administrations. Implementation of many policies was handed to the states, including the Clean Air Act Amendments of 1970, the Pollution Control Act Amendments of 1972 (regarding water pollution), and others. James Lester (1990) assessed this trend and concluded that the states varied significantly in their abilities, economically and organizationally, to maintain commitments consistent with the original intent of the U.S. Congress. Many state governments lack the expertise available to the national government, tend toward parochialism, may be unwilling to make needed commitments, or are dominated by conservative elites. These problems can be overcome if states make commitments to upgrade their organizational capabilities. Lester (1990) classified the states, according to how well they implemented selected national environmental policies, as progressives, strugglers, delayers, or regressives. Progressives (Lester cited, for example, Washington) have high commitment and strong organizational capabilities. Strugglers (such as Montana) have a high commitment but weak organizational capabilities. Delayers (such as Texas) have a weak commitment and strong organizational capabilities. And regressives (such as Wyoming) have both a weak commitment and weak organizational capability. Lester (1990:74) concluded that for regressive states "decentralization of environmental programs will likely be a disaster. They may fail to adequately implement federal laws in this area, and they are unlikely to take independent actions." Policy makers clearly need to take these considerations into account before turning national policy implementation over to state governments.

All these forces and factors converged in the specifics of the ferret rescue effort. The next eight chapters (Part I) examine some of the participants, their perspectives, situations, and strategies, and the events, processes, and outcomes of the ferret recovery program in an effort to define those small and large problems in a way that is analytically rigorous and practically useful. This review helps us understand why current programs fail to meet their potential and why so few species have actually recovered. It also provides a more realistic and well-grounded basis for suggesting how we might reconstruct the process by which we protect species. Readers may, as a result, be impelled to consider some different options. Part II suggests an alternative for reform, a strategy for constructive learning, innovation, and adaptation.

Some readers may find this book messy, for two reasons. First, it transcends the established niches of natural resource work and the legitimate boundaries of many recognized academic and professional disciplines. Wildlife management, conservation biology, sociology, political science, and organization and management are brought together, reflecting the complexity of actual conservation processes. This approach may alarm those who want to contain endangered species restoration as a strictly biological, technical, and apolitical matter. A second reason for the apparent messiness is that it addresses multiple audiences: university students and instructors, conservationists both in and out of government, and professionals in the fields of natural resource management, organization design and behavior, and the policy sciences. For all these people, there are lessons to be learned from the ferret experience about ways to improve public policy processes in natural resource management.

I have several reasons for writing this book. First is my firm conviction that those of us concerned with conservation make our job harder than it should be. We create unintentional road blocks that greatly complicate our work. Saving species is not a clear-cut, straightforward undertaking by any means. Yet this account shows that there is a considerable gap between what we *know* about saving species and what we in fact *do* about saving species. Many of the barriers to achieving our goal are a direct consequence of how we understand the task and how we organize ourselves for action — that is, how organizations are structured and how people work within and through organizations. We are largely ignorant of better organizational alternatives, methods of solving problems, or points of leverage we may have in affecting overall decision processes. This book was written to help bring the professional, organizational, and policy dimensions of conservation work into clearer focus. I do not advance any new theory about professionalism, organizations, or the policy process. I draw on existing bodies of knowledge and experience — off-the-shelf theory, if you will — heavily substantiated with citations, to demonstrate that pervasive problems are not unique to nature conservation. They have been observed, analyzed, explained, and even solved in other realms. Moreover, these other disciplines, bodies of knowledge, and tried-and-applied ideas have enormous power to improve the implementation of endangered species policy or, for that matter, natural resource management in general.

This book describes disorders within the ferret program and for that reason may be criticized as disparaging. But, like the sick patient who needs a doctor to diagnose his illness, understand its causes, and treat it, endangered species programs need description, diagnosis, functional understanding, and appropriate treatment. The intent of this book is not to dwell on the disorders of the ferret program but to use them to analyze larger problems. The primary goal is to improve the problem-solving capabilities of the people and organizations responsible for saving species.

My second reason for undertaking this project is to encourage participants in other endangered species programs to write case histories of them — not just detail the biological challenges but, more important, draw the "human envelope" around species, as Ron Westrum (1994) called it. If participants could describe their experiences with reference to a useful paradigm — such frameworks already exist — then we could make progress in saving endangered species. But the subjects of professionalism, organizations, and policy are seldom recorded and analyzed systematically by those with firsthand experience in restoration programs, and so the accumulated experience and insights are lost as a basis for community-wide learning and improvement.

A third reason for writing this book is to urge universities to develop curricula in conservation biology and natural resources management that embrace organizational studies and policy sciences as well as conservation sciences. Training of natural resource specialists at present is limited to technical subjects and positivistic problem-solving approaches. Despite their obvious benefits, these methods tend to obscure the insights, experience, and problem solving skills from other areas of knowledge. Universities too often fail to teach the inter- or transdisciplinary perspectives, knowledge, and skills needed, nor do they develop the ability of graduates to think comprehensively and practically about how to solve problems. I support Albert Worrel's (1970) admonition that natural resource professionals need to explore the social sciences for concepts to understand their own working world, even though, as Charles Perrow (1970) noted, it requires a trek into what biologists disdain as the "mushy marshes."

My involvement in ferret conservation goes back many years. In 1973, I set out working nearly full time to find ferrets. The next eight years took me to ten states in pursuit of the elusive creature, but my searches were centered in

Wyoming. These efforts were conducted under the auspices of nongovernmental and university organizations. In late 1981, when the species was "rediscovered" by a Meeteetse rancher, I was invited by the rancher and by state wildlife officials to become involved. I organized a team of volunteers to assist in the government-led program that eventually developed around the newly discovered ferret population. Since 1986, my participation has greatly decreased. In the late 1980s, I promoted the establishment of relocation sites and encouraged successful reintroductions, primarily in Montana, where probably the best single reintroduction site in the nation exists. I have continued to follow the program closely through the popular and technical literature as well as conversations with participants. Thus, this account is based on long-term, firsthand experience as well as the written public record.

The variables involved in such an analysis are numerous, sometimes elusive, and difficult to isolate and interrelate. But this reflects the reality, complexity, and uncertainty of today's conservation challenges. Even though this book strives to map rationally and objectively some of the factors pertinent to ferret preservation and to organize and treat them systematically, a bias is naturally present. The only weapon against ubiquitous biases is to be sensitive to the differences among people and to try to include the input of all participants in an evolving portrayal of a problem and its possible solutions. But, of course, all opinions are not equally valid: critical standards exist to distinguish among arguments that make various claims to rationality, practical politics, and morality (Lasswell and McDougal 1992). Such a perspective is crucial to the functioning of a democracy and the public control of state bureaucracies and policy processes.

This account is not intended to fan the flames of controversy. I describe my vantage point as an analyst so that readers can understand it in relation to other actors' viewpoints. Although I have a bias against the weaknesses manifest in the ferret case, such as the waste of time and money, I have tried to compensate by documenting heavily from the case material and related literature. The availability of surviving case materials provides uneven support for my analysis; in some places it is strong and in others less so. But through the actions and statements made by the participants over the years, clear patterns emerged in their perspectives, demands, and strategies.

There are many different perspectives on the functioning of the ferret program; several have been published. This *Rashomon* of views exists because individuals occupy different positions in programs and have different access to information and other resources. People also differ in personality, intellect, and experience and in the interpretive lenses through which they examine and give meaning to their experiences. Organizations differ, too, in their cultures and interests, power and authority structures, and resource bases. There is no single correct way to understand the program. I have tried to describe its dynamics as I experienced and understood them. I hope other participants will write their accounts, with their insights, from a thoughtful, systematic, and analytical perspective, so that we can, as a community, build a broad base of case material for examination and learning.

Even with the intention to remain sensitive to biases, however, methodological challenges remain in examining such a complex, lengthy, and convoluted program. An adequate conceptual framework is needed to guide exploration to make the analysis both comprehensive and comprehensible. The framework must be well grounded in human experience and rest on a strong intellectual foundation (Lasswell and McDougal 1992). This also requires an understanding of what constitutes an explanation, which is to say that underlying the relationship of facts is a required logic of explanation. There are various forms of reasoning, and adequate explanations must describe the mechanisms that cause or are responsible for observed events (Harré 1972).

Traditional science — "hypothetico-deductive" or true experimentation in rigorously controlled settings — is not possible in analyses like this because randomization, control groups, and replication are not possible. But in seeking explanations of events, outcomes, and effects, the mere possibility of alternative explanations is not enough to invalidate conceptually sound explanations. Rival hypotheses must be plausible and must be based on a thorough contextual analysis and problem orientation as described by Lasswell (1970, 1971a), Brunner (1982), Brewer and deLeon (1983), Lasswell and McDougal (1992), and others. This approach may have limitations and may not satisfy some strict, "positivistic" scientists, but we have to deal with real-life problems as they come to us and as we construct them. This is the approach used here.

There are two perspectives that can be taken of any event or outcome, as described by Bruno Latour (1987), a sociologist of science. He labels these the "black box" (or "ready-made science") perspective and the "open controversy" (or "science in the making") perspective. The black-box view sees an event or outcome in a summary, completed, de facto way from a "certain, cold, unproblematic" perspective. The open-controversy view examines the process of the work, people, complexity, unknowns, surprises, decisions, competition, and controversy:

> When we approach the places where facts and machines are made, we get into the midst of controversies. The closer we are, the more controversial they become. When we go from "daily life" to scientific activity, from the man in

the street to the men in the laboratory, from politics to expert opinion, we do not go from noise to quiet, from passion to reason, from heat to cold. We go from controversies to fiercer controversies. It is like reading a law book and then going to court to watch a jury wavering under the impact of contradictory evidence. Still better, it is like moving from a law book to Parliament when the law is still a bill. More noise, indeed, not less. (Latour 1987:30)

Examining a situation as complex and important as the ferret program from these two perspectives produces two very different understandings of what happened. On one hand, conventional scientists and agency administrators tend to "shy away from the disorderly mixture revealed by science in action and prefer the orderly pattern of scientific method and rationality" (Latour 1987:15). Their accounts of the ferret program clearly reflect this (U.S. Fish and Wildlife Service 1983, Biggins and Thorne 1994). On the other hand, historians, sociologists of science, policy researchers, and philosophers tend to open the black boxes to give outsiders a glimpse. That approach is also taken in this book: it promises to provide many lessons for improving ESA implementation, but it also raises more controversies.

Species and ecosystem conservation and restoration are vitally important tasks — among the most important ones facing humanity today. It requires all our knowledge and skills — technical, scientific, social, and political — and our highest moral commitment. We must all learn from our collective experience and find better ways to work together. My motives for writing this book are focused on improving our individual and collective performance in this essential work.

PART I

The Ferret Program and Its Behavior

These eight chapters describe and analyze efforts to restore the endangered black-footed ferret during the first few years after the species' discovery in Wyoming in 1981. They look not just at the changing content of the story — laws and regulations, agency activities, dollars spent, decisions and events, numbers of ferrets — but at the *process* of conservation. As Giandomenico Majone (1989:19) notes, "knowledge of process is . . . essential for purposes of evaluation and learning since it provides information that outcome measures are almost sure to miss." These chapters do just that: they provide the specifics about the workings of the ferret program necessary for a constructive evaluation of the program. This information — added to that from numerous other cases — is also vital for evaluating and ultimately reconstructing the process by which we restore species under the Endangered Species Act.

This is a story of public policy — of how problems of various kinds were addressed or ignored, how participants perceived problems and solutions differently, as well as what strategies they used, what outcomes they sought, and what effects occurred. The story reveals disagreement about what the ferret conservation challenge was, what ought to be done about it, by whom, how, where, and when.

Like narrative stories, policy stories tell of the struggle between different forces to transform the world. Just as people interpret novels, movies, and the stories that unfold in the daily news in different ways (especially as they are complicated by real-life details or secondary story lines), so too do people differ in how they understand the meaning of policy stories (Stone 1988).

The unit of analysis in this story is the organizations that participated in ferret recovery. The account attempts to discern their aggregate characteristics or central tendencies over time via their actual behavior. Organizations play a pervasive role in modern society, and they are among the principal targets for effecting change in the outcomes and effects of public policy processes. There is much precedent in this century for their study and management.

Not everyone is aware of the significance of processes of interaction in the field of conservation. If the issues brought up by this story are appreciated at all by most participants or observers, they are usually conveyed in war stories about people, events, and circumstances and explained with words like "personality," "politics," "luck," "lack of commitment," or "bureaucracy." But this kind of conventional analysis — simply an accumulation of events — fails to crystallize actual organizational and decisional processes; its meanings are unique to particular situations (Lasswell and McDougal 1992). Conventional analysis emphasizes *content*. This book takes a more functional analytical approach to the ferret story. Functional analysis focuses on *context* as well as content and the meanings and roles of events and decisions in larger organizational and policy systems. It looks, for instance, not so much at the membership, meeting minutes, and recommendations of the Black-Footed Ferret Advisory Team but instead at how the team functioned as an instrument of enlightenment in providing advice — as its name suggested — or as a means to consolidate and concentrate power, or as a way to promote certain other values.

The case material on some aspects of the program is limited; many issues covered in this book were not addressed openly and explicitly at the time. Structural and process features, concerning the relation of the ferret program to the task at hand and to its operating environment, are more often suggested obliquely, rather than directly addressed, in the available case material. Future research may bring to light more information on these subjects. Although the case material supporting this analysis is uneven, a clear pattern of behavior for the whole program emerges which can be described and analyzed. Thus, the case material is balanced with literature from the fields of organizational design, behavior, and learning and the policy sciences, which is brought in to clarify functional relationships and performance standards. This approach is not fully satisfactory, but it is the best possible under the circumstances.

It is not the task of the analyst to lay to rest questions about fundamental disagreements or standards of evaluation and accountability. The uncertainty of a case can never be completely removed, no matter how well crafted the analysis. Only the political process can make determinations about standards and performance. The job of the analyst is to "contribute to societal learning by refining the standards of appraisal of public programs and by encouraging a more sophisticated understanding of public policies than is possible from a single perspective. The need today is less to develop 'objective' measures of outcomes — the traditional aim of evaluation research — than to facilitate a wide-ranging dialogue among advocates of different criteria" (Majone 1989: 183). This is the analytic guide used here to tell the policy story of the black-footed ferret program's formative years.

EDSON FICHTER

Black-Footed Ferrets
From Near Extinction to Near Recovery

The black-footed ferret is one of the world's most endangered mammals, and with its nocturnal and ground-dwelling habits it is one of the most elusive. But upon its discovery in 1981, the ferret population of Meeteetse, Wyoming, was thrown into the limelight and caught the attention of many conservationists, wildlife managers, and biologists, as well as the American public. The ferret restoration program, ongoing since discovery of the Wyoming population, has been covered in many newspapers and magazines, on radio and television, and in the scientific literature. The ferret is thus one of the best-known American endangered species, and many people are closely following efforts to restore it. At the least, these efforts are expected to rescue the ferret from impending extinction. At best, the ferret recovery program might be a model conservation program. Regardless of how it plays out, the evolution of this program has implications for national endangered species policy. This chapter provides a brief introduction to the history of the species as well as the Meeteetse population in the first five years after its discovery.

History of the Black-Footed Ferret

The black-footed ferret, order *Carnivora* (meat-eating mammals), family *Mustelidae* (weasel-like mammals), is one of about fourteen living species worldwide in the genus *Mustela*. It is the only ferret native to North America. Its nearest living relative is the steppe polecat or Siberian ferret (*M. eversmanni*) of Eurasia. As late as the 1920s, the ferret was widespread and at least locally abundant, if not common, throughout much of its former range — nearly 100 million acres over twelve Great Plains and Rocky Mountain states, two Canadian provinces, and Mexico.

Ferrets appear to be obligatory predators on prairie dogs (*Cynomys* sp.) and once occupied a range essentially identical to that of prairie dogs. They prey on these squirrel-like rodents and use their burrows for shelter and nesting. No litter of young ferrets has ever been found outside prairie dog colonies. Prior to white settlement prairie dogs numbered in the hundreds of millions. Their colonies covered thousands of square miles; one in Texas was 250 miles long and 100 miles wide. The Lewis and Clark expedition reported the existence of prairie dog colonies on its way across the upper Great Plains.

Because of their burrows, the vegetation they consume, and their clearing of colony sites, prairie dogs have been considered agricultural pests and competitors with livestock since white settlement first began in the American West. Large-scale rodent control programs were demanded by livestock and agricultural interests and were conducted and funded largely by federal and state governments. They drastically reduced the number of prairie dogs (and other species associated with the "prairie dog ecosystem") through trapping, shooting, gassing, flooding, and — primarily — poisoning. Although poisoning began in the late nineteenth century, the federal government initiated a concerted, coordinated, national effort in 1915. Poisoning with strychnine, 1080, and zinc phosphide continues today on a smaller but still significant scale. Although prairie dogs still occupy much of their former range, their population is but a minute fraction of that which existed in the 1920s, and their colonies are small and widely scattered.

These poisoning programs are considered the major cause of the ferret's demise. Some ferrets were killed directly by the poisoning and trapping aimed at prairie dogs, but the primary cause of their demise was loss of their prey base and of appropriate habitat. Their remaining habitat was fragmented into smaller and smaller patches, thus rendering isolated ferret populations highly vulnerable to extinction from various causes, including demographic events (such as inability to find mates), genetic events (such as inbreeding depression), and environmental events (such as drought or flood), as well as local catastrophes (such as disease in either the ferrets or their prey).

Several Indian tribes knew about or used ferrets, and ferrets began appearing in fur-trapping records in the 1830s, but the species was not described scientifically until 1851, when John Audubon and the Reverend John Bachman gave a brief account in *The Quadrupeds of North America*. The first full description of the species was not published until 1877, and the species was not studied scientifically in its natural habitat until 1964 in Mellette County, South Dakota. About ninety individuals, including eleven litters, were observed in this population over the next eleven years, and nine ferrets were taken into captivity. Much was learned about ferret biology, ecology, and husbandry from the South Dakota studies, although the first efforts at captive breeding were unsuccessful. This last known surviving population died out by 1974; its extremely small size probably resulted in demographic and genetic problems that magnified the effect of limited available habitat. Nevertheless, the U.S. Fish and Wildlife Service (FWS) established a recovery team in 1975 in the hope of locating additional ferrets.

Conservation measures for the ferret have been complex. Protection of the ferret ranked high in the "Redbook" list of endangered wildlife compiled in 1964 by the Committee on Rare and Endangered Species within the Bureau of Sport Fisheries and Wildlife, and it was again listed in an FWS list of endangered species priorities in 1966. By 1980, with the loss of the South Dakota population and with no others known despite extensive searches, the ferret was presumed gone from most of its former range and was generally considered by the FWS to be "unrecoverable," a euphemism for extinct. The 1981 discovery of ferrets in Wyoming—which occurred strictly by chance when a ranch dog killed an unusual animal eating from its food dish and the rancher took the carcass to a knowledgeable taxidermist—was viewed as a rare second chance to recover the species.

The Ferrets of Meeteetse

At the time of their discovery, the Meeteetse ferrets were expected to occur in low numbers as a result of ongoing systematic pressures (primarily loss of habitat) as well as chance events. Given this perspective and the initial paucity of information about ferret demographics, behavior, and habitat requirements, the situation called for careful, timely, elective conservation research focused on understanding those key aspects of ferret biology needed to recover the species. Field studies were designed to yield practical, conservation-relevant data. All efforts were intended to avoid disturbing the ferrets, to maximize data needed for conservation and recovery, and to provide the basis for cooperative studies. Study methods included direct observation of the ferrets' behavior both night and day, radio collaring of some individuals to monitor their locations and movements, and studies of prey, habitat, and environment. Researchers also followed tracks in fresh snow that the ferrets had made the previous night. Snowtracking allowed them to determine the animals' movements and above-ground behaviors, such as digging and scent marking. Spotlighting was conducted at night year round, but especially in the summer, to locate and count the ferrets. The lights, mounted on trucks or carried by researchers on foot, were shined repeatedly across the landscape to locate the ferrets' characteristic green eyeshine, which could be seen at a distance of a few hundred yards. This technique permitted researchers to count individuals and family groups. A census was taken in mid-summer for about four to six weeks. At that time the young were old enough to be active above ground, yet family groups of mothers and young were still together. The juveniles began dispersing in September. The population was also estimated by a mark/recapture method, in which animals were safely trapped live, marked with a small eartag, and quickly released. Trapping was conducted again a few weeks later, and the ratio of tagged to untagged animals was used to generate an estimate of the total population. Mark/recapture sampling was conducted in late summer and early fall.

The ferret killed by the dog was discovered on September 26, 1981. Scientific research and recovery efforts followed almost immediately, involving several federal, state, and nongovernmental organizations. Researchers at once sought the wild population from which that animal had originated. Prairie dog colonies in the region were systematically surveyed for sight and sign of ferrets. The thirty-seven white-tailed prairie dog (*C. leucurus*) colonies found to be occupied by ferrets were dynamic, reflecting yearly changes in prairie dog populations; in 1982, the region contained seven thousand acres of live prairie dog colonies. Historical evidence suggested there may have been over seventy-five thousand acres of prairie dogs in this area in the 1930s, when large-scale prairie dog poisoning programs began.

From 1981 through 1985, at least 282 ferrets were observed. Minimum ferret numbers observed during spotlighting were 61 in 1982, 88 in 1983, 129 in 1984, and 58 in 1985 (the 1982 total is not comparable to other years because not all colonies had been located). The mark/recapture population estimates in the fall of 1983, 1984, and 1985 were similar to the counts from spotlighting. Each August the population comprised about two-thirds juveniles and one-third adults. From 1982 through 1985, sixty-eight litters were found with a mean size of 3.3 (range 1–5).

Large numbers of ferrets disappeared each year because of mortality and emigration. Of sixty-one ferrets counted in the summer of 1982, only twenty-eight survived until the following summer, while thirty-three disappeared—a loss of 54 percent. Sixty juveniles were added to the survivors in summer 1983, for a total of eighty-eight. Forty-five of these animals—51 percent—

were lost over the next winter, while forty-three survived. In summer 1984, eighty-six juveniles were added, bringing the total population to 129. But by summer 1985, only twenty of these animals survived, while 109 had disappeared — a staggering loss of 85 percent. Thirty-eight young were counted in summer 1985, but by fall they and the twenty survivors had been severely reduced: twelve animals had been taken into captivity, while about forty more had simply disappeared. Only between four and ten individuals remained in the wild that fall.

The 1982, 1983, and 1984 population counts contrasted markedly with the early August 1985 spotlight count of fifty-eight and subsequent declining numbers over the summer and fall of 1985. Repeated mark/recapture estimates in 1985 also showed the dramatic and persistent decline in numbers. Although juveniles typically leave home and disperse from September to late October, the 1985 losses could not be attributed to successful dispersal because there was no suitable habitat (no large unoccupied prairie dog colonies) nearby for ferrets to colonize. If any of the disappearing ferrets had dispersed, they would have died.

The large population decline in 1985 was ultimately attributed to canine distemper (*Morbilivirus*), which is invariably fatal to ferrets and may have been introduced by other native carnivores. A simultaneous outbreak of sylvatic plague (*Yersinia pestis*) in the prairie dog population may have also contributed to the ferrets' demise directly and indirectly. Similar to bubonic plague in humans, sylvatic plague is a bacterial disease widespread in wild mammals; it often decimates prairie dogs. Plague was diagnosed in May and June 1985 in several Meeteetse colonies by the Center for Disease Control in Fort Collins, Colorado. Surveys in 1986 and 1987 showed that plague had reduced the Meeteetse prairie dog complex to a level that could have supported few if any ferrets.

Ferrets in Captivity

Captive breeding of endangered species is a widely recognized — albeit extremely costly and risky — recovery technique, in which captive animals are bred to increase numbers rapidly. It provides control of a reservoir of animals to protect against extinction in the wild, to produce stock for release into the wild, to gather life history and behavior information critical for future conservation and reintroduction efforts, and to inform the public and enlist its support of recovery programs. One of the principal conservation research questions posed in 1981 was whether the Meeteetse ferrets produced an annual surplus that could be used for captive breeding or relocation to other sites

(Clark 1981). By late summer 1983, all data indicated that a surplus did exist. In a report first issued in 1983 (Richardson et al. 1986), it was strongly recommended that captive-rearing and reintroduction efforts be undertaken for ferrets soon. The report proposed a scenario for captive breeding and concluded that it was highly likely that Meeteetse ferrets could be successfully maintained and propagated in captivity. In 1984, several captive propagation facilities were made available to breed ferrets and finance the operation—the FWS's Patuxent Wildlife Research Center in Maryland, a National Zoo captive-breeding facility in Virginia, and a large, empty mustelid breeding facility at Washington State University in Pullman. Several other facilities also expressed an interest in helping, among them the Bronx, Brookfield, and Denver zoos. Unfortunately, no ferrets were taken into captivity until after their catastrophic decline in mid-1985.

Only one previous attempt to propagate ferrets in captivity had been undertaken, using South Dakota ferrets, although individual ferrets had been held in zoos over the previous eighty years. Much was learned from the South Dakota effort, and since then many new techniques have been developed which could aid captive propagation of ferrets: artificial insemination, embryo manipulation, genetic engineering, gamete and embryo storage, endocrine control of reproduction, and encouragement of successful lactation and neonatal survival.

Because of the precipitous decline in numbers documented in the summer of 1985, ferrets were taken into captivity beginning in September 1985. The first six individuals captured (two adult males, one juvenile male, one adult female, and two juvenile females) all died of canine distemper in a facility run by the Wyoming Game and Fish Department (WGF), probably because of inadequate quarantine procedures (Peterson 1985, Thorne and Williams 1988, Thorne and Oakleaf 1991, Miller et al. 1996). Miller et al. (1996) describe the capture of the first six ferrets from September 13 to October 12, 1985, the first death on October 22, and the final death on January 6, 1986. A second group of six (two juvenile males, two adult females, and two juvenile females) was taken between October 25 and 31, 1985, and housed individually; four or five of these ferrets may have been closely related.

In late 1985, the Captive Breeding Specialist Group (CBSG) of the International Union for the Conservation of Nature and Natural Resources (IUCN, now the World Conservation Union) became involved in advising, formulating, and virtually directing WGF and the FWS in the captive breeding of ferrets. (The CBSG role and captive breeding are reviewed in Clark 1989, Seal et al. 1989, Thorne and Oakleaf 1991, Williams et al. 1991, Miller et al. 1996.) By the end of 1985, the CBSG had reviewed the state's facilities, resources, personnel, support, and plans and made numerous recommendations for upgrading efforts (see Miller et al. 1996). The CBSG concluded that it would be genetically desirable to have at least twenty breeders as founders of the captive population for maximum retention of genetic diversity. On this basis, and because two of the males in captivity were immature and unlikely to breed in 1986, the CBSG strongly recommended bringing in at least three additional animals immediately, especially adult males. Without them, prospects of successful captive rearing were remote. (The success rate was estimated at less than 10 percent.) About six ferrets were thought to remain in the wild at Meeteetse at this time, including one known adult male. Action on the CBSG's recommendation was deferred by government officials until summer 1986. As predicted, the six captive ferrets did not breed in 1986.

The CBSG recommended that if fewer than ten ferrets were found at Meeteetse in summer 1986, all animals should be brought in for the captive propagation program. Fortunately, four ferrets persisted in the wild and that summer produced two litters of five kits each. By early 1987, twelve of these (four adults and eight offspring) had been added to the captive population. No additional wild ferrets have been found since early 1987, and the species is presumed extinct in the wild at Meeteetse. One female caught in 1985 died in January 1987, leaving seventeen Meeteetse ferrets captured in 1985–87 to form the nucleus of the captive population. However, the entire captive-bred population relied on only seven founders; of the original eighteen ferrets taken into captivity, eleven left no surviving offspring (Reading et al. 1996). It is highly likely that some of these seven fertile ferrets were closely related.

We have now had two "last chances" to save the black-footed ferret — first with the South Dakota population and then with the Wyoming ferrets. If decision makers had intervened earlier in the Wyoming case and had begun captive breeding or translocation in 1983 or 1984, we might not have come so dangerously close to losing the species a second time. Nor would the effort to restore it have been so costly in terms of money, time, and stress. As it is, the black-footed ferret will require careful management for decades to come both in captivity and in the reintroduced populations. This will require an adequate program — the subject of this book.

2

Participants and Perspectives
Complexity of Joint Action

Endangered species conservation is always an interdependent enterprise. In the ferret restoration effort, some persons supplied information needed by others, some provided working permits needed by others, some gave access to the animals needed by others, and so on. In late 1981 and early 1982, only a few participants were involved, but as the years passed, more organizations and individuals joined the effort. In 1987, a Wildlife Preservation Trust newsletter listed seven major organizations and twenty-four key individuals.

A critical event early in the program that affected all subsequent aspects was the transfer of administrative leadership of the recovery effort from the federal government to the State of Wyoming (Strickland 1983, Schroeder 1987). Section 6 of the Endangered Species Act addresses U.S. Fish and Wildlife Service cooperation with the states and directs the secretary of the interior to "cooperate to the maximum extent practicable with the States" (U.S. Congress 1983: 14). FWS administrators have tremendous discretion to interpret this phrase, as they do in many other parts of the ESA (Houck 1993). The ideal is to strike a balance between federal and state interests in order to achieve a cooperative and effective program that accounts for the differing concerns of the two levels of government. Initially in this case, the FWS had control over the kind of contractual arrangements possible with the Wyoming Game and Fish Department, and it had a range of options. The FWS decided that cooperation "to the maximum extent practicable" meant giving WGF the lead role.

In this chapter I describe the variety of participants involved in ferret conservation and touch on their perspectives and strategies in the years while the Meeteetse population survived. I examine key organizational participants, recount the transfer of lead authority from the federal government to WGF and some important consequences of this action, and suggest why cooperative joint action among participants was difficult.

The Participants

Organizational participants in ferret restoration included federal land and wildlife management agencies, state agencies, and a variety of nongovernmental organizations. Three units of the U.S. Fish and Wildlife Service (Department of the Interior) were involved along with the Bureau of Land Management (BLM, Department of the Interior), and the Forest Service (Department of Agriculture). These agencies differed in their congressionally mandated missions, histories, organizational cultures, and operating styles (see Clarke and McCool 1985). In the state government, the Wyoming Game and Fish Department, the State Lands Board, and the University of Wyoming (primarily the Cooperative Research Unit) participated in ferret recovery. They also had different characteristics and interests relative to each other and to other actors. In addition, some nongovernmental organizations (NGOs) participated. Ferrets were located on seven private Meeteetse-area ranches, whose operations were affected by the ferret program. Several oil and gas exploration and extraction companies operated on both private and government land in the area. There was also the small team that I assembled to conduct conservation research on ferrets, which was partially supported by a dozen local, regional, and national NGOs. Despite its early loose, informal, and changing connections, this coalition of participants nevertheless formed a system with many interdependent structural and functional properties similar to formally constituted organizations. While understanding that coalitions and organizations have many distinct features, such as different constraints and opportunities for action, this book recognizes the ferret coalition as a real entity and uses policy and organizational theory to elucidate the participants' behaviors and roles in the coalition.

These several groups represented a wide range of organizational perspectives, values, strategies, histories, cultures, and needs to manage their external environments. Patterns in perspectives and strategies began to form and diverge early in the ferret program. Differences became clearer over time as actors positioned themselves in relation to one another, carried out independent and joint activities, and created and fulfilled various roles. Two major, deeply embedded determinants of each participant's perspective were its sense of urgency about how quickly the ferret program should proceed and its definition of the geographic boundaries in which the recovery effort should occur. Some actors demonstrated little sense of urgency. The WGF coordinator spoke in terms of a fifty-plus-year program and said there was no hurry to begin. Whenever the NGO research team advocated moving ahead quickly with field studies and captive breeding, the notion was met with no response or with rejection by WGF administrators (see Carr 1986, D. Weinberg 1986). The FWS expressed no formal position on this issue at first, and thus the pace of the entire national recovery effort was set by WGF.

The geographic boundary of the ferret recovery effort varied initially, too. From the beginning the NGO research team and its supporters promoted a national perspective, using facilities and resources across the United States and ultimately reintroducing ferrets to all or nearly all states within their former range. State officials, on the other hand, focused their attention at the state level. In 1983, for example, they announced that no ferrets would leave the state for captive breeding (e.g., Carr 1986, D. Weinberg 1986) and then rejected early offers of holding and captive-breeding facilities at the National Zoo and elsewhere. Despite its appearance of territoriality, this focus of attention is understandable: state agencies exist to serve state needs and protect state interests. Nevertheless, fundamental differences in perspective on the basic elements of time and space had lasting consequences for the program's behavior.

Each participant behaved rationally according to its own assumptions and self-constructed views of the situation. In turn, each developed its own expectations based on its own understanding of reality. These differences in perspective reflected the values and cultural identity of each group. Each participant's resource holdings, experience with ferrets and ferret searches, and ferret-related problems varied, too. The histories of the participating organizations varied, as did historical relationships among them. They represented different types of organizations — government research, government regulatory, government management, private profit-making corporate, and not-for-profit research, among others. The organizational goals (or operating theories), the means of achieving those goals, and the measures of success varied among them; in addition, policy specialists have noted the potential for conflicting goals *within* organizations (e.g., Yaffee 1982, Tobin 1990). The critical issues for each organization, prompted by unique cultures, also led to different expectations and demands as well as behaviors.

Differential power holdings and uses of power were clearly visible in the strategies employed by each group over the first few years of the program. Some had power through legal mandates, some through property rights, some through their information holdings, some through their expertise, and some through the financial or political resources they commanded. Power was used strategically to persuade, control, or coerce other actors.

The participants in the ferret program were accountable to different constituencies or clients, that is, other groups or organized interests that supported, financed, or otherwise legitimized the participants. These ranged from specialized interests in limited locales to national publics. Since approval and legitimacy are matters of prime importance to all organizations — without them they cease to operate — most actors in the ferret program were highly responsive to their constituents. One major source of legitimacy is a good relationship with the press: any group with an influential contact can ensure that its views are presented favorably to the public. In the ferret program, perceived organizational legitimacy varied among the participants, as did the kind and degree of accountability to which each was subject. Another related difference among the ferret program's participants concerned the beneficiaries of each organization's activities.

Prominent Participants in Ferret Conservation

U.S. FISH AND WILDLIFE SERVICE

The U.S. Fish and Wildlife Service is a federal bureau charged with managing and conserving the nation's wildlife and inland and anadromous sport fisheries, within certain constraints relative to the states. It has long been considered, along with the National Park Service, the country's premier conservation agency. The FWS has had more than a century of responsibility for America's wildlife in managing refuges, protecting habitat, conducting research, enforcing fish and wildlife laws, providing recreational fishing, advising other agencies, and protecting endangered species (Reed and Drabelle 1984). The FWS and its predecessor, the Division of the Biological Survey, have tended historically to be conservation and game oriented (see Yaffee 1982, Reed and Drabelle 1984). The agency remains strongly committed to waterfowl management, for example. These wildlife protection goals, however, have conflicted with other mandates of the agency, such as sport hunting on many wildlife refuges and animal damage control to destroy pest species. The extermination of prairie dogs by the agency's large predator and rodent control branch is one of the main reasons ferrets are endangered (this program has since been transferred to the Department of Agriculture).

Three separate units of the FWS were involved in early ferret recovery. The Denver Regional Office (Region 6) is one of several major offices around the country that manage wildlife refuges, provide ecological services, and administer the ESA as well as handling all the other responsibilities of the agency in that region. The Montana/Wyoming Field Office in Helena, Montana, largely administered the ESA through Section 7, which requires federal agencies and all federal projects to consult with the FWS concerning possible effects on endangered species; the FWS renders a decision in the form of a "biological opinion." This brought them in close contact with many other state and federal agencies. The Denver Wildlife Research Center, based in Fort Collins, Colorado (with a field office in Sheridan, Wyoming), was a subunit of the regional office which in the late 1970s and early 1980s had contracted with the Bureau of Land Management to conduct large-scale ferret "clearance surveys" on potential coal fields. When ferrets were located in Wyoming, this unit conducted radio telemetry and other research on them. Within these three participating branches of the FWS, there were differences in outlook and expectations. Since the early years of the ferret program the FWS has been internally reorganized.

WYOMING GAME AND FISH DEPARTMENT

The Wyoming Game and Fish Department is a state agency, which, like the FWS, has certain legal and jurisdictional responsibilities for wildlife in Wyoming. Involved in the ferret program were senior administrators in Cheyenne, a Black-Footed Ferret Advisory Team (BFAT) established by the department after mid-1982 (consisting of representatives of state and federal agencies and ranchers), a ferret coordinator, a local warden and his district superiors, and, later on, field personnel.

WGF's responsibility for the state's wildlife grew from the need to protect game animals after the wholesale overexploitation by commercial hunters and poachers in the late 1800s and early 1900s (Edgerly 1983, Blair 1987). In fact, the states are credited with taking the initiative in wildlife protection. WGF has done very well by developing strong law enforcement capabilities. The department historically emphasized game management, maximizing wildlife numbers for economic reasons to serve its clientele of in-state and out-of-state hunters. The agency derives most of its income from hunting license fees and is therefore highly responsive to state hunting interests and other state concerns (see Blair 1987).

Like all organizations, WGF needed to manage its external operating environment, including bolstering public perceptions of its legitimacy, protecting its clients, and establishing a good relationship with elected officials. Perhaps as a consequence, WGF assumed a very visible role in public relations for the ferret program. The agency also had to protect its relationship with ranchers, one of the most powerful organized interests in the state. Their cooperation was needed to allow hunters access to their lands, conduct cooperative projects, and, of course, provide access to the ferrets.

As the ferret program progressed, WGF relied more and more on the Cooperative Research Unit at the University of Wyoming. This unit is a joint operation cosponsored by the U.S. Fish and Wildlife Service, Wyoming Game and Fish, and the university. The unit eventually carried out important research and survey tasks for the state.

ISU/BIOTA RESEARCH TEAM

The nongovernmental research team that I organized was formally affiliated with the Department of Biology at Idaho State University in Pocatello and with Biota Research and Consulting, Inc., of Jackson, Wyoming. The ISU/Biota research efforts grew out of my searches for ferrets in Wyoming since 1973 (supported by various NGO research and conservation groups) and Biota's research and consulting work, which included numerous searches for ferrets, some in clearance surveys for both government and private organizations. The ISU/Biota research team entered the program in part because of invitations from ranchers and WGF. This team carried out field work on the wild ferrets from 1981 to 1985, participated in numerous meetings with other organizations, and produced many popular and peer-reviewed scientific publications.

Although Biota was not legally a nonprofit organization, its participation in the ferret program was entirely funded by private grants and contributions, and all labor was volunteered. In short, it behaved like a not-for-profit group. The research team was responsible to a large number of funders and supporters, including ten local, regional, national, and international conservation organizations.

For the ISU/Biota team, legitimacy derived from recognition not only from the university and conservation communities and the public but also from scientific peers. This required that the team maintain a role for itself in the ferret coalition, stay on good terms with other participants, and satisfy its financial supporters with practical results. The team was concerned with exercising professional skills.

RANCHERS

Seven private ranches were home to black-footed ferrets; they were formally represented on BFAT beginning in mid-1982 by the rancher who worked the largest, oldest ranch with the greatest number of ferrets. The ranching community in the Meeteetse region, which stockmen and settlers first reached in the 1870s, has a proud history. Its relationship with wildlife has been mixed. On one hand, ranchers led efforts to eliminate several wildlife forms, particularly predators such as bears and wolves, which preyed on live-stock, and pests such as prairie dogs, which were believed to compete directly with livestock for forage. On the other hand, ranchers have cooperated in the protection of many big-game species, such as deer, elk, and bighorn sheep.

Ranchers' values and views were predominantly derived from the local ranch community. For the Meeteetse ranchers, legitimacy and accountability were tied to their success in the marketplace and to their families or the direc-tors of their ranch corporations; but they also paid heed to the larger ranching community and, in some cases, to the livestock industry of the state. Ranchers tended to maximize sustainable livestock production and oil/gas production, which began in the Meeteetse area in the 1950s. A critical issue of concern for them was economic efficiency and effectiveness as measured by the market, but they also wanted to be seen as cooperating, contributing partners in the ferret program.

Both state and federal agencies and the ISU/Biota team welcomed ranchers' participation in order to build local support — hence legitimacy — for ferret conservation. It seems probable that ranchers joined the effort in part because they feared that if they did not act, their interests might be infringed upon by governmental regulations, or their private activities and their use of public lands might be significantly constrained. Ranchers seemed most concerned with getting back to life as it had existed before ferrets were discovered.

Transfer of Leadership from the Federal Government to the State

National policy for endangered species management is embodied in the Endangered Species Act of 1973, and Congress designated the FWS and the National Marine Fisheries Service as the lead legal agencies in such activities. The FWS, however, transferred leadership to the State of Wyoming's Game and Fish Department shortly after the discovery of the Meeteetse ferrets. The transfer was described by Gilbert (1984:75):

> With subjects once again available as grist, the federal ferret machine com-menced grinding, the first motions being essentially political ones. In keeping with the strong states'-rights convictions of Secretary of Interior James Watt, the animals were effectively defederalized a few months after their discovery. Wyoming was encouraged to create a ferret advisory committee (on which there is one federal representative) and management of the creatures found near Meeteetse — or subsequently elsewhere in the state — was transferred from the U.S. Fish and Wildlife Service to the state body.

The force of "strong states'-rights convictions" was to play a major role in the subsequent unfolding of the ferret program. (This issue was alive and well in the 1994 Wyoming gubernatorial primary, as demonstrated by one office seeker, who claimed that "filing lawsuits against federal agencies, defying federal mandates, and other forms of conflict with the federal government would be a major focus of his administration" [Jackson 1994:A1].)

The transfer surprised some observers and raised many questions about how or if, and under what authority, Wyoming could organize, manage, and coordinate a national recovery effort. Such an effort would, by any reasonable definition, require input from many other state, national, and nongovernmental organizations and would need to be closely coordinated for decades. Although federal-state cooperation was necessary and beneficial, the wholesale transfer to the state would have worked only if the surrogate state agency responded with fidelity to the federal policy (Carr 1986, Lester 1990).

WGF acknowledged some of the challenges it faced when it stated that "critical decisions had to be made [by Wyoming] without the benefit of a national planning perspective" and that the existing federal recovery plan gave "no answers" to many key strategic and tactical questions necessary for national ferret recovery (Thorne and Oakleaf 1991:249). WGF was in the unenviable position of flying blind. Although there may have been political and public relations advantages for the agency to assume leadership, it is also possible that it was driven more by the disadvantages of not assuming leadership, since other groups would then be operating in its domain without its control. According to a top WGF official, the reasons for the transfer included recognition by the FWS that the ferrets were a population unique to Wyoming, which is responsible for its resident wildlife, and that WGF "probably was in the best position to carry out a ferret research and management program" (Strickland 1983:5). Other officials wrote that the transfer was warranted "by the site-specific nature of the recovery effort, the numerous local problems, and the willingness of WGFD to commit personnel and funding to the recovery programme" (Thorne and Oakleaf 1991:256). WGF officials quickly noted that the agency had "a very limited budget" with which to conduct needed research, management, and conservation. To compound matters, WGF had at the inception of the program few staff members experienced with ferrets, prairie dogs, or the conservation biology of small populations (such as stochastic population modeling, genetic considerations, captive breeding), and it had a limited administrative organ capable of handling a complex national program requiring joint action by multiple, interdependent participants over many years. Once the federal transfer of leadership was complete, the program's

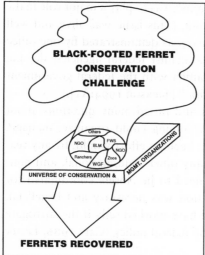

Figure 1. Ideal working arrangement of organizations involved in conserving ferrets.

Figure 2. Actual working arrangement of organizations involved in conserving ferrets.

scope and execution were limited by the conception, skills, and resources
applied to it by WGF.

There are two ways to visualize the interactions of the network of organizations involved in ferret restoration. Figure 1 shows the universe of conservation and management organizations tightly clustered and mutually sharing the
vision and the task of ferret conservation; as the program proceeded, the ferret
conservation challenge would be practically and quickly processed by this
collective. In such an arrangement, organizations would relate to one another
in ways that maximized attainment of the primary goal. Establishing goals,
inventing alternative ways to meet the goals, obtaining and allocating resources, and continuously appraising performance would be the shared responsibilities of all participants in an open, flexible, and largely democratic,
consensual process. This was an ideal for the program — a partnership. Figure
2, on the other hand, shows how the program worked in reality. It included the
same universe of organizations with the same overall task, but without a
shared vision or commitment to an interdependent partnership. Here a single
organization served as the hub with all other organizations relating to it like
spokes on a wheel. Organizations related to one another only through the hub.
The hub possessed very few resources of its own, and because it could function
only if such resources as skills, information, and money were available to it,
the hub was vitally concerned with controlling these essential items. In this

second model, the ferret challenge was processed through the much smaller aperture formed by the single hub organization.

Just as the hub's resources were significantly less than the total that would have been available from all the participating organizations, so too its constituencies and supporters were less than the total served by the other participants. For example, despite its major land holdings in the area occupied by ferrets, the Bureau of Land Management (BLM) was limited in its participation in the ferret program. Reading speculated on the reasons for this; although his description covers a later period, it also pertains to the BLM's lack of participation in the early years:

> In addition to interagency problems, several seemingly important agencies played limited roles in the BFF [black-footed ferret] reintroduction program in Wyoming. Perhaps most important of these was the Wyoming BLM. Although initial releases [of reintroduced ferrets] focused on BLM administered public lands, the BLM's role was primarily constrained to pre-release activities (i.e., assistance in preparing necessary documents). The BLM could have remained an active participant, assisting with livestock operator relations, habitat monitoring, etc. Instead, the BLM's role in Wyoming consists solely of providing financial support for prairie dog monitoring. The reasons for this limited involvement were probably 1) a lack of interest in further participation by the BLM and 2) WGF's desire to limit participation to as few individuals and agencies as possible to facilitate logistics and control. (Reading 1991:5, citations in original omitted)

Because of the enormous responsibility placed on WGF, its organizational characteristics and outlook, and its limited resources to meet that responsibility, it is possible that WGF was unable to envision or consider the first arrangement described above (figure 1). Beginning with a March 1982 meeting, for example, WGF informed all participants that they were expected to turn over their financial resources to WGF, which would assume responsibility for them as well as for all decision making and activities related to the ferret program. This probably seemed to WGF to be the necessary and logical course of action. It is likely that WGF officials tried to simplify and structure their responsibility by falling back on the cultural norms and standard operating procedures used in the past by their agency (see Westrum 1986, J. Wilson 1989). They proceeded, quite reasonably, to structure a program with themselves as the hub, holding on to decision-making authority and control of resources. This functioned to centralize and control all program elements and activities, including the scope of participation, ideas, and actions of other participants (see Lindblom 1980, Brayton 1983).

The WGF-administered ferret program seemed to be on a path laden with the pitfalls described by Fesler (1980), who observed that policy implementation can become far more complex when state governments are delegated authority and allotted (or not allotted) funds to administer national programs: failures may occur if states fall prey to inappropriate control by narrow, parochial self-interests and managerial deficiencies. Bailey and Mosher (1968:99) noted that when major national policy was administered through state and local instrumentalities by an understaffed agency with structural limitations beset by demands for clarification of its actions, "the wonder is not that mistakes are made — the wonder is that the law is implemented at all" (see also Pressman and Wildavsky 1973, Nakamura and Smallwood 1980).

The transfer was politically attractive during the term of President Reagan and tenure of Secretary Watt, although WGF had assumed strong states'-rights positions in other interagency programs, including bighorn sheep, grizzlies, and wolves (e.g., Harvey 1987, Keiter and Holscher 1990). But the FWS may not have understood or adequately considered the implications of its action for the actual work of ferret recovery. The transfer functionally subordinated the FWS to the position of a silent partner, although on several occasions the FWS retained the public appearance of coequal program management with WGF (e.g., Carr 1986, D. Weinberg 1986). Ekey (1992:8) concluded that "the FWS has abdicated its responsibility by passing along its responsibility to recover species to states, as with black-footed ferrets in Wyoming."

The ferret program began with excitement over the rediscovery of the species and widespread agreement to save ferrets. But the federal government's transfer of leadership to WGF was seen by some observers as the single most important "mistake" made in the entire ferret program (e.g., Gilbert 1984, Carr 1986). Under WGF's lead, the program seemed unable to move quickly enough to capture agreements while they existed. Nor did it create the necessary organizational machinery for a successful implementation effort. Understanding and agreements soon gave ground as the decision-making process got under way, field actions were initiated, and people, organizations, and conditions evolved. The ferret program was not as simple and straightforward a task as it may have appeared at first to many participants and observers. Part of its extreme complexity was the result of its multiple and very different — yet interdependent — organizational participants. All these factors and forces greatly reduced the possibility of quick success that most participants had originally anticipated.

The Complexity of Joint Action

If all participants agreed with the overall policy aim of recovering the ferret, then why did the program evidence so many weaknesses? Simply, participants disagreed on means, not ends. But in real life, ends and means are complexly interwoven aspects of a single unit, and distinctions between them are somewhat artificial. The ends for one participant (for example, to collect accurate data on ferret habitat) might have been the means for another participant (to protect that habitat from loss). Conflict is often about means, since means are here and now, while ends are somewhere in the future.

There are many reasons why participants oppose, or merely fail to facilitate, cooperative means to achieve a mutually shared goal. Pressman and Wildavsky (1973:99–102) listed seven reasons, and hints of all of them were evident in the ferret program. The first reason is "direct incompatibility with other commitments" (p. 99). The goal of saving ferrets may have been agreed upon by all the participants, but the means of achieving it may have been contrary to other organizational goals. For instance, ranchers throughout the West expressed concern that the discovery of black-footed ferrets might inhibit their ability to clear their lands (including undeeded public grazing lands) of prairie dogs. Although poisoning programs in the Meeteetse area were minimal in the early 1980s, ranchers did not want their options curtailed. In addition, WGF annually provided tens of thousands of dollars to the state Department of Agriculture for pest animal poisoning. WGF also permitted predator trapping to continue very near the ferret-occupied area. Another instance of direct incompatibility was the enforcement of a two-year moratorium on oil and gas field development in the ferret-occupied area by the Bureau of Land Management (with concurrence from WGF and the FWS). This raised the ire of many local Meeteetse residents, whose livelihoods depended on that industry.

A second reason for opposing cooperation may be "no direct incompatibility, but a preference for other programs" (p. 99). Some participants seemed to show higher concerns for other programs in which they were involved. Since WGF's funding and public support came largely from hunters, their attention to game management programs over nongame or endangered species programs, for instance, was understandable.

A third reason may be "simultaneous commitments to other projects" (p. 99). Clearly, all the groups that participated in the ferret program had prior commitments to other, ongoing programs; ferrets were a new concern. These simultaneous commitments limited what resources — including knowledge, skills, funds, time, attention, and information-processing abilities of agency officials — could be devoted to ferret conservation. In fact, the work loads of government agencies may become overwhelming when they are mandated to carry out increasing numbers of programs within limited budgets. As a result, too many commitments may lead bureaucrats to give inadequate attention to some key projects. Grizzly bear management in the Yellowstone region in the early 1980s, for instance, was a much higher profile, longer-term issue with potentially greater rewards for WGF. As a result, the agency may simply not have been able to turn its attention to a new program, especially when combined with officials' lack of urgency about ferret restoration.

A fourth reason for opposing or neglecting cooperation may be "dependence on others who lack a sense of urgency in the project" (p. 100). The early ferret program grew around several participants who could not act without each other, yet varied in their sense of urgency about achieving various goals. For example, WGF showed no urgency early in the program to employ captive breeding as a means to ferret restoration. Although other participants wanted an early captive-breeding effort, they were dependent on WGF to undertake this activity and constrained by its lack of a facility or inclination to build one and by its veto of the plan to move ferrets to existing facilities in other states.

A fifth reason may be "differences of opinion on leadership and proper organizational roles" (p. 100). Leadership in the ferret program was muddled or weak from the beginning, and Forrest (1987:1) exhorted the FWS "to clarify the roles of the various program participants." One major, persistent source of confusion was the roles of the federal and state governments: Which of the two had ultimate authority over decisions if the two disagreed? Despite the transfer of leadership, FWS clearly could not abandon its legal responsibilities as the nation's chief protector of wildlife. Confusion about leadership, responsibility, and accountability led to conflict that was especially apparent at the field level in the mixed-organization field team in numerous decisions regarding capturing, radio-tagging, and monitoring ferrets.

A sixth reason may be "legal and procedural differences" (p. 100). Many such differences existed between participants in the ferret program, stemming largely from the different organizational types (service, business, government). This was especially evident in the permitting process for field work, which determined what could be done to the ferrets, by whom, and when (direct observation, prey studies, habitat surveys, live-trapping, attachment of radio collars, inoculations, and transport of ferrets within Wyoming and to other states). Once in the field, some participants relied on professional experience and judgment, while others were bound to clear most of their decisions with distant superiors along a chain of authority.

A seventh reason may be "agreement coupled with lack of power" (p. 101). There was agreement among some participants, for instance, to undertake captive breeding at an early date, but their collective power was insufficient to sway the lead agency.

Conclusions

By necessity, the program to recover ferrets included several governmental and nongovernmental organizations. No one of these organizations could have fulfilled all the needs of the program during its first few years. The whole depended on the lawful authority and management of the agencies, on the expertise of the field teams, on the accord of the landowners, on the funding of both governmental and nongovernmental supporters, and on the willingness of these and all other groups to cooperate. Participants acted under varying legal, professional, economic, organizational, or ethical norms that were clearly different for each group and changed somewhat over time. Participants also varied in their sense of urgency for ferret recovery and the geographic focus for various activities, including captive breeding. Initially, the wealth of knowledge, skills, and resources available for ferret recovery offered promise for a model program. In the critical early years, however, the need was not recognized nor the mechanisms created to meld these varied, interdependent groups into a well-integrated coalition for timely, effective decision making and cooperative yet role-differentiated action.

No one in the coalition demonstrated an explicit awareness of the organizational demands of a task like saving ferrets. No one seemed to possess a professional knowledge of what organizational designs might meet those needs, what management and leadership functions the organization must perform to succeed, or what roles each participant could or should constructively contribute. Each group seemed to be caught up in immediate concerns, and each responded as opportunities and threats arose in ways that seemed best to serve its immediate interests. Some of these "satisficing" responses were helpful in meeting the task of ferret recovery; others were not. Lindblom (1980) called this mode of operation "muddling through" or, as it applies in this and many other cases, "still muddling, but not yet through." The effect of this less than ideal approach can be seen by examining how information — that is, intelligence — about the ferrets was generated and used. The next chapter looks at the use of intelligence and the timeliness of some key decisions.

3

Intelligence Failures and Delays
Two Program Pathologies

Two major kinds of problems plague the decision-making process in complex programs. Intelligence failures, most often associated with national defense policy, are perceived breakdowns in the system by which strategically important information is collected, analyzed and understood, and acted on. Intelligence is needed to predict or warn authorities of events, to judge the results of ongoing operations, and to plan policies and forces for future "deterrence and defense." Richard Betts (1978) noted that intelligence failures can be conceptualized in three ways. One is that mistakes are bound to happen in any human endeavor and must be kept in perspective (although it is difficult to measure the rate of success to failure in intelligence systems). Intelligence failures can also be viewed as "pathologies of communication," as breakdowns in the "process of amassing timely data, communicating them to decision makers, and impressing the latter with the validity or relevance of the information" (pp. 62–63) — the implication being that simple procedural changes can correct the problems. A third way of understanding intelligence failures is as "paradoxes of perception," which Betts described as "unresolvable trade-offs and dilemmas," whereby fixing one part of the intelligence system only creates problems in other parts. All three of these conceptions can help illuminate two intelligence failures, both with drastic consequences, that occurred in the ferret program.

Delays are another common problem in implementation. Like intelligence failures, the causes, methods, outcomes, and effects of delays can be difficult to untangle from the larger web of decisions that make up any complex program. Program delays, in fact, can be hard to separate from program failures: at what point does a delay become a failure? Certainly, as Jeffrey Pressman and Aaron Wildavsky (1973:116) pointed out, "No genius is required to make programs operative if we don't care how long they take, how much money they require, how often the objectives are altered or the means for obtaining them are changed." Yet many programs have an inherent urgency, a brief window of opportunity, that demands timely action, and timeliness must be considered one of the criteria for judging the success or adequacy of programs.

In this chapter I focus on a few major examples of intelligence failures and delays that significantly weakened the ferret program's ability to recover the species in a timely, efficient manner. Two intelligence failures and their probable causes are examined, the structure of intelligence failures and barriers to improvements are outlined, and suggestions are offered for avoiding such failures. I also take a look at the delays in captive breeding and offer a model to explain them.

Intelligence Failures

All decision making depends on the use of information (Lasswell 1955, 1956), that is, "acquisition, analysis, and *appreciation* of relevant data" (Betts 1978:61; emphasis in original). Without good intelligence, estimation of problems and selection and implementation of successful solutions are unlikely (Brewer and deLeon 1983). Failure to gather or use intelligence in problem solving is common. Major mistakes are more often made by decision makers and policy makers who consume intelligence than by the professionals who produce it. The reason for this, according to Betts (1978), is that decision makers operate under premises that constrict their perceptions, leading to "selective inattention," a kind of "boundedness" and outright "blindness" in some instances (Lasswell 1971a, Schön 1971, 1983). In Betts' words (p. 61), "intelligence failure is political and psychological more often than organizational." In addition, heavy administrative workloads limit insightful reflection on complex situations. Basically, intelligence failure is a problem of misperception, miscalculation, and misjudgment.

Two major disasters rooted in intelligence failures stood out, both in 1985. First was the catastrophic loss of most ferrets at Meeteetse, in which mortality in the wild was so great and so rapid that extinction seemed inevitable. Second was the death of the first six captured ferrets that were to serve as the nucleus of the breeding population. The necessary intelligence, generated by the field teams or based on earlier experience, was in place in both instances, yet little was done by decision makers to minimize the losses until the situations were critical (Maguire 1991). Falling calamitously back to back, these two intelligence failures raised profound questions in the minds of many participants and observers about the ability of the program and of the agencies entrusted with it to save endangered species.

INTELLIGENCE FAILURE #1:
NEAR EXTINCTION OF THE WILD MEETEETSE FERRETS

Events in the summer of 1985 unfolded like a nightmare. In late 1984, 129 ferrets had been counted at Meeteetse. But in late June 1985, two people from the FWS Montana/Wyoming Field Office and the ISU/Biota team did an initial survey: "We looked for about three or four hours. Neither of us saw a ferret. I think that night Steve and I about cried. It was like walking into a mortuary. We knew something was starting then" (cited in Zimmerman 1986:6). A catastrophic decline in the population was documented over the next few months (Forrest et al. 1988). The total field survey effort that summer, in both hours and days, exceeded that expended in each of the previous years, and so surveyors felt confident of their results (Forrest et al. 1985a, 1985b). The FWS Wildlife Research Center carried out 43 percent of the survey work, the ISU/Biota team 39 percent, WGF 11 percent, and others 7 percent. The ferret decline was real, rapid, and unlikely to end until the last ferret died unless something were done quickly. Verbal reports from the field were issued nearly daily to federal and state officials. The ISU/Biota team made a written interim report to WGF on August 6, summarizing the July survey of 94 percent of the known ferret-occupied area. It showed a substantial decline in ferret numbers from 1984 to 1985 on all prairie dog colonies except one. One large key colony showed an 89 percent decline, on the basis of search efforts equivalent to those of previous years. The total decline was estimated at 68 percent (Forrest et al. 1985b). The cause was unknown at the time, but one or more diseases, including plague, were suspected (Clark et al. 1985a, 1985b).

In May, a month before the major decline was detected, a volunteer with the FWS Wildlife Research Center had identified sylvatic plague in the prairie dog population. This disease persists in wildlife (especially rodents) and sometimes flares up in epidemics that may devastate populations within short periods. When prairie dogs are affected, ferrets may also succumb to the disease but are more often lost because their food supply dies out (see Maguire and Clark 1985). By early August, it was estimated that plague had destroyed more than

13 percent of the prairie dog complex at Meeteetse (D. Biggins, 1986, personal communication). Also in May, agency officials had agreed, after considerable urging, to bring six ferrets into captivity under WGF management as the foundation of a captive breeding program *if an adequate surplus of young were found in the wild,* although the number that constituted an adequate surplus was unspecified (Thorne 1987, Miller et al. 1996).

The August 6 interim report and its cover letter noted that the ferrets were more vulnerable to extinction than ever before and predicted that even more ferrets could be lost to the unknown factor or factors within the next few weeks. The report pointed out pitfalls of the wishful thinking that seemed to underlie agency officials' lack of action:

> At the best, the reduced ferret population will eventually recover with mini-mal management, retarding recovery efforts for the next few years because few animals will be available for captive rearing efforts. At the worst, ferret numbers will continue to decline potentially to extinction. We suspect local extinctions of ferrets probably occurred at times in the past with the disrup-tion of their local prey base. We do not have the luxury of awaiting such a potential outcome. We must guard against acting on only best-outcome as-sumptions. (Clark et al. 1985a:2)

The cover letter recommended that, to corroborate this information, "a writ-ten assessment of the ferret/prairie dog situation be called for *immediately*" from the FWS Wildlife Research Center field team leader and also from WGF's own field personnel (Clark et al. 1985a:2). There is no evidence that this assessment was requested within the next few weeks by administrators or carried out either by WGF or the FWS. Accompanying the ISU/Biota report were six pages of recommendations, including steps to protect the declining prairie dog population as well as the ferret population and ideas for organizing the program more appropriately for better intelligence to clarify causes for the ferret decline. There were also suggestions to institute more intense field moni-toring immediately, to identify the cause of the ferret decline, and to bring in additional expertise in this time of crisis.

The letter, report, and recommendations — directed at obtaining more reli-able intelligence and closing feedback loops between field data and decision makers — seemed to fall on deaf ears within WGF and the FWS. But when this same intelligence reached the press, the declining ferret population and the implications of the loss were quickly reported. Also noted were the growing discrepancies between, on one hand, the field-generated intelligence on the ferrets' status and recommended conservation actions and, on the other hand, state and federal government assessment of the intelligence and of the overall situation. Two sets of recriminating articles appeared. Newspaper headlines from mid-July 1985 to spring 1986 highlighted the dichotomy: "State says ferret scare unnecessary" (Ontiveroz 1985), "Black-footed ferret 'plagued' by columnists" (Skinner 1985), "Ferrets, fleas, and false alarm" (Audubon Magazine 1985), "Wyoming expert doubts ferret-decline report" (Howard 1985), "Ferrets safe from disease" (Cody Enterprise 1985), and "Federal officials praise G&F [WGF] for ferret efforts" (White 1985a). In sharp contrast were other stories: "Last ferrets are dying while government fails to act" (Bauman 1985), "Ferrets nearly extinct? It's too late for 'I-told-you-so'" (Bauman 1986), "Ferret colony edges closer to extinction" (Marston 1986), "G&F mishandled recovery of ferret" (Hampton 1986), and "Wyoming was urged to handle ferrets better" (Krumm 1986). Finally, as a result of the agency's decision in May and mounting public pressure, six black-footed ferrets were captured between September 12 and October 11, 1985, by the joint program led by WGF.

In the midst of the controversy, on October 11, the ISU/Biota field team released its final survey report to WGF and FWS Regional Office officials. The cover letter stressed that "ferret numbers continue to decline precipitously, further establishing the downward trend identified in our 'Interim Report' to you of August 5 and 6, 1985. . . . We feel that the alarming decline in ferret numbers, compounded by plague, represents a sincere threat to the Meeteetse population as well as to the success of ferret recovery" (Clark et al. 1985b) The report itself concluded that "these data indicate a strong immediate need to evaluate current conservation and recovery strategies at Meeteetse" (Forrest et al. 1985b:14). But both WGF and FWS Regional Office officials still seemed to underappreciate and discount the field data, even though their own personnel had helped gather it. Publicly (even in its own publication), WGF dismissed the intelligence as erroneous: "The whole thing is an overblown crisis. We are doing everything possible to protect the ferrets. And we still cannot see these ferrets as being in serious danger" (Ontiveroz 1985:1); "There is no doubt that fewer ferrets have been seen this year, but the situation is not as bad as the newspapers indicated" (Skinner 1985:38). By mid-October nearly all the wild ferrets were dead.

It is difficult to understand the agencies' dismissal, considering the high stakes — survival or extinction for a species and acclaim or condemnation for the agencies' handling of the program. The field data were consistent, the research effort had been comprehensive, and the conclusion seemed unassailable. Moreover, prior to the catastrophe, WGF staff had written that "diseases are a profound threat to any animal whose population is as small and self-contained as the ferrets'," with specific mention of canine distemper (Thorne

1984:11). Only a decade earlier, captive ferrets from the South Dakota population had died of canine distemper contracted through inoculations, and its 100 percent fatality rate was known to participants in the Wyoming program. In addition, conservation biology theory and direct observations of small populations had all led to the same conclusion—that disease can at any time devastate small populations (e.g., May 1986). Yet with these several lines of intelligence in place and with enormous risks, officials maintained that ferrets had persisted at Meeteetse to the present and would, therefore, survive well into the future (Wertz 1984, Wildlife Conservation International 1986). No decisions were made or actions taken to monitor individual animals closely enough to learn whether they were dying or dispersing; to find the new locations, if the animals were dispersing; to collect and autopsy bodies, if the animals were dying, so that the causes of their deaths could be identified; and to take countermeasures against any detectable disease (if possible, in the field) or to bring all the surviving animals into protective captivity for quarantine or treatment.

INTELLIGENCE FAILURE #2: LOSS OF THE FIRST SIX CAPTIVE FERRETS

The second major intelligence failure resulted in the deaths of the six ferrets taken into captivity between mid-September and mid-October. All six were housed in close proximity in a WGF holding facility; it is believed that two carried canine distemper from Meeteetse and transmitted it to the four healthy individuals (Thorne 1985, personal communication; Miller et al. 1996). All six died between October 22, 1985, and January 6, 1986. Dick Randall (1986:9) reported on the disaster:

> Dr. [Tom] Thorne [the WGF veterinarian largely in charge of the facility and animal care] looks back sadly on events of the last few months. "No one is more disappointed than I am about what's happened," he says, "but it doesn't do any good to go around finger-pointing when it's so precarious right now. Along with others, I recommended against capturing any ferrets last year. At the time, I thought that would have been the wrong recommendation."
>
> Wyoming has taken a lot of heat for placing the first six ferrets captured last fall in one enclosure, and thereby exposing them all to distemper. . . . Critics say experienced hands with captive animals would have known better. "Every zoo in the country," says [one zoo authority], "when it has precious animals like our snow leopards, for instance, places them all over the country. Feline distemper or some other disease could come in and knock out the group. Even a house cat walking through could cause a disaster. So you separate animals." WGF staff members admit that the ferrets' prospects would probably be better today if the breeding program had been started a year to two ago. . . .

> We're at a point now where our options with wild ferrets have been pretty
> much foreclosed by this disease.

Although quarantines and standard animal husbandry techniques were widely
known, WGF held one fatally wrong assumption which led them to house all
six ferrets together: "I thought, well, they're all from the same population, so I
didn't isolate them. It's something I wish I hadn't done" (a WGF official cited
in Peterson 1985:30).

These deaths in WGF's facility beginning in late October finally and firmly
caught administrators' attention. It also permitted positive identification of
the unknown mortality factor as canine distemper, which prompted agency
officials to admit that the wild population was indeed undergoing a real decline and that action was necessary. Official press releases indicated the change
in the stories: "Disease threatens rare ferret colony, says G&F" (White 1985b)
and "Ferrets' future hangs by a slender thread" (Daily Times 1986). Despite
this dramatic about-face, there was no official acknowledgment that administrators had been terribly wrong only days or weeks earlier, based on essentially
the same intelligence (plus the identity of the previously unknown disease
factor). Although regret was expressed, there apparently was no retroactive
examination of the intelligence failure as such. Agency officials proceeded as if
it had been merely a case of bad luck, as if they had made the best decisions
possible from the available information.

With the wild population rapidly dying and all captive ferrets dead or dying,
the next step was to capture more wild ferrets. A second group of six was
brought in during the last week of October. This time the ferrets were housed
separately. "We're doing what, in hindsight, we should have done in the first
place," said one WGF official (cited in Peterson 1985:30). The year closed
with the second group of six ferrets alive in captivity, apparently all healthy,
and an estimated five or six ferrets remaining in the wild at Meeteetse (possibly as few as four; Miller 1996, personal communication). Recovery looked
bleak, to say the least. A world-renowned group of experts, the Captive Breeding Specialists Group of the International Union for the Conservation of Nature and Natural Resources (IUCN), estimated that the six captive ferrets were
unlikely to reproduce successfully. All the remaining wild animals were also
highly likely to be lost, according to previous field studies at Meeteetse, which
showed that most ferrets die over winter, computer modeling on the prospects
for the few surviving wild animals, and expert opinion. If these assessments
proved to be correct, the ferret would be functionally extinct. This was enough
for Chuck Carr (1986:7) to conclude at the time that the Endangered Species
Act had "failed the ferret." And Pamela Parker (1989:ix) marveled, "How we

came to have, and nearly lose, not just one, but two chances to avoid the extinction of such a prominent species is a remarkable story. How banana peels of biology and bureaucracy could slip the ferret to the edge of extinction despite active support of the public backed by the power of the Endangered Species Act is yet another wonder."

CAUSES OF INTELLIGENCE FAILURES

Three major difficulties obstruct the good collection and use of intelligence. But as Betts (1978:72) pointed out, "None of these three barriers are accidents of structure or process. They are inherent in the nature of intelligence and the dynamics of work" and are therefore extremely difficult to eradicate. The first barrier is the "ambiguity of evidence": "It is the role of intelligence to extract certainty from uncertainty and to facilitate coherent decision in an incoherent environment" (p. 69). But to accomplish this task, intelligence analysts must extrapolate from inadequate, contradictory, too little, or too much evidence, often with too little time, without oversimplifying or confusing the picture for decision makers. Faced with ambiguous and fragmentary data, analysts too often indulge in wishful thinking or rely on intuition or ideology to make their interpretations.

During the summer of 1985, as the ferret population was decreasing by about 50 percent each month, agency administrators dismissed the indicators that a major problem was unfolding before them. The Meeteetse field data were considered very reliable by the experienced field personnel who collected it but suspect by agency officials, who indicated that at times they were deluged with more information than they could process (Williams 1986). The developing intelligence contradicted assumptions that officials held, and sheer disbelief made it easy to discount the intelligence. Although the loss of about 150 ferrets was documented from late 1984 through fall 1985, the fact that a few ferrets persisted was held up by WGF as evidence that the population was not in jeopardy. (Indeed, positive information can be dredged up in almost any situation, regardless of performance.) The agency failed to recognize that in some instances a single intelligence failure can lead to overall disaster. Using only the positive information, or overemphasizing it, both reflected and contributed to wishful thinking. Closely associated with this phenomenon was probably oversimplification, or failing to grasp the complexity of the situation. These seemed to converge to create a highly misleading picture of how well the ferrets were doing and how well the program was functioning. Moreover, as Zimmerman (1986) reported, when government officials finally realized there was a disaster in the making, the time that they had previously said could be used for a rescue had largely gone.

Compare this case to official reactions to reports of ozone thinning over Antarctica in the late 1970s and early 1980s. Westrum (1988:5–6) pointed out that, in that case, data "were *withheld* because of their anomalous character," satellite computer programs "had been *programmed to ignore*" a certain range of measurements, and "*expectations* led to structural pressures against the flow of information" (emphasis added). Westrum's explanation of such situations — "The norms of science dictate caution about the transmission of anomalous results" (p. 5) — is a fair description of what happened in the ferret program.

The second barrier to analytical accuracy in use of intelligence is "ambivalence of judgment." This is a question of how to assess less than conclusive evidence, how to be honest, accurate, and neither overly cautious nor overly rash. Such ambivalence was shown in WGF's alternative explanations of the events of 1985 — that low numbers were a normal annual fluctuation, or that ferrets had dispersed elsewhere and were, by implication, fine, or that the field methods and data were in error (e.g., Williams 1986, Prendergast 1986): "The Wyoming administrators adopted the most sanguine view of the situation, one that coincidentally permitted them to do nothing. Ferret numbers seemed to be dropping because the young were dispersing from their parents' territories, officials declared. Confronted with evidence that in the previous three years ferret young had not dispersed so early, the administrators simply dismissed the dispersal research" (D. Weinberg 1986:63) Administrators seemed to have assumed that because the tiny population had survived the ravages of diseases, predation, and changes in land use over the previous decades, no special management was needed now (such as ongoing disease monitoring in the wild). They seemed to cling to premises that hindered learning about their own intelligence failures or adapting the program to the rapidly changing circumstances.

Intelligence and policy are closely linked here, as are analysis and advocacy: discussions about intelligence rapidly turn into debates about policy options. The decision-making process in the ferret program does not lend itself to an easy separation between intelligence failures and policy failures. The evaluation of intelligence in this case seems to have been colored by the biases of past assumptions (for example, states' rights and bureaucratic management), and administrators seemed suspicious of any intelligence that exposed the limitations of their standpoint.

The third barrier is organizational structure and procedures. Authority structures and hierarchy, centralization, specialization, and the allocation of time and resources all constrain an organization's ability to process information. Betts (1978:67) added the related problem of "the dominance of operational authorities [those groups who respond to perceived threats] over intelligence specialists, and the trade-off between objectivity and influence. Operators have more influence in decision making but are less capable of unbiased interpretation of evidence because they have a vested interest in the success of their operations." In the ferret case, WGF, the agency that was responsible for an official response, was clearly dominant over the field researchers (intelligence gatherers) in terms of public visibility, legitimacy (as perceived both by the agency itself and the public), legal authority, and power. As a result, the agency's interpretation took precedence and the agency did nothing to respond to the threat until September 1985. Officials appeared to indulge their preference not to take animals into captivity and to justify their inaction by issuing overly optimistic assessments. They criticized the intelligence gatherers as "alarmists" and questioned their integrity, objectivity, motives, and professional qualifications privately and publicly (Williams 1986).

This is a common problem where intelligence evaluation is tightly coupled with operational authority and action—that is, where the same people are responsible both for interpreting intelligence and for acting on it. Those who have a stake in carrying out a program in a certain way may be biased in how they interpret intelligence. When WGF took over leadership of the program, it was in charge of interpretation, operations—everything, in fact, but intelligence gathering, for which it was still dependent on the research teams (ISU/Biota and the FWS Wildlife Research Center). There are numerous examples of disastrous military campaigns in which intelligence assessments and operational responses were tightly linked. The problems of this arrangement in a military context were summarized by Betts (1978:67), and they appear equally valid for the ferret case:

> In most cases of mistakes in predicting . . . or assessing operations, the inadequacy of critical data or their submergence in a viscous bureaucracy were at the best the proximate causes of failure. The ultimate causes of error in most cases have been wishful thinking, cavalier disregard of professional analysts, and, above all, the premises and preconceptions of policy makers. Fewer fiascoes have occurred in the stages of acquisition and presentation of facts than in the stages of interpretation and response. Producers of intelligence have been culprits less often than consumers. Policy perspectives tend to constrain objectivity, and authorities often fail to use intelligence properly.

Many aspects of organizational process also confound good analysis of intelligence. Betts observed that "in a crisis, both data and policy outpace analysis" (p. 68). The time to scrutinize data is usually limited, as is the money for additional collection or analysis and the expertise to provide in-depth analyses. Good analysis may also be inhibited by bureaucrats' tendencies to pass decisions up the hierarchy, centralize decision making, and use fixed criteria in decision making. Unfortunately, reorganization or procedural reforms to improve the use of intelligence are difficult and may not necessarily eliminate intelligence failures. Day-to-day business may override mechanisms that are set up to prevent the rare catastrophic intelligence failure so that the potential for intelligence failures persists. WGF's failure to go outside the agency for expert consultation, its wishful thinking, and its basic premises about the status of the ferrets and the unreliability of the field researchers all led to a significant breakdown of its intelligence system.

AVOIDING INTELLIGENCE FAILURES

Because of the formidable barriers and inherent paradoxes in intelligence systems, there are no quick and easy resolutions, but some recommendations have been made. Betts (1978) reviewed six common suggestions to avoid intelligence failures. First, assume the worst and act on it. Second, institutionalize multiple advocacy so that one set of preconceptions will not totally dominate decision making. Third, streamline the intelligence process and spend more resources on analysis. Fourth, institutionalize dissent by assigning one or more people to play the devil's advocate. Fifth, if failures stem from dishonest reporting or the intellectual mediocrity of analysts, penalize the former and replace the latter. And sixth, "force decision makers to make explicit rather than unconscious choices, to exercise judgment rather than engage in automatic perception, and to enhance their awareness of their own preconceptions" (p. 83). Agency officials in the ferret program obviously did not assume the worst and act on it, nor is there any evidence that they fostered devil's advocates within their ranks. WGF stifled dissenting voices by controlling meeting agendas, shouting down contrary views, not recording other views in meeting minutes, discrediting the ISU/Biota research team publicly, and other means; evidence of these is given in later chapters.

It is only from honest self-examination that mistaken preconceptions and unexamined assumptions can be identified and corrected. The uniformity of WGF and FWS behavior over several years suggests that neither agency conducted such self-examinations. There are many possible reasons why this did not happen, among them one put forth by Betts (1978:83), who observed that "intelligence consumers are political men who have risen by being more decisive than reflective, more aggressive than introspective, and confident as much as cautious." And he warned that this kind of cognitive change is extremely unlikely. Indeed, he concluded, and experience tells us, that none of these remedies will be panaceas for reforming the intelligence process in programs like ferret recovery; each has intrinsic potential dangers of making the process too cumbersome, insensitive, routinized, or costly. Ultimately, ambiguities and ambivalence can never be completely overcome, and the human limitations of perception, predisposition, and time can be only marginally improved. Agency officials charged with protecting endangered species will certainly make mistakes and must bear responsibility for them. Still, there are two ideals to strive for: "anything that facilitates dissent and access to authorities by intelligence producers, and anything that facilitates skepticism and scrutiny by consumers" (p. 88).

Delays

There were clearly different perspectives from the beginning of the program on if, when, where, and how to begin the captive breeding of ferrets. One view judged that the time was right in 1983 or 1984, while the other considered it premature. The ISU/Biota team, backed by a larger NGO conservation community, repeatedly urged government authorities to begin to establish a second, buffer colony of ferrets to protect against disaster. WGF's veterinarian, Tom Thorne, was also an early proponent of captive breeding, but only in Wyoming (Miller et al. 1996). Because of bureaucratic delays such recommendations were ignored: "Time passed. The field work continued. Searches for ferrets were begun in other states. Litters of ferrets were recorded at Meeteetse. Data were published. Letters were written. No progress was made toward captive breeding during 1982 and 1983" (Carr 1986:5–6).

By late 1984, when the wild ferret population stood at a high of 129, "there didn't seem to be a better chance to get a captive breeding program started" (D. Weinberg 1986:64). And it was in this year that WGF began moving in this direction. A committee, including "experts in zoo management and captive breeding," was set up to develop a captive-breeding plan to present to the Black-Footed Ferret Advisory Team (Wyoming Game and Fish 1984). But it wasn't until January 1985 that WGF was granted permission by the Game and Fish Commission to begin captive breeding contingent on funding from FWS and private contributions to build a facility and operate the program in Wyoming (Wyoming Game and Fish 1985). It was apparently not until May 1985 that the decision was made to do so later that year.

In December 1983, the ISU/Biota team had issued a report, "Black-Footed Ferret Recovery: A Discussion of Some Options and Considerations," with a cover letter asking government agencies to convene a meeting soon to discuss captive-breeding options (Richardson et al. 1986). Carr (1986:5–6) described these events in 1984:

Finally, at the request of the nongovernmental conservation community, a meeting was called by the Wyoming Game and Fish Department in the spring of 1984 in Cheyenne. Jim Doherty and I were invited to participate. The meeting would include field biologists, veterinarians, and administrators representing federal, state, and private agencies, essentially the extended network of people responsible for the survival of the black-footed ferret.

Sure enough, captive management became the focus of the meeting just as soon as the introductory material was set aside....

The 1983 figure [population count] and the abundance of youngsters every fall relative to the number of adults, were strong indications that ferrets could be captured without jeopardizing the Meeteetse colony. Thinking back to that large gathering in Cheyenne, I recall a universal consensus that establishment of one or more captive colonies was of utmost urgency. The chief justifications were (a) to provide a strategic cushion in the event of a disease—an epizootic—struck the little Meeteetse population and (b) to provide, in the course of time, the stock for recolonization of suitable ferret habitat. It was sound, if belated, reasoning. The only dissension came in deciding how to do it....

At Cheyenne we began to see the hang-up on captive breeding as an element in the survival process. State officials, while concurring with the captive propagation tactic, announced firmly that no ferrets would leave Wyoming to achieve the purpose. Simultaneously they declared that their own Sybille Canyon Wildlife Research Unit was unsatisfactory as a captive breeding facility, an ironic viewpoint as things turned out; and they concluded that federal and/or private agencies should pay for the cost of building and staffing a proper facility in Wyoming.

In view of the availability of well-equipped, well-staffed, well-funded facilities in several locations around the U.S., this pronouncement by the lead agency for ferret recovery was met with consternation by both federal and private nonprofit organization representatives. The 1984 capture season (September–October, when young of the year are weaned and dispersing) came and went, but the Cheyenne impasse prevailed despite the probabilistic certainty of the consequences.

David Weinberg (1986:64) recorded that nothing happened in the summer of 1984, "and so the arguments were repeated, this time more emphatically, at a ferret workshop held in Laramie in September." The chief of the ecology branch of the FWS Wildlife Research Center recalled: "At the April, 1984, ferret meeting in Cheyenne and the workshop in Laramie that September, ... I spoke for captive breeding" (cited in Randall 1986:9). Another FWS representative, affiliated with the FWS captive-breeding center in Maryland and experienced in trying to captive-breed ferrets, also spoke:

> Many captive-breeding experts and field biologists were urging that some of the young be taken into captivity. The state said, "We don't have enough

biological data to know what percentage we're losing." Some of us replied, "We agree, but based on other small-mammal populations, we're probably losing 50 or 60 percent of the young of the year." We said we felt some animals could be taken in without jeopardizing the wild population. (Cited in Randall 1986:9)

"That was the last anyone heard about captive breeding that year," reported Weinberg (1986:65). WGF's delays continued: "The urgency to captivate [*sic*] ferrets has been overemphasized. If the concern is to avert unforeseen demise of the Meeteetse ferret population, then the captivation of ferrets can be accomplished when, and if, such an emergency occurs" (WGF official cited in Zimmerman 1986:6). Carr (1986:6) reported that "in May of 1985 a decision was made by state and federal officers to attempt to capture ferrets in October, provided the scheduled summer counts showed an acceptable but unspecified surplus. Sybille Canyon was agreed upon as a holding facility, but no specific breeding facility was identified."

This only partly answered the nagging questions about captive breeding as part of an overall restoration strategy. Would enough animals be taken into captivity to provide a viable breeding nucleus? Would the program pursue the recovery goal aggressively and increase numbers rapidly, or would it remain small, cautious, and experimental in nature? What would be the fate of the remaining wild animals? And then, of course, in 1985 the Meeteetse ferret population did not show the "acceptable but unspecified surplus."

Why did WGF, with the support of the FWS Regional Office, not initiate captive breeding a year or more earlier? It is necessary to review some of the answers that program participants and observers offered to this question at the time. Wyoming officials claimed — after the events of 1985 — "that they have never been against captive breeding as a way to enhance wild populations" (D. Weinberg 1986:65). Randall (1986:9), however, thought that "in trying to understand WGF's delay in acting, it helps to recall that it is a state agency oriented toward preserving animals in the wild, with no previous experience in captive breeding." One WGF official said that the state "had a 'commitment' to leaving the animals in the wild if possible. 'We manage wild populations. . . . We do not manage zoo populations here'" (Prendergast 1986:40). In an article about the legacy of Bill Morris, who became director of WGF in late 1985, Neal (1995:E4) described the decision that faced policy makers:

The matter was debated by the department's top staff in a larger atmosphere of harsh criticism against the department. Environmental groups and some scientists were howling at the department for not having brought in some of the ferrets earlier.

No one at the department knew if they could even breed the little weasels successfully once they were brought in. . . .

In an interview with the *Star-Tribune* after he retired, Morris said the decision was the most difficult he had to make as director.

"I have no compunction about killing an animal," he said, "but I have a helluva time putting one in a cage."

Weinberg (1986:65) offered a third observation about WGF's motives:

They simply resented the pressure that they were getting. "We were being stampeded," says [one state official]. "The pressure was on and we weren't going to be pushed into it." . . . Other state officials offer a variety of reasons for not pursuing the idea that year. They didn't feel that the ferrets were in any imminent danger; besides, institutions, such as the National Zoological Park, that offered to take ferrets were not capable of managing a large captive breeding program for these animals. . . . [One state official added,] "No one, but no one, suggested taking ferrets for nonselfish reasons."

May (1986:14) noted that "although this [selfish motives] may be true, it may reveal more about the accuser than the accused." Weinberg (1986:65–66) went on:

In fact, it may have been the state of Wyoming that was being selfish. For, as officials acknowledge, they never seriously considered allowing ferrets to leave the state. "We'd have no control over them," [an official] says. Instead, Wyoming wanted to build its own captive breeding facility, and at the time there was no money to do so. . . . To [him] and other Wyoming managers, the prospect of pulling together a complex, controlled breeding program for black-footed ferrets in less than a year may have seemed overly ambitious or even impossible. Wyoming is a conservative, fiercely independent state whose public officials are certainly not quicker than other bureaucrats to introduce change. They didn't believe captive breeding was an urgent matter — even though their own wildlife veterinarian . . . had warned them from the beginning that canine distemper could devastate the Meeteetse ferrets. At any rate, they were willing to take a slight gamble, which they just happened to lose. This outcome raises yet another question — whether local people, who may not see that sending some ferrets to Virginia [to the National Zoo] may be far superior to letting them die in Wyoming, should be running endangered species programs.

"It was a missed opportunity," concluded a FWS Regional official (cited in D. Weinberg 1986:66) regarding the captive breeding of ferrets in 1984. Nevertheless, the director of the FWS Endangered Species Office publicly declared that the FWS had "no reservation about the decision in 1981 to give Wyoming the lead role" (cited in Randall 1986:9).

By late 1986, a strange twist crept into WGF's perspective: it now wanted credit for initiating and leading the captive breeding effort (Wyoming Game and Fish Department 1987). In response Steve Forrest (1987:2) noted:

> There is no evidence, either in BFAT minutes, the Wyoming Research Plan of 1982, public press releases, or my recollections that Wyoming ever proposed, supported, or "took the initiative" . . . for captive propagation until 1984, long after others had forced their hand. In fact, it is my recollection that opposition to captive propagation from Wyoming was so intense that no ferrets were removed in 1984, when such an action could have been critical to survival of the species. I do not think it should be the position of the U.S. Fish and Wildlife Service to offer a revisionist history of the facts.

Delays occurred in other aspects of the program, too, as illustrated by two brief examples. (See also Miller et al. 1996.) The IUCN's Captive Breeding Specialist Group first entered the picture after ferrets were taken into captivity, and team members urged WGF to breed the ferrets as quickly as possible:

> Acutely aware of the importance of time, they wanted to move quickly. When reproduction is delayed, genetic diversity dwindles. Additionally, each new generation in captivity can further erode behavioral and physiological traits necessary for survival in the wild.
>
> Wyoming, however, maintained its cautious approach. For example, a technique using vaginal cytology to determine when a female black-footed ferret was in estrus had been developed 10 years earlier by Jim Carpenter at the U.S. Fish and Wildlife Service's Patuxent Wildlife Research Center, Patuxent, yet Wyoming did not employ it in 1986. At the start of the 1987 breeding season, the technique was used only once a week. By March, when time was slipping away with little evidence of potential reproduction, Wyoming began using it several times a week. Knowing when females were in estrus was critical to the success of captive breeding. That knowledge, and the arrival of the wild-caught adult male from Meeteetse on 1 March 1987, produced the first living litter of captive black-footed ferrets, a grand event. (Miller et al. 1996:99–100)

In another case of delay, Miller (1992:8) noted that the 1987 recovery plan called for use of an experimental approach to learn how best to restore ferrets to the wild. He described a significant delay in this process:

> Montana was scheduled to reintroduce black-footed ferrets in 1992 and wanted to compare conditioned animals to cage-raised animals. Wyoming, however, through its governor, requested Montana to delay that state's 1992 black-footed ferret reintroduction until 1993. Wyoming wanted to test the effects of telemetry on survival and claimed they needed 40 animals in each group (telemetered and nontelemetered). That would require the whole stock

of black-footed ferrets available for reintroduction. It was an election year, and black-footed ferrets were a political issue (because many ranchers dislike prairie dogs and endangered species), so the governor of Montana readily agreed. The delay also gave Montana, in its governor's words, "time to make concrete strides toward control [poison] of prairie dogs to the 1988 levels as they have agreed to do." He added, "I am appreciative that we could have extra time granted by Wyoming's proposal to see results in this area." (Citations in original omitted)

A MODEL FOR PROGRAM DELAYS

Understanding delays as a policy tactic is important in order to improve endangered species restoration programs. Delays are lost opportunities that come about as "a function of the number of decision points, the number of participants at each point, and the intensity of their preferences" (Pressman and Wildavsky 1973:118).

The if, when, where, and how of captive breeding were points of contention in the ferret program. WGF set the condition initially that if ferrets were ever bred in captivity, it had to be done in Wyoming and under the agency's control. The FWS seemed to concur. But because WGF had no adequate facility, no resources to build one, and no personnel to staff one, no progress could be made. In contrast, other participants (such as the ISU/Biota team and their NGO conservation community backers) set no boundary conditions and encouraged captive breeding in regional and national facilities whose staff and funding were already in place.

When there are differences of opinion, the price of coming to an agreement, according to Pressman and Wildavsky (1973), is delay or modification of existing programs. These authors characterized participants in disagreements by their preferences (are they for or against the issue?), the intensity of their preferences (do they care or are they indifferent?), and the resources they bring to bear to effect the outcome (are they powerful or weak?). When progress depends on getting "clearances" from key participants, a program will be delayed if a participant has an intense aversion to it and mobilizes abundant resources to block it. In this case, the ISU/Biota team might be characterized by a strong preference for captive breeding but with few resources to put it into effect.

WGF, on the other hand, was initially strongly against captive breeding outside the state and had considerable resources to block it. The agency's lead status afforded it a key resource — control of access to the ferrets — which it used to veto the removal of ferrets outside the state until 1989. But in Pressman and Wildavsky's words, "Vetoes are not permanent but conditional. Accommodations may be made, bargains entered into, resistances weakened" (p. 116). The essential policy problem in such situations is to provide incentives for participants to change their behavior. And so, extensive bargaining with WGF was necessary for captive breeding to proceed. After the FWS provided about $250,000 for a captive breeding facility and assured the state that captive breeding would not dilute its control of the program, WGF agreed that it was time to begin a limited captive-breeding program. The disappearance of the wild population at about the same time left few other options open. Subsequently, the federal government provided large sums annually to WGF's ferret program; the *Casper Star-Tribune* (1995a) reported that "state and federal agencies have spent $10 million in seven years to breed and release the rare black-footed ferrets." In short, the price of agreement in this case was quite high.

Combinations of numerous minor delays, as well as the major captive-breeding delay, kept the program from realizing its potential. Even though some delays appeared to be intentional, others were certainly unplanned. Some delays were procedural, a result of the time required to process plans or request and receive funding (see Thorne and Oakleaf 1991). Still other delays were caused by necessary attention to other activities by participants, all of whom had many other projects in addition to ferret recovery.

Time is, of course, a widely acknowledged scarce resource. (Its expenditure should receive the same attention as the expenditure of money, but seldom does.) "If you want to know what matters most to an organization," advised Pressman and Wildavsky (1973:121), "chart the activities on which its members spend their precious allotment of hours." How people and organizations use time indicates the centrality or peripherality of an issue to them, but even when a program is central, the time available may be limited. Thus, the opportunities for delays in complex programs proliferate: "Multiply the number of participants, give them varying degrees of centrality, arrange their time budgets differently, and you have set up a typical pattern of stop and start characterized by a little forward movement and a lot of delay" (p. 121).

Does WGF's ultimate decision to captive-breed ferrets, even though perhaps one to three years late, count as a failure or a success? Those who emphasized the timeliness of recovery and who understood the very narrow limits of the opportunity available tended to see it as a failure. Some, with different goals and measures of success, believed it was "better late than never."

Conclusions

I have identified and illustrated two program pathologies that significantly reduced the ferret program's adequacy, effectiveness, and efficiency. Intelligence failures and delays are relatively common organizational pathologies, especially in bureaucracies. Recognizing these problems while they are happening is not easy, and preventing them is even more difficult. Because intelligence failures often result from the assumptions and biases of top-level decision makers, one option to prevent or correct them is a sophisticated leadership that identifies and examines its assumptions and carries out adequate, ongoing reality checks. To avoid delays in restoration programs, no one organization should have veto power over events necessary to move a program forward. Abundant financial resources would, of course, also help avoid delays in many instances.

Programs can also be structured and operated in ways that minimize the chances that these two pathologies can occur. It is clear to many observers that the very structure of WGF's program made it highly vulnerable to these and other difficulties. A host of assumptions about organizational relationships, professional roles, and integrating mechanisms did not, unfortunately, fit the reality of the participating organizations or the demands of ferret restoration. Thus, the structure itself became a major cause of additional problems, making ferret recovery harder rather than easier.

4

Program Structure as Political Process
Designing for Control

As the lead agency, Wyoming Game and Fish had authority to establish
the structure of the black-footed ferret program, its modes of operation, spa-
tial and temporal boundaries of program action, and patterns of participation.
Not surprisingly, these reflected the state organization's perspective and expectations. In general, program structure — the patterns of relationships among
positions and roles in an organization — appears to be both a determinant and
an outcome of power and influence. Jeffrey Pfeffer (1978:26) described what is
involved:

> Structure involves relationships, including authorizations to evaluate, the dif-
> ferential distribution of the right to reward and punish, the unequal allocation
> of information, resources, and the capability of coping with uncertainty, and
> as a consequence, differences in power, influence, and control within organi-
> zations. Assuming conflicts over preferences and goals, as well as over beliefs
> about the consequences of actions, structures become one focus for the con-
> test over control, and at a given time, provide differential governance to
> various organizational participants.

Pfeffer explained that the contest over who in organizations makes decisions
and why, who benefits, and who controls is fought through structural arrangements (see also Nadler and Tushman 1980). In programs where there are

differences among participants over definitions of situation, goals, and strategies, control of the coalition or program is a vital issue (Child 1972). Because governance, control, and political process are directly related to organizational structure, understanding the ferret program's structure and function is essential.

In this chapter I focus on the structure of the ferret program and some of the consequences. I describe the program's structural evolution, examine some implications of this structure for the program's behavior, and describe organizational interdependencies in the coalition and the appropriateness of WGF's program with regard to these relationships. Finally, I examine the complex roles of professionals and bureaucrats and relations between them.

Evolution of the Ferret Program's Structure

Soon after it assumed leadership, WGF convened several meetings of participants, through which the structure of the program largely evolved. There was, however, no constitutive process. At no time did the agency specify, through either visual or verbal models, the structure of the coalition of organizations or the relationships among them. Hints emerged, though, from the dialogues and interactions of participants. The relationships of the participating groups moved through four phases in a sequence that was largely predictable, given the context. From an informal association prior to discovery of the Meeteetse ferrets, a hierarchical bureaucracy evolved within a year after WGF assumed leadership (figure 3). This development had numerous implications for how the program operated and what, when, where, and by whom actions were undertaken to restore ferrets.

Before the Meeteetse discovery, there was no formal program to restore ferrets because no ferrets were known to exist. Nevertheless, several organizations that had some interest in ferrets related to one another informally and infrequently through arrangements best described as a simple matrix (figure 3a). Also at this time, a little-used formal channel existed between federal and state agencies concerning ferrets, although there seems to have been no contingency planning by either federal or state officials in case ferrets were located.

The second phase, a complex matrix, existed only briefly (figure 3b). When ferrets were first found, the simple matrix rapidly grew both in the number of organizations involved and in the frequency and type of communications among them. The significance of the discovery demanded action, including getting organized. The FWS Regional Office was the focus of the increased volume of communication, as in the earlier simple matrix, since it was the federal agency responsible for recovering listed species. The FWS called two meetings in Meeteetse within about a month after the ferrets were found, one closed and one open to the public. The objectives of both were ostensibly to identify likely participants in ferret recovery, meet local ranchers, foster a climate of cooperation, and determine a course of action. Discussions were very general, and the relative merits of various ways to organize a program were not discussed. Shortly thereafter, the FWS began to transfer leadership to WGF. Neither agency acknowledged the need to establish an effective structure for the program in order to proceed with ferret recovery. Instead, the program's organizational arrangements remained in limbo for the next few months until the formal transfer of lead authority was completed in early 1982.

The third phase was a sharp move to a traditional bureaucracy once WGF assumed the lead (figure 3c). The agency's intentions concerning the program's structure were announced in a meeting about six months after ferrets were found. WGF officials expected to be in charge of the program, including the collective financial resources of the coalition, and would be making all important decisions. For example, Brayton (1983:21) reported that "one of the major concerns of the Wyoming Game and Fish Department is to develop a centralized research fund . . . [which] would allow . . . a better integrated operation." A number of assumptions stood behind such a structure, and there was no opportunity to discuss these or alternative structures or funding mechanisms and administration.

By the time this first meeting was convened by WGF in March 1982, the agency had appointed a Black-Footed Ferret Advisory Team (BFAT, described in chapter 6). The initial members included representatives of WGF, the FWS Regional Office, the State Lands Board, the Forest Service, the Bureau of Land Management, the University of Wyoming, and ranchers. Advisory boards for special projects are often set up by government agencies, and they are frequently limited, as in this case, to other government agencies plus any particularly powerful outside interests. The founding agency thereby signals that the selected members are the ones it recognizes as being directly affected by the program and therefore are the ones it recognizes as legitimate players. Other groups (nongovernmental researchers or the Meeteetse community, for instance) are thus delegitimized while the agency maintains the appearance of being cooperative, well-advised, and responsive to outside concerns.

The fourth phase in the evolution of the program's structure was a move toward stricter bureaucracy (figure 3d). WGF took on more and more control activities and insisted on frequent reports (that is, intelligence gathering) from all formal and informal participants over subsequent months. This phase was fully institutionalized when WGF hired a ferret coordinator. Late in 1982, the

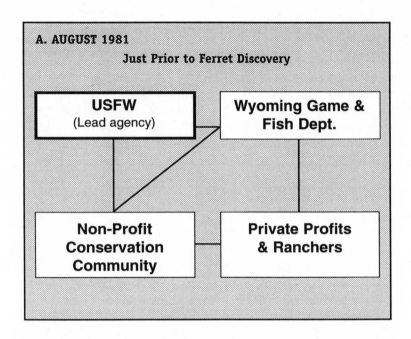

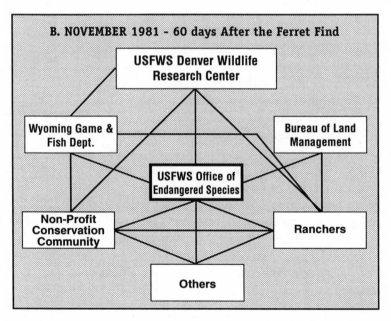

Figure 3. Organizational arrangements for recovery of the Meeteetse black-footed ferrets: *A,* simple matrix; *B,* complex matrix; *C,* bureaucracy; *D,* heightened bureaucracy. (Reprinted with permission from Clark and Harvey 1988.)

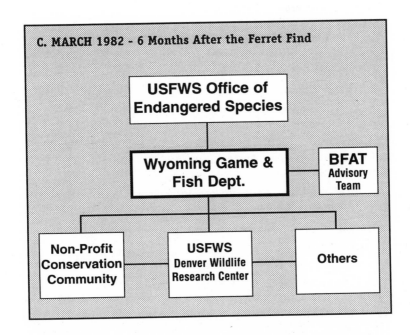

C. MARCH 1982 - 6 Months After the Ferret Find

USFWS Office of Endangered Species

Wyoming Game & Fish Dept.

BFAT Advisory Team

Non-Profit Conservation Community

USFWS Denver Wildlife Research Center

Others

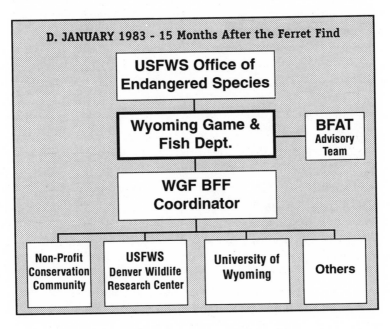

D. JANUARY 1983 - 15 Months After the Ferret Find

USFWS Office of Endangered Species

Wyoming Game & Fish Dept.

BFAT Advisory Team

WGF BFF Coordinator

Non-Profit Conservation Community

USFWS Denver Wildlife Research Center

University of Wyoming

Others

FWS Regional Office, under Section 6 of the Endangered Species Act, which permits cost sharing in such programs, provided about $20,000 to WGF in a two-thirds federal to one-third state cost-sharing arrangement to fund this position. The coordinator role is generally expected to facilitate, integrate, and coordinate participants and to increase trust and communication. The ferret coordinator, however, oversaw field workers in the ISU/Biota and FWS Research Center teams, reported on them to supervisors, gathered and centralized information within his organization, and enforced directives from WGF administration in Cheyenne. As a result, this role served to further lengthen and stratify hierarchical arrangements. In addition, WGF's veterinarian was active in field regulation, often making independent decisions on monitoring, telemetry, and trapping. WGF thereby largely solidified its bureaucratic control of the program.

Implicit throughout this evolution were certain assumptions about how power, authority, and roles were distributed, how information should flow, how interdependencies among the actors were structured, how decisions should be made, and other vital structural issues — all of which determined how the program could function. In the end, the ferret program reflected WGF's assumptions, and it was set up and operated under principles of traditional bureaucratic management.

The bureaucratic model, originally described by Max Weber (1947), offers many advantages for both government and private organizations and for society. It is so commonplace today that few people realize that it is a twentieth-century invention or that other models, better suited to certain problem-solving situations, are available. Bureaucracies have rules and standard operating procedures and a clear division of labor. They have a hierarchical structure of authority, or chain of command. Technical competence — as opposed to "friendship, family ties, and favoritism" (Daft 1983:124) — is required as a basis for getting a job. In the private sector, owners are distinct from workers. Workers do not appropriate the rights or property of their positions or use them for personal advantage. And the bureaucracy keeps written records of its activities, decisions, and rules. These characteristics promise authority, dependability, efficiency, competence, predictability, reliability, stability, rationality, impersonality, objectivity, task orientation, and continuity — all necessary in complex societies (Daft 1983). But bureaucracies have many limitations and perform best in stable environments with little change or uncertainty. Daft (1983: 145) observed that "bureaucracy certainly has its benefits, but should not be used when organizations are small, when employees are highly professional, or when the environment is unstable." Bureaucracy today connotes hierarchical structures with power at the top, a reliance on rules, roles, and regulations, and an aversion to risk taking or change.

According to Robert Nakamura and Frank Smallwood (1980:7–12), this classical, mechanistic model of bureaucratic administration was based on "a centralized, hierarchical pyramid . . . [with] a highly rationalized, legalistic kind of authority and structure" (p. 7), a belief in the separation of politics and administration and in the neutrality, professionalism, and nonpoliticality of administration, and the acceptance of efficiency as the criterion on which to measure performance. Nakamura and Smallwood pointed out that two assumptions underlie this model. First is that *decision making* is a rational process of clarifying and organizing goals and values, investigating means of achieving them and their consequences, and finally choosing the path most likely to bring the desired results. Second is that *policy implementation* follows this same pattern: policy makers choose an agent to implement policy on the basis of technical criteria and give specific instructions to the agent. The implementer then carries out the instructions with results near those expected by policy makers because he or she possesses "the technical capability, the obedience, and the will to carry out the policies" (p. 10). But recent studies have shown these assumptions to be unfounded. Policy formulation is more complex, incremental, and uncertain than previously thought. And policy implementation is "compounded by an intricate variety of psychological norms and bureaucratic pressures that take on a complex political life of their own . . . because administrators are involved in the process of making policy when they apply policy 'at successively less abstract levels' " (p. 11). Steven Bissell (1994:323) offered a general explanation: "As with any policy there are increasingly defined limits. The outer limits are marked by legal constraints and judicial proscriptions. The next level is legislative constraints, followed by regulatory issues determined within some sort of political process by commissions or committees. The innermost level of policy and that at which the vast majority of decisions are made is the administrative level within the management agencies themselves."

How administrators perceive their organization's operating environment largely determines the organization's subsequent behavior. According to Charles Perrow (1970:112), "the environment is always both a threat and a resource" because of the other organizations present. There are three basic ways an organization can interact with others in its environment, depending on whether it perceives them as a threat or as a resource. The first type of relationship is *reciprocity,* which is extensive among organizations in the profit sector, especially in highly uncertain environments. In these cases, other organizations are seen as potential resources, and cooperation among them can increase the efficiency of all. Big consortiums have grown, for example, around the oil industry and the microcomputer industry. Such linkages introduce valuable areas of predictability and certainty. The second type of interaction is *competition,* which occurs when organizations view others as threats to their own existence. Competition feeds and sustains uncertainty, reduces efficiency, and precludes cooperation. Mechanisms of competition include predation on others' resources or attacks on their legitimacy. The third way organizations relate is through *co-optation.* One organization co-opts another that threatens it (or contributes to its uncertainty) by bringing the threatening organization into its own realm of influence, thereby defusing the threat and gaining legitimacy. Co-opted groups might be either formal or informal participants, but they are always subordinate and controlled.

The evolving ferret program was a complex mix of reciprocal, competitive, and co-optive relationships in response to various perceived threats or opportunities. Some organizations perceived others as both threats and opportunities. The state and federal agencies treated each other more or less reciprocally in that they often supported one another against outside criticism. But they also competed for legitimacy. The relationship between the two research teams was also largely reciprocal, although there was also an element of competition between them. WGF competed with the ISU/Biota team by applying for funding from some of the same sources.

WGF's eventual incorporation of certain other groups into BFAT seems to exemplify co-optation. These were the National Wildlife Federation, a Washington, D.C.–based conservation group historically known to support state wildlife claims, and University of Wyoming researchers. In co-optation, according to Perrow (1970:114), someone "may be brought into higher positions in order to 'buy him off' or, to put it less bluntly, to socialize him to the legitimacy of the policies of the dominant faction in the organization." These outside groups were brought in only after WGF had stabilized and simplified its operating environment and secured its control of the program. Through co-optation it was able to answer, on its own terms, long-standing calls to represent conservation and research interests on BFAT. Such a relationship may partially eliminate conflict but also may give rise to apparent inconsistencies in knowledge, skills, personnel, or resources:

> Such inconsistencies may involve duplicate activities or functions, or subunits apparently working at cross-purposes. A rationalist perspective would argue that such inconsistencies reduce organizational performance and should be eliminated. Such a view, however, neglects the possibility that these structural inconsistencies may be a reasonable response to the conflicting demands and interests of organizational participants. (Pfeffer 1978:240)

The refusal to share decision making, the co-optation of some groups and competition with others, and the political alliances formed with still others were clearly "rational" efforts by the lead agency (in keeping with its assumptions about organizational structure) to deal with the complexity of its operating environment.

Because organizations are goal-directed, social entities, program administrators should pay close attention to the ways in which people contribute to, function within, and limit or are limited by organizations (Jelinek et al. 1981). In the ferret case, attention to organizational issues seemed to concentrate on maintaining control. The state's increasingly rigid program led to a poorer congruence of various program functions with the actual requirements of saving ferrets in a timely, effective, and equitable fashion, and conflict grew.

Some Consequences of Program Structure for Program Behavior

PRESSURE TO BUREAUCRATIZE

The organizational and policy literature is full of descriptions and explanations of why complex organizations organize and manage as they do (Miles et al. 1974). For example, Paul Bracken (1984:221, 227) observed that when an organization's operating environment is uncertain, as it was for WGF upon discovery of the ferrets, complex organizations "have certain built-in tendencies, directions they naturally move toward when subjected to different constraints and levels of excitement. We can think of these tendencies as their internal dynamic response to outside stimuli. . . . Any organization contains a body of systematic knowledge, based on precepts, procedure, and rules programmed into it. As precepts, procedures, and rules evolve and accumulate over time, they may lead to decisions and reactions being taken without full comprehension of the rationale or justification." Bracken's observations accurately capture the agencies' responses to the ferret find and to new relationships with participants in the recovery effort. The bureaucratic form that the ferret program assumed was an automatic, understandable, and predictable response from both the state and federal standpoints.

Another component in understanding WGF's response, is that in times of organizational change, when the environment "acts up" or when change is rapid, nearly all organizations are affected by political issues, and some organizations feel threatened (see Stein and Kanter 1980). WGF may well have feared the possibility of relinquishing or sharing its traditional autonomy, control, and stewardship over wildlife in Wyoming to the FWS or outside conservation groups. It is easy to imagine that WGF's administrators proceeded almost automatically to maintain or even strengthen the agency's control in the uncertain aftermath of the ferret discovery. Underlying premises play themselves out in actual practices. In such situations, "it is not difficult for an administrator ... to conclude that cooperation with another agency, unless it is on his own terms, will threaten his autonomy and threaten the wisdom of his approach or program" (Perrow 1970:128). In such situations, as Perrow (1979) noted, the atmosphere of fear and loss of control may influence administrators' decisions. James Q. Wilson (1980:376–377) observed that, in general,

> government agencies are more risk averse than imperialistic. They prefer security to rapid growth, autonomy to competition, stability to change. Exceptions exist, but they tend to be found among agencies with specially benign environments — strong public support and popular leadership. Much of what otherwise might seem puzzling about these agencies becomes clearer once we understand how they define the nature and source of potential threats to their security and support — in short, once they determine what constitutes a threatening crisis. ...
>
> That agencies are risk averse does not mean they are timid. Quite the contrary: their desire for autonomy, for a stable environment, and for freedom for blame gives these agencies a strong incentive to make rules and to exercise authority in all aspects of their mission. No agency wishes to be accused of "doing nothing" with respect to a real or imagined problem; hence every agency proliferates rules to cover all possible contingencies. The process is known familiarly in the bureaucracy as "covering your flanks." The more diverse the organized constituencies with which an agency must deal, the more flanks there are to be covered.

It was clearly in the interests of WGF to lead the high-profile ferret recovery program successfully, and it is reasonable to expect that the agency, like any other group, would use all the tools at its disposal to secure its own interests. The organization with the most power largely decides whose interests are served (Pfeffer 1978, Perrow 1979). Program structure simply reflects the distribution of power; it is the institutionalization of power. Once institutionalized, program structure is very difficult to rearrange, even when programs perform poorly.

Pfeffer (1978:224) noted that decision authority "makes it possible for those in control to take actions to facilitate their maintenance of power." Of the widely recognized mechanisms to institutionalize power, WGF exercised several in its ferret program. First, it designated all positions of power to be filled by its own members: WGF chaired its advisory team, WGF recorded meeting minutes, WGF served as ferret "coordinator," WGF or its ally, the University of Wyoming, chaired other committees such as the ferret captive-breeding committee in 1984. This domination of the power setting was reflected in WGF news releases (see Langston 1982, Northern Wyoming Daily News 1982).

Second, WGF structured the information flows to control public access to field data. For example, WGF's media plan placed it in charge of all contact with the public and the media. Program accomplishments were reported to the public, and the wording of news releases maximized WGF's public recognition and enhanced its role while it minimized the importance of other actors' roles and accomplishments (see Casper Star-Tribune 1982, Wyoming Game and Fish Department 1983).

Third, WGF limited the distribution of rewards, and with them recognition, to its own members and supporters while withholding them from other actors, especially those who maintained different views (see WGF's press releases and newsletters over the years, also Casper Star-Tribune 1982, Wyoming Game and Fish Department 1983, Langston 1983). This self-legitimizing technique was discussed by Salancik and Pfeffer (1977), who noted that the key to institutionalizing power is creating mechanisms that legitimate the organization's own authority and decrease that of others.

The longer the ferret program continued, the more institutionalized WGF's power became; but the more institutionalized power becomes, the more likely it is that an organization will be out of phase with its environment (Salancik and Pfeffer 1977). This state of affairs showed up as a mismatch between the program's structure and management and the changing status of the ferret "problem." This was most evident in 1985 and 1986, when WGF delayed rescue actions despite the drastic reduction in numbers of ferrets observed. As Lawrence Hrebiniak (1978:192) concluded, "Whatever the real facts, it can be said with certainty that the organization is likely to use its power to eliminate, control, or otherwise affect actual or potential environmental problems or sources of uncertainty. It will try to decrease its own vulnerability, while increasing that of others, if possible." Thus, for the organization in a powerful but threatened position, the focus of action becomes not the task at hand, but its own survival or legitimization. Given this understanding of organizations, it would appear that WGF's program structure and behavior served its interests well over the first several years of the ferret restoration effort. But how well did it serve the common interest of ferret recovery?

WGF's response was not an uncommon or unexpected one for government agencies in such situations. Donald Warwick (1975) states that the strongest pressures for maintaining bureaucratic structures and operating procedures lie in the external environment of the agencies. For a public bureaucracy, survival and effectiveness depend on the public's perception of its legitimacy and on forming alliances with other agencies and groups. Agencies typically institutionalize favorable alliances, thereby "proving" their legitimacy. In the ferret program, WGF's operating environment contained other organizations, groups, and individuals who acted as outside authorities (FWS), monitors

(FWS, NGO conservation groups, the public), clientele groups (hunters, Wyoming citizens), allies (ranchers, Bureau of Land Management, University of Wyoming), or adversaries (potentially all of the above). Individually and collectively, these organizations, groups, and individuals possessed considerable power, thus making WGF's external environment highly threatening. In any coalition, the actions of one group have significant ramifications for the actions of others, adding uncertainty to each participant's environment.

An organization's need to manage its environment may contribute to rigidifying bureaucratic hierarchies and rules in three ways (Warwick 1975). First, in complex environments, the strong need for communication creates pressure within an organization to centralize its structures and operations. This means that important decisions tend to be passed up the hierarchy, and in uncertain and complex environments nearly all decisions are seen as important by subordinates. Superiors expect to receive key information needed for decisions and to exercise their discretion in the process. Second, the resulting upward flow of messages can create an overload. WGF's coordinator in part managed information flow both up and down the hierarchy. This role helped to centralize information and power, thus institutionalizing WGF's position and managing a significant part of WGF's external environment. Third, Warwick (1975) noted that as pressures for coordination grow, a need to reinforce hierarchy is felt by bureaucrats. Also, the larger and more diverse the set of participants, the greater the pressure to devise and institutionalize explicit rules to govern the actions of all participants. Because many organizations were "trespassing" in WGF's domain, WGF simplified its environment by subordinating, controlling, or ousting other participants.

There were many advantages for WGF to develop rules, regulations, and formal procedures in circumstances like the discovery of ferrets (see Diver 1983)—that is, in operating environments that are uncertain, unstable, risky, complex, and threatening. Individuals within bureaucracies are most protected from the shifting tides of internal and external environments by rigid bureaucracy. Bureaucracy allows agencies to maintain a sense of security, effectiveness, control, and autonomy. Unfortunately, adherence to bureaucratic incentives also sabotages a program's ability to learn, change, or adapt quickly to changing circumstances (see Westrum 1986, 1988, 1992). This may be what happened in the early years of the ferret program.

PROGRAM CONSEQUENCES

Bureaucratization of the ferret program had ramifications for every aspect of its functioning. Organizational structure always has implications for functioning, according to Robert Daft (1983). Not only does structure assign tasks and responsibilities, describe the levels of hierarchy, and identify functional groups within the organization, but it also governs the systems of communication, coordination, and integration. These critical systems include how information moves within the organization, how decisions are made and by whom, how conflict is resolved, how the external environment is interpreted, and many other facets of organizational livelihood. Numerous mechanisms link groups vertically within an organization (or, in this case, within a coalition), including referral up the chain of command, rules and standard operating procedures, planning and scheduling, and special information systems (Daft 1983). Horizontal linkages between groups, which are especially important when groups are functionally interdependent, as they were in the ferret program, are accomplished not only through paperwork and direct contact, but also by the use of liaison roles, task forces, permanent teams, or coordinators.

Structural weaknesses show up in several ways (Daft 1983). Poor decision making is a strong sign of structural deficiencies, such as the intelligence failures and delays in the ferret case described previously. When information does not get to the right people, when diverse interests are not integrated into decision making, or when there is inadequate communication between top-level decision makers and hands-on workers, there are structural problems. Another symptom is failure of an organization to respond innovatively to changes in its environment, as in WGF's unwillingness or inability to accept the crash of the ferret population in mid-1985. Excessive conflict, which was rife in the ferret program, is a third indication that an organization's structure has not adequately integrated conflicting goals. The lead agency did not clearly and effectively assign tasks, delegate responsibilities, identify functional needs of the program, or describe how all the groups fit realistically into the whole. No formal linkages were established. Communication between groups was most often informal, even opportunistic. As WGF wrested control of the structure, it assumed control over virtually every function of the program — that is, behavior was largely determined by structure.

Among the behavioral consequences of the ferret program's structure was that it significantly restricted orientation to the "problem" of ferret recovery and exploration of the means that might be used to achieve it. The context of the recovery problem was not analyzed and realistically updated. The very limited contextual discussions did not acknowledge the common interest: that ferrets were a national resource and that national institutions (such as the National Zoo) could be involved early on. The membership of BFAT was limited to representation of those agencies and special interests that were immediately and directly affected by the ferret program. The program reflected a narrow understanding of the scope of the recovery goal, the scope of the work to be accomplished, the organizational designs needed, and the best use of knowledge, skills, and people. For example, apparently no nationally recognized, experienced conservation biologists or administrators were initially consulted by the agencies to aid in developing a state-of-the-art conservation program or plan. Nor were experts who would ultimately be needed (for example, captive-breeding specialists) called in until late 1985. Nor were outside experts asked to review and upgrade the program's decision and policy processes, as is often done in the business world (but seldom in government) by organizational consultants and policy analysts.

A second consequence was what Virginia Schein and Larry Greiner (1977: 56) called "functional myopia and suboptimization." Each of the functional groups within the coalition (researchers, managers, landowners, BFAT advisers, etc.) tended to emphasize its own activities and interests and thus "suboptimized" for the program as a whole—that is, paid less attention to the whole than to separate parts. Each had particular knowledge, skills, and even vocabularies that were not shared with other functional groups. The lack of practical, structural mechanisms for coordinating planning, building teams, setting common goals, convening meetings between leaders of all functions, and addressing other needs led to poor integration and poor problem solving. BFAT was widely seen as filling the need for cooperation, but it served largely to represent various (mostly agency) interests, not functional groups.

Another aspect of this narrow problem orientation was that most program participants were biologists and thus, like all disciplinary specialists, bounded in their thinking. Their purview did not include systematic knowledge and skill in the functions of organizations or decision processes. Few in the program asked the larger questions about how well the ongoing, overall processes were actually meeting the goal of ferret recovery. This reflects the functional separations that usually exist in bureaucracies. Advancement too often depends on seniority alone, with the result that higher echelons are staffed by people with specialized knowledge, who continue to emphasize the perspective of their specialty instead of seeking a broader view of the program.

A third consequence of bureaucratic structure was rigidity in the face of changing circumstances. The pyramidal authority structures and routinization of work that make bureaucracies so efficient in stable situations can also render them insensitive to emerging problems and changes in the status of the problem. Schein and Greiner (1977:56) pointed out that "top-management decision making based on past experience, while also being insulated from lower levels, can paralyze or blind management from dealing effectively with nonroutine issues. Minor problems can grow into major crises before coming to top management's attention." The ferret program never "put its ear to the ground" and never developed mechanisms to anticipate political problems (such as the consequences of not involving conservation groups from the beginning) or cultural problems (such as conflict between the tradition and preference for managing animals in the wild and the possible need for more intrusive and manipulative management techniques). In short, the bureaucratic structure itself made the ferret recovery process harder for the coalition rather than easier.

Organizational Interdependencies and Their Mismanagement

A striking feature of WGF's operating environment was the multiple interdependencies that existed among the organizations. Interdependence is "the extent to which employees or departments depend upon each other to accomplish their tasks" (Daft 1983:182) or a condition where actions taken within one unit affect actions and work outcomes of another unit (McCann and Ferry 1979). For example, from 1981 until 1985 WGF was dependent on the ISU/Biota field team, as well as the FWS field team, for nearly all the basic data on ferrets in the wild. WGF depended on the FWS for permits and public money. The ISU/Biota and FWS field teams were dependent on WGF for research permits. The ISU/Biota team depended on outside funding. And all actors were dependent on ranchers for access to the ferrets on their private lands. Although most of these interdependencies and their programmatic implications were not acknowledged publicly, they were knowingly exploited by many participants:

> [The key rancher] is determined to keep the scale of the research effort small. . . . He has told the Fish and Wildlife Service that if there is a large influx of people in the search area, all outsiders, including biologists, will be asked to leave. On private land, [the rancher] and five other ranchers with ferrets on their property are in control, says [a] Fish and Wildlife Service biologist. (Nice 1982:107)

> The bureaucrats keep on good terms with the private landowners, lest they lose access to their prize. Meanwhile, the ranchers want to get along with the government to safeguard grazing and other private privileges on public lands. (Nice 1983:19)

> [In early winter 1981/1982] officials at the Fish and Wildlife Service — charged with the protection of endangered species — were deciding who

should manage the ferret project. And they handed it over to the Wyoming Game and Fish Department. . . . But when the state was unable to come up with funds, some observers questioned its commitment. . . .

[One state official said], "Coming up with extra dollars is not very easy. We're facing some major financial problems as it is." . . .

[BFAT] requested a joint research proposal [from the ISU/Biota and FWS field teams]. (Nice 1982:108)

Progress in the entire program was dependent on WGF:

The state-run advisory team has spent more than a year trying to decide how to handle its delicate biological treasure. (Nice 1983:18)

[Two FWS biologists] are working on the vital logistics of ferret research to coordinate and mesh federal, state and private functions. Sometimes, when there is a need for rapid, responsible decision-making, one government agency can be seen passing the other going in the opposite direction, though both are supposed to be heading for the same place. The private sector is left scratching its head in wonder. (Randall 1983:6)

These interdependencies were greatest in the early years of the ferret program, when there was the greatest uncertainty about what to do and how to do it. But as biological, organizational, and political uncertainty was reduced, the kinds of interdependencies changed. By late 1985, for example, the field teams had provided considerable data on the ferrets, their biology, and management needs. This relative abundance of information — not to mention the demise of the wild ferret population — markedly changed the interdependencies, especially WGF's dependence on the field teams. By the summer of 1986 WGF had functionally displaced the ISU/Biota team by hiring the University of Wyoming Cooperative Research Unit to conduct the summer spotlighting (although very few ferrets were believed to remain in the Meeteetse area, and the Coop Unit had limited prior experience with ferrets). The ISU/Biota team's request for a permit to advise and train the new workers so that data collection would be standardized was denied by the WGF director (Morris 1986a, 1986b). These changes simplified WGF's operating environment.

In any coalition organized around a common enterprise, the outcome will be a product of the complex web of relationships among the organizations and the status of the problem. The task requires integration, achieved through coordination and control. Without recognition of the interdependencies that actually exist and without explicit management of them, coordination and control — and thus integration — will be problematic, and the program will tend to develop debilitating pathologies.

COORDINATING THE PROGRAM

The ferret program, with its large array of participants, was what James D. Thompson and Robert Hawkes (1962) called a "synthetic organization," a collection of interdependent organizations that each brought different resources, skills, and knowledge to bear on a single task. The high degree of interdependence called for considerable interaction, consultation, or exchange of information. Thompson (1967) described three types of interdependencies that are possible among organizations. First is "pooled interdependence," in which each organization must render a discrete contribution to the whole and each is supported by the whole. An example is manufacturing, where different parts are made in different factories and shipped to a central point for assembly. Second is "sequential interdependence," in which each organization or unit must contribute to the overall task in a specific sequence. An example is an assembly line. In both pooled and sequential interdependence, outputs of the units accumulate in one place—in one factory or in the offices of a select group of decision makers. Third is "reciprocal interdependence," in which the output of certain organizations or units becomes the input for others, and vice versa, because they are mutually related. An example is an airline that has both maintenance and operations units: the output of maintenance is flyable aircraft and the output of operations is aircraft in need of maintenance. Obviously, neither unit can perform its duties without the input of the other. In reciprocal interdependence, each organization must be "penetrated" by other organizations through cooperative goal setting and joint decision making. Each must have reciprocal contingencies for cooperating with the others.

Collective action comes through coordination, and different types of interdependence require different coordinating mechanisms (Thompson 1967). First is "standardization," which establishes rules, roles, regulations, and routines that constrain the activities of individuals and units to make their outputs consistent with those of other units. A managing body originates the standards, imposes them equally on all units, and accumulates all the outputs. Standardization works most effectively in stable environments where predictability is high. It is most suited to pooled interdependence. The second type of coordinating mechanism is "planning." It establishes schedules of outputs for individuals and organizations in sequentially interdependent settings. Here again, planning is done by a managing body that accumulates the outputs. It is most useful in environments that are more complex than those found in pooled interdependence, but still relatively predictable or stable. Planning is necessary in sequential interdependence. The third coordinating mechanism is "mutual adjustment," in which information is actively exchanged between participants. This coordinating mechanism is essential in reciprocally interdependent coalitions. There are no managing bodies as such, and feedbacks between organizations or units are coordinated through extensive and constant communication, cooperative decision making, and joint action — in other words, close teamwork or partnerships. Communication and action take place both across hierarchical lines and between organizations. The more uncertain a situation is, the greater the reliance on mutual adjustment (Thompson 1967). "Since decision-making, communication, and coordination problems are greatest for reciprocal interdependence, it should receive priority in organization structure" (Daft 1983: 183).

The ferret coalition was composed of reciprocally interdependent participants. Separately, each group had its own authorization, mandates, funding, and operations. As a coalition for restoring ferrets, however, with reciprocal contributions to a joint enterprise, these groups required mutual adjustment in coordinating their activities. Extensive and constant exchange should have been the norm among all participants. But the lead agency advanced a program in which it accumulated all program outputs and decided on their meaning and use. Agency administrators seemed to assume that a pooled interdependence existed: they expected data to be generated at the bottom and to flow upward, and decisions to be generated at the top and to flow downward. Standardized coordination and planning, appropriate for bureaucracies operating in relatively stable, certain, and low-risk environments, were not successful in coordinating the ferret coalition. Inappropriate coordination and controls generated distrust, negatively affected participants' commitment, and reduced their motivation to work cooperatively, especially among professionals. Alienation developed quickly, as is common when highly skilled professionals are required to formulate and execute solutions to problems but are overly controlled by bureaucrats (see Yaffee 1982). The minutes of BFAT meetings (e.g., August 1985) show continuing difficulties in integrating the coalition as evidenced by several participants' comments.

CONTROLLING THE PROGRAM

In addition to coordination, appropriate control mechanisms were also necessary (Clark and Cragun 1994). Control is the process of directing and shaping the behavior of individuals, departments, or organizations toward certain ends by setting goals and standards, measuring and monitoring performance, evaluating performance, and providing feedback to workers (Hrebiniak 1978). Like coordinating mechanisms, control tools must fit the situation. In pooled interdependencies requiring standardization, top-down regulation by the managing body is the appropriate control. In sequential interdependencies needing extensive planning, a managing body sets overall plans and distributes them to the units, which carry them out in sequence. In reciprocal interdependencies requiring mutual adjustment, however, the control tool is fundamentally different. It is not top-down but lateral, consisting of mutual acts of autonomy and cooperation with mutual attitudes of trust and respect.

Control is a normal and necessary organizational function, although it is frequently viewed negatively as "coercion and restraint" (Hrebiniak 1978: 211). Hrebiniak describes control as an organizational system that depends on context, technology, tasks, level (institutional, managerial, or technical), interdependencies, and people. All these factors determine whether control will be exerted from the top down or will be self-imposed and whether the system will be risk-avoiding or risk-embracing. These characteristics, in turn, foster certain tendencies in the behavior and attitudes of both workers and the organization itself (Hrebiniak 1978). For example, under top-down control systems, there is a tendency among employees to play it safe, to think only of their own jobs, and to do only what they are paid to do. In this system, workers tend to seek guidance only from their superiors and to interact with clients, customers, and coworkers in an impersonal manner. They are largely concerned with security and social needs rather than "higher" needs. They often lose interest in the work and seldom try to expand their knowledge or skills. Under systems of self-control, the tendency is to take more risks, to see how jobs and tasks are interrelated and to seek new expertise and responsibility. Self-control systems foster motivation, satisfaction, and an orientation toward "higher" needs. Workers tend to deal with colleagues, clients, and customers on a more personal, individual basis. They seek advice not only from superiors, but also from subordinates and peers (Hrebiniak 1978).

Dysfunction in an organization's control system may occur at any stage of the cycle — in the goal-setting stage (perhaps the wrong people are setting the goals, or standards are too high or too low, or the context has changed), in the monitoring stage (measurement procedures may not provide useful information), in the review and evaluation stage (discrepancies between expected and actual performance may be caused by accidental or uncontrollable factors), or in the feedback stage (rewards and punishments may be inappropriate) (Hrebiniak 1978). A dysfunctional control system can result in distrust, withdrawal of commitment and involvement, lowered motivation, alienation, dissatisfaction, resentment, resistance, striking back, high turnover, competition, or conflict. In the ferret program, the exclusive rather than participative goal setting, the lack of performance standards, the arbitrariness of evaluation, the immoderate "punishments" and disincentives, and the rejection of self-control all led to many of these negative reactions to WGF's overcontrol.

The control system that WGF exerted on the ferret program may well have been a natural consequence of its bureaucratic presuppositions. In addition to pooled rather than reciprocal interdependencies, for instance, the lead agency seems to have assumed that field work was a technician-level job and that these lower-level, less centralized workers needed to be closely supervised and even distrusted. Despite the many professionals who staffed both research teams, researchers were not asked to participate in decision making; they were expected only to report their findings. WGF also seems to have assumed that the environment was stable and tasks routine, rather than acknowledging the uncertainty of the environment and the subsequent need for flexible responses.

Differences in how organizations and people understood control systems can be added to the many differences that separated groups in the black-footed ferret coalition. To WGF, the growing schisms among participants and the ensuing conflict must have indicated that it was losing control, to which it responded by applying even more control (tightly scheduling work, threatening arrest, declining to renew permits for continued field work). Thus was launched a self-perpetuating cycle of bureaucratic controls, lack of cooperation, and persistent conflict. In such a setting, it was impossible to institutionalize mutual adjustment coordination and professional self-controls, although they might briefly have been possible at the onset of the program.

Managing Professional and Bureaucratic Roles

The interaction of professionals and bureaucrats is a major component of any complex, joint program. There are definite similarities between the two roles: both rely on assumptions about their own objectivity and neutrality, both use established norms to guide behavior, and both depend on expertise, knowledge, or skill for advancement (Hrebiniak 1978). Yet there are also great differences between them, and conflict between the two is often evident in wildlife conservation (Clark 1986, Clark et al. 1994). According to Wilson (1980), professionals relate to norms and styles set by others in the same occupation; these norms generally cut laterally across organizational boundaries. Rewards to professionals come from the profession itself and not from the employing bureaucracy or organization. The professional role usually commands little power in bureaucracies. Hrebiniak (1978) further distinguished professionals as "locals," who tend to be more loyal to their organizations and agree with top-down control systems, and "cosmopolitans," whose loyalty is first to their professions and who view organizational control as restrictive.

Wildlife management agencies at both state and federal levels, for instance, are often staffed by people with professional training in wildlife management, biology, or other resource management fields. Yet some of these workers often have a stronger orientation to the cultures, interests, procedures, and structures of their employing organizations than to the norms of their professions, and they often appeal to scientific standards and arguments to advance their organization's interests.

In contrast, bureaucrats relate primarily to the rules, hierarchy, and authority of the bureaucracy. They are "careerists or politicians," to use Wilson's (1980) terms. Careerists receive rewards largely from their employing agency and hence define their primary identities, expectations, and loyalties vertically up the agency hierarchy and career ladder. These people seek to promote the agency's agenda and their position within it. Politicians primarily relate to the external environment of the agency, managing outside political relationships. They occupy the highest levels in bureaucracies and see their future in the same or similar positions in bureaucracies or in appointed or elected office.

Hrebiniak (1978:242) noted that "there are cognitive, emotional, and attitudinal differences" among people in professional and bureaucratic roles that can cause conflicts and other problems (see also Yaffee 1982). Two major characteristics distinguish the two roles. The first is differences in how they deal with "error," the possibility of making mistakes. Hrebiniak (1978) offers a very telling comparison of risk-embracing and risk-avoiding tendencies. Professionals tend to "embrace error," seeking challenges on which to test their professional skills, accepting error as part of professional problem solving. In fact, professionals search for problems, sometimes hard problems, where the probability of success may be low. Bureaucrats, on the other hand, tend to "avoid error," as in the well-known warnings to "cover your flanks" and "leave a paper trail to protect yourself." In the first several months of the ferret program, a professional researcher who had studied ferrets a decade earlier in South Dakota recommended that "qualified scientists should try to learn about the Meeteetse ferrets as quickly as they can, lest the animals disappear as the ones he was studying did" (Nice 1982:109). A bureaucrat with WGF, however, was "more conservative: 'We don't know what could happen. We do know that the last ferret population that was studied doesn't exist. Nobody can tell us why it disappeared, but it did. We have to be very cautious'" (p. 109). Markedly different responses!

A second and closely related characteristic is that professionals tend to rely on "self-control" while bureaucrats tend to use "top-down control." Hrebiniak (1978:232) described some of the difficulties that arise because of this difference:

Systems heavily reliant on self-control demand a high degree of participation. But persons with influence might see widespread participation, involvement, and shared responsibility as a threat to their own self-interest. People with formal power may feel that systems of self-control can hurt them and ultimately destroy their influence.

These beliefs are supported by two interrelated assumptions. One is the all-or-none law of power. This holds that one either controls or is controlled, leads or is led. The other is the fixed-pie notion of power or influence. Here individuals believe that an increase in power or control for some individuals must reduce the influence and control of others. These perceptions naturally increase resistance to processes of control that seemingly diminish power and the ability to control others.

Such attitudes are probably most common in organizations that place an emphasis on hierarchy and the authority and status indicated by it. (citations in original omitted)

The ferret program involved bureaucrats as well as professionals. Many workers in both WGF and the federal agencies were trained as wildlife managers or biologists but seemed to identify more strongly with their organizations than with the professions. They largely served as managers and administrators in offices distant from the Meeteetse field site and, for the most part, did not visit Meeteetse or work with collection or interpretation of data. They seemed to emphasize top-down control based on legal authority and bureaucratic hierarchies.

There were also professionals involved in the program both within and outside the agencies who possessed specialized knowledge and skills to meet ferret recovery. This included not only experience in conducting field surveys, population measurements of various kinds, habitat assessments, and the like, but also expertise in net assessment, synthesis of large amounts of information, modeling, and interpretation and use of information in devising strategies and tactics for species restoration. There were expectations among this group to exercise self-control based on professional standards and judgment, since the group saw itself as an innovator and problem solver.

Bureaucrats in the program sought to avoid errors. They actively discouraged or prevented risky action, such as early captive breeding. Professionals, on the other hand, saw this tendency as a constraint that diminished the program's problem-solving options. Such disagreements led to growing conflict, which WGF attempted to reduce by applying more controls on the professionals, which generated resentment, distrust, and greater fragmentation of the program. "Conflict is inevitable in systems which face the need simultaneously to avoid and embrace error" (Hrebiniak 1978:243), a dilemma that certainly characterized the ferret program.

Bureaucrats also tend to separate planning and goal setting from doing the work. They are apt to take on planning and goal setting themselves and to assign the implementation work to professionals. This has serious consequences in highly uncertain situations. First, there is a great potential for communication distortion as professional information is passed up a bureaucratic hierarchy where it takes on a different meaning. Second, professionals are not allowed to exercise their full complement of problem-solving skills. These two circumstances have been evident in many wildlife conservation programs (Craighead 1979, Yaffee 1982, Hornocker 1982, Finley 1983, Jonkel 1984, Clark et al. 1994, to mention only a few). Bureaucrats in the ferret program, regardless of which agency employed them, were disinclined to share power with professionals through joint decision making, planning, or other cooperative actions. This only sharpened the traditional bureaucrat-professional and manager-staff dichotomy typical in bureaucracies. The special coordination and control mechanisms needed to maximize cooperation between the two roles were never employed by either WGF or federal officials.

Conclusions

In a very short time after its inception, the ferret restoration program changed from a loose association of interested groups to a fairly rigid and hierarchical bureaucracy, with WGF at the apex. There were many pressures from within and outside the agency to bureaucratize the program, and there was little appreciation of the interdependence that existed among participants. In addition, mismanagement of the inherent tension between professional and bureaucratic roles only added to the mounting burden of unresolved difficulties under which the program operated. Collectively, these failings made the task of saving ferrets much more difficult than the relatively simple biological circumstances alone indicated, and they prevented the flexible but cohesive, responsive but controlled, joint action that would have best served the task of saving ferrets.

Pfeffer (1978) noted that there are two approaches to analyzing organizational structure and its consequences. The first examines the appropriateness of the structure for coordinating interdependencies in order to accomplish a given task. The bureaucratic form of the ferret program was only minimally successful in this regard. The second approach looks at "why and how structure is a result of organizational influence processes and the consequences of a given structure for the distribution of control and power within organizations" (p. 26). It seems clear that, under strong internal and external pressures to bureaucratize, WGF used its formal power (authority) and effective power (control) to decide who to include in the program and who to exclude; who to co-opt, compete against, or form reciprocal alliances with; who to legitimate and who to delegitimate; which control and enforcement systems to institute; how to coordinate the different roles, functions, activities, and participants; who to authorize to direct and evaluate research; who to authorize to judge the program; and many other decisions at both high and low levels. This process (and its severely constricted outcome, the bureaucratic structure) not only had repercussions for the distribution of control and power within the coalition, but also had major impacts on the quality of the program and its ability to achieve the goal of recovering black-footed ferrets.

Designing program structures and integrating participants are, without a doubt, difficult. But if essential elements like these are ignored or misunderstood, many crippling weaknesses can be expected to plague the program. That is why professional, task-oriented, organizational management must be applied to endangered species conservation, as it is employed in innumerable other complex and uncertain societal enterprises. The ferret program is a prime example of the inadequate suboptimal result of inattention to vital programmatic issues.

5

Goals, Power, and Conflict
Making Decisions

When several organizations work side by side in a coalition where each has essential but unique contributions to make, they had better agree on a clear, formal goal. The unanimous goal in the case under examination was to save the black-footed ferret from extinction. Everyone acknowledged numerous subgoals (such as preservation of the wild population, recovery of the species throughout its former range, establishment of viable numbers of individuals and populations, timeliness) and smaller-scale objectives (for example, determining mortality factors through radio telemetry, modeling habitat needs, and population and habitat management plans). Yet discerning how these goals and objectives were constituted by the coalition, which of the groups, individuals, or levels of authority set them, and how these task-oriented goals related to other organizational goals is not straightforward.

All decision making reflects the distribution of power among interests. The decision process involves collecting information, assessing its reliability, promoting or recommending various interests, building consensus, determining how the decision will be carried out (perhaps repeatedly), and assessing the success of the decision. Power can be asserted to manipulate, control, or influence how these decision-making functions are carried out. As in goal setting, how the decision-making process is handled by an organization or coalition helps determine the character and success of that group.

In any program that depends on a diversity of skills, knowledge, people, groups, and actions to solve problems, conflict is to be expected. Problems in the decision process, in goal setting, in the structure of complex programs, and in a host of other areas can generate conflict. A certain level of conflict can be good, in fact, if it motivates better problem solving, but it is bad if it destroys morale and cooperation and deters accomplishment of the task. Goals, power issues, and conflict management can all be addressed in ways that maximize chances of clarifying and securing the common interest, in this case a successful conservation program.

In this chapter I describe the multiple competing goals sought by key participants and their consequences for the ferret restoration task, the program, and relationships among participants. I look at the use of power in the decision-making process to see how and for whom this process worked in the ferret program, and examine the causes and consequences of conflict in the program as well as conflict management strategies.

Multiple Competing Goals and Goal Displacement

Organizations are created for the purpose of attaining goals. Formal goals impart purpose and direction to an organization's activities. There are three general classes of interrelated organizational goals: order goals to control participants, economic goals to produce commodities or services, and cultural goals to maintain an organization's mythology and values (Etzioni 1961). Goals serve many functions, according to Hrebiniak (1978) and Etzioni (1964). They provide orientation and direction for the organization's activities. They legitimize the organization. They serve as constraints on both organizational and individual behavior, yet help spur actors on to greater creativity and achievement. Goals help develop workers' commitment to the organization. They reduce uncertainty in the organization's future. They provide standards by which to judge the organization's success. And, when compared to performance, they foster organizational learning and adaptation. The site or location of goal setting often determines what types of goals are set.

What an organization says or thinks it is, however, may not reflect its actual role or how others perceive it. Many organizations deliberately or unwittingly come to pursue goals other than their official, stated ones (Etzioni 1964). These so-called "real" or "operating" goals are those ends "sought through the actual operating policies of the organization; they tell us what the organization is trying to do, regardless of what the official goals say are the aims" (Perrow 1961:855). They are revealed by the actual "distribution of manpower and material resources" (Etzioni 1964:6). Operating goals are the outcome of a complicated play of power between individuals, groups, and organizations, and they are vitally important to policy implementation (Hrebiniak 1978). William Ascher and Robert Healy (1990:177–178) described some of the competing goals of government employees in particular, which also come to play in development of organizational goals:

> These interests are varying and complex. In various combinations, their motivations are to:
>
> (a) enhance the standing of the agencies in which they work
> (b) promote their own careers within these agencies (or elsewhere)
> (c) adhere to the highest professional standards, either for the sake of professionalism per se or to attain respect from professional peers
> (d) pursue partisan political objectives
> (e) pursue a particular *a priori* policy objective (such as environmental protection at any cost).
>
> Thus, any official's reactions can be understood in the context of weighing these motivations. Although any observer might frown on these motivations as detracting from the simple pursuit of the public interest, in the eyes of the individual official these objectives may well be seen as compatible with placing him or her in the position of having the greatest scope to "do good." ...
>
> Natural resource policies always imply benefits and costs for various socioeconomic groups (including state enterprise personnel and even government officials). Even though natural resource policy obviously addresses the question of how to pursue the "public good," the fact that particular policies will indulge or deprive specific groups tends to mobilize them to shape the policies in their interests. Even the ideally honest and impartial public servant will find that the definition of the public good is too vague to specify precisely what must be done, thus giving wide range to varying interpretations of how to proceed.

Since operating goals are generally not stated, an examination of both the formal goals and the organization's actions is often the best way to assess the efficiency and fitness of the real goals:

> The stated goals of an organization can serve as a clue to the actual goals of the organization. But a researcher cannot uncritically accept the stated goals of the organization as its actual sociological goals, since organizations tend to hold "public" goals for "front" purposes. [A researcher seeking real goals cannot] elicit this information from the top elites of the organization since they may not be free to communicate these goals to the researcher. Hence, the need to draw on an examination and extrapolation of ongoing organizational processes, especially "production," in the study of organizational goals. (Etzioni 1961:72)

The degree of correspondence between formal and operating goals is often an apt indicator of how well an organization "fits" its task environment, which is the work to be done as well as the total context of that work, including other organizations (Hrebiniak 1978, Daft 1983). If formal goals are developed from a correct assessment of the task, and if the ensuing actions efficiently achieve those goals, then the operating goals are the same as the formal goals. If, however, the actions belie the stated goals, or if the formal structure of the organization is such that the goals cannot be met or are stymied, then operating and formal goals differ. Byars (1984) noted that one major cause of an organization's failure to meet its goals — assuming the goals are appropriate initially — is that the wrong organizational structure is used to implement them.

ORGANIZATIONAL GOALS IN THE FERRET PROGRAM

The operating goals of organizations in the ferret coalition seemed at times to differ from their formal goals. There is evidence that WGF sought control of the program in addition to restoring ferrets and, possibly, achieving other goals. But what happened when the formal goal came into conflict with the operating goal? Although in many instances the two were compatible, even complementary, when one sequence of decisions and actions could not serve both goals simultaneously, the result was that control goals seemed to dominate task goals — with serious consequences for the program. The program's goals were not set jointly by all participants, contrary to Hrebiniak's (1978:50) recommendation that a "coalition or the combination of organizations for a single purpose requires a commitment for joint decision making." Goals in the ferret program were primarily determined by WGF's senior administrators, who were removed both spatially and contextually from events in the field. It is easy to see how control goals could become separated from formal goals and run a course of their own.

Goal displacement or inversion, as it is known, is not uncommon in organizations that have an authoritarian tendency (Hrebiniak 1978, Daft 1983). There is no doubt that WGF sincerely desired and worked toward ferret recovery, but its contextual understanding of the situation compelled the agency also to seek control of decision making, problem definition, allocation of resources, definition of participant roles, and timing and location of operational efforts. That the agency continued to insist on control is illustrated by these excerpts from WGF's response to the draft ferret recovery plan produced by the FWS (Wyoming Game and Fish Department 1987:5–7):

> We have taken the lead in black-footed ferret management, and intend to retain control over the species in the near term future. . . . We can find no place

that [the plan] acknowledges Wyoming will maintain control of black-footed ferrets within the state (and within constraints of Federal permits). We believe this should be corrected. . . . The Wyoming Game and Fish Department, which has taken the initiative in capture of black-footed ferrets and implementation of the captive breeding program, will continue to maintain responsibility for control of the captive breeding program within constraints of Federal permits. . . . It appears to us that portions of the Recovery Plan are designed to turn control of this program over to private interests. We would not agree to that.

Forrest's (1987) rebuttal to WGF's response to the draft recovery plan (of which he was co-author) also recognizes WGF's penchant for control:

The statements that Wyoming "intend(s) to retain control over the species in the near term future" and "the captive breeding program" demonstrate Wyoming's ongoing reluctance to participate in open and collaborative discussions of problem-solving on ferret recovery. I do not believe recovery can succeed in this kind of management environment. Recovery is likely to succeed only if a national approach is taken. I believe that the U.S. Fish and Wildlife Service must firmly grasp the leadership role to ensure that the program remains open and receptive to the talents and support [of] those with an interest in the welfare of the species. (Citations in original omitted)

These few excerpts suggest that one of the state's issues of critical concern was control and that WGF viewed federal oversight as a "constraint" on its actions.

   This kind of goal inversion within agencies is not unique to the ferret program (Alvarez 1993, Clark et al. 1994, Yaffee 1994b). Steven Yaffee (1982) studied conflicting goals in implementation of the Endangered Species Act, with a focus on the FWS's Endangered Species Office in Washington, D.C. He noted that the disparate goals and histories of participants created more problems than the sheer number of participants and program components. Typically, responsibility for implementing new programs is given to existing sets of organizations and people. New programs are absorbed into the existing agendas of established agencies and are most often made up from parts of old programs. Not surprisingly, new programs tend to perform like old ones:

Individuals and organizations have goals and traditions that hinder new programs. Individuals in bureaucracies strive to achieve rewards that are defined by the disciplines or professions they belong to or by the organization itself. Organizations develop traditions about how things are done and what is important; these become norms to guide individual behavior. Networks of groups of individuals and organizations form through time and serve to structure intergroup and interagency behavior. (Yaffee 1982:106)

Thus, new programs start in an environment that is already largely fixed as to which program elements will be featured, which actors will participate and how, and what operating goals will dominate. Programs may be given to agencies or bureaucrats who do not understand them, care little about them, or are even hostile to them. New people are generally added only at low levels in the program (technicians, for example). In such situations, new programs are reshaped during implementation in terms of existing institutions. Unfortunately, old goals and traditions can impede new ways of solving problems. Yaffee (1982:107) concluded, with regard to the many conflicting goals that surface in endangered species programs and the problem of goal inversion, that "if there is one observation that shines out in reviewing the list of institutions involved in implementing the ESA, it is the limited number of groups that really care about the preservation of endangered species."

Like most new programs, the ferret program required the interaction of multiple agencies and organizations with long-standing, conflicting goals and histories. The program included the usual cast of state and federal agencies in oft-repeated relationships, the customary modes of operation, and the habitual problems, including perennial state-federal tensions.

The Use of Power in Decision Making

Many chains of decisions are required to solve complex problems, such as restoring endangered species. Some are naturally of a higher order than others, and thus some decision sequences are nested inside more general ones. The whole course by which decisions are made — from recognition of problems to discovery of their solutions — is called the decision process. Studies have shown that this process consists of seven activities, or functions (Lasswell 1971a, Lasswell and McDougal 1992): intelligence (collecting information, assessing its reliability), promotion (making recommendations), prescription (setting the rules to be followed), invocation (enforcing the rules), application (implementing the rules), termination (ending or modifying the process), and appraisal (assessing the success of the decision). This process does not always move ahead in a straightforward manner. The functions of the decision process can help clarify complex social, political, and organizational situations.

The decision process is most successful when democratic mechanisms exist to deal realistically with issues of import and complexity. This requires good intelligence and a flow of high-quality information, among other essential ingredients. It is most successful when there is interdisciplinary involvement and when evaluation is open, independent, and ongoing. Although government often figures prominently in decision making in such arenas as endangered species conservation, participation by authorities outside government and by people directly affected by the decision process can help avoid over-centralization and poor performance of programs (for example, intelligence failures and delays; Brewer and deLeon 1983, Ascher and Healy 1990).

The entire decision process can be subverted by coercive strategies (Lasswell 1956, Lasswell and McDougal 1992). Decision functions can be monopolized and concentrated in the hands of the few and activities channeled in ways that are congenial to the most powerful agency. In such instances, participants who seek other arrangements are stifled and eventually excluded. "Often the outcome is the result of an overwhelming ownership element" (Lasswell 1956: 14). Any group's efforts to concentrate or share decision functions reveals its values, perspectives, and strategies. This description of the use of power in decision processes can help illuminate what happened in the ferret case. When WGF denied a research permit to the ISU/Biota team for continuing work in mid-1986, it largely captured the scientific intelligence function for itself. The agency inserted the University of Wyoming Cooperative Research Unit, which it had hired, into the vacant niche it had created and further relegated the FWS field team to a more limited role in the field and in interagency transactions. With these acts, WGF increased its control over the decision process simply by gaining greater control over the intelligence function. WGF sought and ultimately achieved control of promotion, prescription, and invocation, too, because it set the standards, laid out the plans, and made final decisions at every level, from monitoring prairie dog colonies to granting permits and limiting the membership of BFAT. Concentrating power seemed to be an end in itself, and the goals that power might legitimately have served — in this case, recovery of ferrets — faded into the background.

The powerful role of bureaucratic discretion has been acknowledged by several authors. "The considerable discretion inevitably left in the hands of administrators requires that they shape outcomes through their decisions, thus creating policy in the most concrete sense" (Ascher and Healy 1990:171). This is confirmed by Yaffee (1982:70): "In implementing the ESA, discretionary judgments were made about what species to review in what order, which experts to talk with, what data to believe, what research to undertake, what degree of regulation to propose, what external interests to consider, and what regulatory exceptions to allow. . . . In fact, the assumptions about prohibitive policy hide enormous amounts of administrative discretion." And Rohlf (1992:144) noted:

> The executive branch of the federal government in theory simply carries out the wishes of Congress, but as a practical matter the views of the incumbent

administration often influence interpretation and implementation of federal legislation. In contrast to the legislative process, this sort of "playing politics" with federal policy occurs with little or no public participation or even public knowledge. O'Connell (1992) correctly notes that agency regulations interpreting the ESA, as well as agency actions implementing the statute, account for many of the reasons why the ESA does not work.

APPRAISAL IN THE FERRET PROGRAM

WGF's actions in regard to appraisal of the ferret program are a particularly good illustration of its efforts to appropriate the decision process. Appraisal, or evaluation, identifies those who are "causally or formally responsible for successes or failures" (Lasswell 1971a:29). Appraisal is essential for two reasons: it identifies whether resources were properly allocated and serves as a basis for rewards. According to Bissell (1994:23), "While there has been a moderate amount of attention paid to the judicial and legislative levels of wildlife policy, the preponderance of policy made by the actions of state and federal agencies has gone more or less without formal analysis." Ideally, appraisal should focus not only on the outcome—whether ferrets are eventually restored to health—but also on the process—what the cost was in dollars, time, and lost opportunities, how well the decision and policy processes worked in achieving the desired outcome, and what effects ensued. However, as Ascher and Healy (1990:172) noted, "the very fact that appraisal is so intimately connected with rewards and punishment frequently leads to distortions in the appraisal function."

No thorough or systematic appraisal of the ferret program, independent or otherwise, was carried out at either state or federal levels during the years covered by this account. Much of the informal self-appraisal by government to date has focused only on partial outcomes and has concluded that, because ferrets have increased in number in captivity and reintroductions have begun, the program has been successful (e.g., Thorne and Oakleaf 1991, Casper Star-Tribune 1993c). To many, especially technically oriented biologists or uncritical observers, this may seem to suffice as an indicator and to justify the conclusion that the increase in ferret numbers resulted directly and largely from WGF's actions. The department has proclaimed the program a success: "The captive breeding effort is being conducted by the Wyoming Game and Fish Department and has been successful, allowing the program to meet established goals" (Oakleaf and Thorne 1992:1; see also Wyoming Game and Fish Department 1992a). The proclamation of success extended to the cooperation of WGF-chosen players:

> After three successful black-footed ferret releases into Wyoming's Shirley Basin, the state's top wildlife administrator is ready to call the recovery effort

the "almost" conservation success story of the century, according to a news release.

Wyoming Game and Fish Department director Francis "Pete" Petera said, "When the black-footed ferret is thriving on its own, dispersing to unoccupied habitat and participating in an ecosystem as a self-sustaining population, it will be the conservation success story of this century. We're not there yet, but I guarantee you, that day will come."

Petera was speaking in Washington, D.C., at ceremonies kicking off a nationwide celebration recognizing the success of captive breeding efforts for the ferret. . . .

Petera used the occasion in the nation's capital to praise the courage of the Wyoming Game and Fish Department leaders who made the decision to take the last wild ferrets into captivity in 1985. He also applaud[ed] the cooperation of ranchers, agencies, private industry and others in the recovery effort, and noted the dedication of state and federal scientists who often worked around the clock to make the operation a success. (Casper Star-Tribune 1993:D1)

The time and financial costs of the ferret program, considered exceedingly great by some observers (although it is difficult to get figures, Miller et al. 1996 cite a total of more than $1.5 million for 1991 alone), were represented by WGF as normal and reasonable:

> The time and effort required to implement a black-footed ferret recovery programme in Wyoming can be documented or predicted: to obtain adequate biological and demographic knowledge of black-footed ferrets required three years (1981–84); obtaining funding and developing a captive breeding facility required three years (1984–86); developing adequate captive propagation techniques required two years (1986–87); development of a relatively secure captive population required four years (1986–89). A minimum of five years (1991–96) will probably be required to attain Wyoming objectives of re-establishing at least two populations in the wild. (Thorne and Oakleaf 1991: 258)

This history gives the impression that everything had proceeded according to some plan and that each step could only have been carried out sequentially.

Critical appraisal of WGF's program from outside the agency was summarily dismissed. Tom Thorne and Bob Oakleaf (1991:246) asserted that "mistakes, both real and alleged, have been described by commentators that were well-intentioned, naive about Federal and State laws and endangered species management, uninformed about actual events surrounding the black-footed ferrets. Most of these authors, however, failed to provide insight into important problems confronted [by WGF] in the black-footed ferret programme and ignored the many lessons and parallels with other endangered species programmes." The agency depicted itself as the victim of unwarranted attacks: "It's been a hard road, and we're to be forgiven if the effort has left its marks. If we're a little paranoid, it's because we've been ambushed so many times. If we seem uninclined to compromise, it's because past compromises have too often led to disasters. If we insist on a passionate commitment to a carefully defined doctrine, it's because we've seen so many efforts to turn conservation philosophy on its head. The psychological quirks of hard-line conservationists are understandable enough. But our quirks are hurting us" (Wyoming Game and Fish Department 1991b:2).

Because of this history of dismissing or ignoring outside appraisals, it is unlikely that the program will ever receive a thorough in-house evaluation. However, independent, non-agency appraisals that look at outcomes, effects, and processes are beginning to appear. Some aspects of the ferret program have been evaluated by the press, scientists, scientific organizations, and conservation organizations. Miller et al. (1996) and Reading and Miller (1994) provided in-depth accounts. For instance, Miller et al. noted that

> sometimes one method of evaluation masks deficiencies that another method reveals. For example, counting only the number of ferrets in captivity and reintroduced has created an impression of success, at least over the short term. These numbers are certainly a source of pride to recovery-program participants, and they represent a tremendous effort on behalf of the species. But they say nothing about efficient use of effort and resources, amount of genetic diversity conserved, unpursued opportunities, public support for the program, public attitudes about habitat destruction, broader issues of biodiversity, or what has been learned about black-footed ferret conservation and reintroduction. (p. 204)

These authors pointed out that recovery programs may actually show progress in outcome measures in spite of "inadequate and ineffective organizational arrangements," lack of "a rigorous use of science, experimental design, or adequate documentation," inefficient use of resources, conflict among participants, "a poor job of assessing and addressing the attitudes of the local public," and lack of public education (pp. 204–206):

> In the future, the program's success may be defined by a few isolated and heavily managed black-footed ferret populations, while the actual species diversity of the prairie dog ecosystem continues to decline. Reintroduction could thus be labeled a success (at least from the perspective of agency self-aggrandizement), but in reality amount only to a cosmetic effort rather than true conservation. (p. 206)

Despite these criticisms, government appraisal in the ferret program seems to be an illustration of success breeding success. A few years' success in meeting specific, easily measured objectives of the recovery plan (raising the number of captive ferrets, reintroducing animals to the wild) has given WGF further advantage in the appraisal function. It has used this leverage to bolster its position to the point that the agency's "success" has been widely accepted. Some of WGF's allies, such as the FWS Regional Office and the Wyoming Chapter of the National Wildlife Federation, have consistently praised the agency's performance despite the drop in ferret numbers in 1985, the chronic conflict, the delays, the high costs, the shaky genetic status of ferrets, the low numbers of surviving reintroduced ferrets, or other facts. Indeed, the program has received accolades in recent years for its performance, including awards from the Society for Conservation Biology and the American Association of Zoological Parks and Aquariums.

Decision-making processes can be manipulated by powerful groups to achieve particular ends. Ferret program participants performed or influenced various decision functions, especially on occasions when they shared activities, values, and interests, thus forming alliances or "political arenas." Nevertheless, one of the outcomes of the overall process was its concentration, centralization, and legitimization of operational control within WGF (see Lasswell 1956). A certain set of values and perspectives was served — namely, those of WGF and its allies — while those of other participants were not met. Those interests with power ultimately gained more power and control through the decision process. By 1986, all seven functions were essentially under WGF influence.

Unproductive Conflict

The black-footed ferret program in Wyoming was riddled with conflict because of the diversity of goals, operating styles, and perspectives among the organizational participants and because those in a position to manage it productively did not do so. Conflict arose in many intergroup relationships — between professionals and bureaucrats, between agencies, between subunits of single organizations, and between individuals. Even after several years, when the program might have been expected to settle into a workable routine, conflict persisted: "Relations between agencies and personnel working on the [ferret] reintroduction program were often strained and conflict laden. This definitely influenced program operations. Although acknowledgment of this problem was widespread, there was little mitigation" (Reading 1991:4).

Conflict is familiar to those who study and analyze organizations and policy processes. When it is out of control, conflict can be costly: it diverts energy from the work to be done, reduces judgment, and produces "loser effects" such as denial, distortion, dissension, and blaming of scapegoats. Too much conflict results in poor coordination in achieving the overall goal because it decreases contact, collaboration, integration, and sympathy between groups, and it results in "poor decisions based on distorted information and low commitment" (Brown 1983:48, Daft 1983). Conflict may cause "coercive tactics of influence" to be used, even sabotage and violence (Brown 1983). Many of these symptoms showed up in the ferret program. However, the program also exhibited symptoms of too little conflict, when it suppressed or avoided differences that should have been confronted, discussed, and resolved: "Such suppression produces decisions based on inadequate information, poor analysis of options, failure to confront outmoded traditions and myths, and little awareness of critical interdependencies. In the long term, conflict suppression is associated with interface overorganization [i.e., too rigid a structure between groups] which encourages inattention to important differences and interdependencies among the parties" (Brown 1983:48–49).

CAUSES OF CONFLICT

Organizational and individual participants may vary dramatically in how they understand the causes of conflict and the means to defuse it. The nearly universal and unfortunate response is to attribute conflict to individual "troublemakers" and then to get rid of them. But conflict is rampant when programs are confused or inadequate, when coordination is lacking, or when control over resources is in dispute. In other words, conflict is usually not the result of "bad" people but of poorly structured and operated programs. If relationships and responsibilities in the ferret program had been cooperatively clarified in the beginning, if resources had been allocated so that each participant could properly carry out its mandate, if appropriate coordination and control mechanisms had been instituted, and if goals had been agreed upon, it is unlikely that the program would have suffered so much conflict. The program's structure and domination of decision functions by WGF was possibly the largest single cause of conflict and also the hardest to manage productively. "Gaining and exercising power," Hrebiniak (1978:247) observed, "are not frictionless processes."

If the origins of conflict are not understood by at least some program participants who are in positions to manage it productively, it will likely fester, increase in intensity, and produce a host of negative consequences. But administrators of the ferret program did little to resolve the many underlying causes of conflict and, in fact, ultimately contributed to it. WGF misattributed the conflict to a few individuals with big "egos" who were "politically maneuvering" the situation to their advantage (Wyoming Game and Fish Department 1991b:2, Thorne and Oakleaf 1991). In one WGF official's view, conflict came from "having disparate groups involved that are constantly throwing rocks at each other [and this] is a damned poor way to run a program. If I had it to do over, the first time I heard someone back-stabbing someone else, I'd kick him the hell out of there immediately" (Zimmerman 1986:7). This focus on *people* as a way to understand and manage conflict is common, according to Jelinek et al. (1981). But such a limited understanding of organizations does little to defuse conflict or rectify its underlying causes (J. Wilson 1989).

It is necessary to understand why conflict can be expected to appear in organizations and what strategies are available to manage it productively. According to Daft (1983), conflict has two ingredients: differences between groups and frustration, that is, a perception by one group that others may block its efforts to achieve its goals. Conflict is a natural consequence of all the inherent differences in a complex program — incompatible goals, competition for resources, power differences, differences in tasks, differences in training and skills, and so on. Conflict may arise between more or less equal groups with different tasks or goals, between hierarchical levels, or between social groups with ethnic, religious, political, or other differences. It increases as uncertainty and complexity in the task environment increase, as the number of participants grows, as interdependencies solidify, and as managers structure programs to increase the differences between groups. It was not long before many participants in the ferret program attributed the worst motives to others in the coalition without appreciation for the situations and constraints that faced other groups or their shared goals.

CONFLICT MANAGEMENT STRATEGIES

Daft (1983:422) has observed that "conflict has to be effectively managed for the organization to perform effectively and to achieve its overall goals." Conflict has been discussed to this point as though it were entirely negative, but recent studies have shown that it can yield numerous positive results — focusing efforts on the task at hand, providing in-group cohesion and satisfaction, balancing disparities among groups, stimulating hard work, producing new superior ideas, and calling attention to fundamental problems needing solution — *if managed within a productive range* (e.g., Thomas 1976, 1977, Daft 1983). Appropriate levels of conflict are demonstrated in two levels of interaction: problem-solving behavior and bargaining behavior. Conflicting groups exhibit problem-solving behavior when they clarify mutual interests as well as differences, openly explore alternative solutions, develop trust and useful communication, and choose options that have benefits for all groups. Such behavior "generate[s] decisions based on accurate and complete information" and builds stable and long-lasting relationships among groups (Brown 1983:51). Appropriate conflict is also shown in bargaining behavior, when groups recognize the benefits of their underlying interdependence on each other but show somewhat less trust and more closely managed information flows than in problem-solving behavior. Bargaining behavior clarifies groups' interests, boundaries, and differences and fosters a forum by which they can continue to negotiate (Brown 1983).

Either "structural" or "process" strategies can be used to manage conflict successfully. Structural strategies call for changes in a program's formal reporting relationships (organizational designs), while process strategies seek changes in individuals' attitudes (interpersonal behavior). Daft (1983) outlined a sequence of nine strategies to reduce conflict; they lie along a continuum from structural to attitudinal changes. First is a strictly structural change: groups can be physically separated. Second, managers can invoke rules to enforce cooperation or separation. Third, interactions among conflicting groups can be limited to common goals. Fourth, attitudinal as well as structural changes can be effected by bringing in integrators (coordinators). Fifth, groups can be compelled to confront conflict and negotiate. Sixth, outside conflict-management consultants can work closely with conflicting groups to change their attitudes. Seventh, rotating members among conflicting groups can lead to helpful changes in attitudes and understanding of out-groups. Eighth, stressing superordinate goals and interdependent tasks can help conflicting groups see their mutual interests. And ninth, group training by psychologists can be very effective in changing attitudes.

L. David Brown (1983) also described four useful intervention strategies for managing conflict productively. First, behavior can be redirected by refocusing attention on different issues or different alternatives, by improving the flow of information (expanding opportunities for communication, guarding against stereotyping, raising "taboo" issues, and creating mechanisms to increase trust), or by offering new options for action (that is, breaking out of destructive patterns of interaction). Second, resources (including personnel, information, and funds) can be reallocated, expanded, or contracted, or their sources changed. Third, perspectives can be refined: changes can be made in the ways groups "understand and assign meaning to events and actions" (Brown 1983: 64). Conflicting groups can do this by reformulating their interests (clarifying differences but stressing superordinate goals), by changing unrealistic stereotypes of their opponents, by "reconceptualizing the situation" (creating alternative theories to explain it), and by seeking to understand better the dynamics of the conflict. And fourth, underlying forces that cause conflict can be realigned by redefining the boundaries of groups or changing their "permeability" relative to other groups, by altering groups' "norms and values," or by changing the rules, standard operating procedures, or incentive systems.

It appears that WGF did not recognize conflict in the ferret program as a manipulable variable—it did not actively, productively manage conflict. The agency, instead, suppressed conflict. It reduced contact among groups by convening few meetings, especially informal ones. It did not actively build either the trust or the reporting mechanisms needed for adequate, two-way information flows. This suggests that the agency settled for poor problem analysis, poor decision making, and conventional approaches rather than managing the conflict appropriately. Despite its powerful position, it exhibited some of the "loser effects" described by Daft (1983)—denial, distortion, and blaming of scapegoats. If the agency can be credited with having made any attempt at conflict management, its strategy was chiefly structural: it promulgated rules and designs by which to isolate groups in the coalition. It introduced a "coordinator" into the program, but his activities did not increase information exchange, trust, credibility, or collaboration. The authority relationships and program structure could not permit the kind of integration of participants or the kind of control (in the sense of direction and leadership) needed to reduce conflict. Daft (1983:433) said it well: "The incentive system governs the degree to which subgroups cooperate or conflict with one another." By not welcoming all participants into the coalition, by not coordinating and directing them, WGF established disincentives to share information and to cooperate. Some participants took it upon themselves to handle the conflict by changing attitudes through socializing with members of other groups. This process strategy was of limited success, for the most part, because some groups refused to participate.

Some of these same general strategies might have been used early in the program to prevent conflict from building. Daft (1983) described four preventive approaches available to managers. First, they could have deflected conflict by emphasizing the primary goal and each group's unique contribution to achieving that goal. Second, they might have defined activities clearly so that each group understood its responsibilities, the limits to its authority, and its role in the larger coalition. Third, they could have stimulated contacts and communication so that misperceptions could not arise. And fourth, they could have avoided win/lose situations by not forcing any group to lose and by stressing joint action and pooling of resources (human as well as financial). But these or similar mechanisms went unrecognized and unused by administrators and coordinators in the ferret program.

Conclusions

The incompatibility of different kinds of goals in the ferret program led to goal inversion, in this case the domination of control goals over task goals, a phenomenon common in bureaucracies. The program's decision processes, those streams of judgments and conclusions on various issues, came to be monopolized by WGF's powerful position. Decision functions came increasingly under its influence until, after some years, the agency largely controlled the entire decision-making process, permitting it to institutionalize and legitimize its program in intractable ways. As a result of these developments, conflict was intense, usually destructive, and chronically misdiagnosed and mismanaged by program leaders. Because professional organizational management was absent, the program suffered and the ferret suffered — almost to extinction. But, as Pressman and Wildavsky (1973:109) observed about new programs, "The cards in this world are stacked against things happening, as so much effort is required to make them move. The remarkable thing is that new programs work at all."

6

Advisory Teams, Coordinators, and Field Teams
Legitimizing and Bureaucratizing

Work as complex, both technically and organizationally, as endangered species restoration usually requires knowledgeable, authoritative advice, well-integrated programs, and effective field teams to be successful. Viewed from a distance, the ferret program appeared to be well assisted, with three formal advisory teams (at times with two in operation simultaneously), two ferret coordinators (one employed by WGF and the other by the FWS Regional Office), and two major field teams. But in fact the roles played by the advisory teams varied considerably: they sometimes offered essential technical and strategic planning advice, but all helped WGF to bureaucratize its program. The coordinating roles also varied, but basically they were conventional managerial linking positions that sought to police field workers and to facilitate top-down command and control. The role of the field teams was to get basic information on the wild ferrets and their conservation needs, but they were maintained in peripheral, technician-level positions and not permitted to participate fully in decision making and ferret recovery. All the advisory teams, coordinators, and field teams legitimized the program and elevated its public profile and, in so doing, facilitated greater government bureaucratization.

In this chapter I briefly examine the structure, function, and significance of the three advisory teams and describe how each related to the overall program. I also look at the two government coordinating positions and appraise their effect on the restoration effort. Finally, I describe the two major field teams active in the first few years of the program and their different, complementary, and sometimes shared activities. In principle, all these subunits of the program could have enhanced its adequacy, effectiveness, efficiency, and equity, but in practice, they deviated significantly from their ideal operations for a variety of reasons.

There were other teams, working groups, workshops, and coordinating committees active at various times in the ferret restoration effort that are not examined here. Most were temporary (such as workshop groups) and others only met once a year (for example, the Interstate Coordinating Committee). Most have never been described in any detail despite their collective influence on the ferret restoration effort. One view of these entities was given by Wyoming Game and Fish (1991a), which highlighted the University of Wyoming and the Cooperative Research Unit in Laramie. Although the behavior and contributions of these additional teams, groups, and committees varied, they all functioned similarly in their legitimization and bureaucratization of the WGF-dominated program.

Advisory Teams

Advisory teams are valuable in endangered species restoration efforts for several reasons. Not all the specialized information needed to restore a species will necessarily reside in the agencies mandated to carry out the recovery program. Broad-based, outside, technical advice can supplement existing knowledge and bring new perspectives to the task. Outside advisers can increase the range of options for action, enhance the profile and legitimacy of the program, and sometimes help garner additional resources. Traditionally, however, advisory teams in endangered species conservation have only provided technical and planning advice and have seldom, if ever, offered organizational and policy process advice. Advisory teams can sometimes cause problems, too. They may provide misleading or incomplete advice, they may contribute to faulty decision making and subsequent actions, and they may be co-opted or captured by powerful interests that use them for purposes other than the ostensible task at hand. Special care is needed to staff teams, to keep them open so that information beyond the team can flow in, and to manage their internal and external dynamics most productively. Robert Culbert and Robert Blair (1989) reviewed the role and utility of recovery teams in endangered species conservation, including their strengths and weaknesses (see also Clark et al. 1994).

In the first five years, ferret recovery was advised, at various times and in various ways, by three separate teams: the FWS Regional Office's Black-Footed Ferret Recovery Team, WGF's Black-Footed Ferret Advisory Team, and the International Union for the Conservation of Nature and Natural Resources' Captive Breeding Specialist Group.

THE BLACK-FOOTED FERRET RECOVERY TEAM

The federal Black-Footed Ferret Recovery Team was established in 1976 and charged with devising a national plan for ferret recovery and updating the plan as needed or every five years. The recovery team comprised representatives of three branches of the FWS, one representative of the U.S. Forest Service, one representative of the National Park Service, one representative of a state fish and game department (South Dakota), and one representative of the National Audubon Society. This team finished its first plan in 1978 and submitted it to the FWS regional director, who eventually approved it. At that time, no wild ferrets were known to exist anywhere, and so the plan was very general. It proved to be of limited utility when the Meeteetse ferrets were found, after which the FWS reactivated the team and directed it to update the 1978 plan. A few meetings took place in 1982, but by 1983 the team fell inactive, presumably at the direction of the FWS regional director. Neither before nor after the 1981 ferret find did the recovery team contribute much to the Meeteetse ferret recovery effort. The team was finally disbanded by the regional director; clear reasons were never given.

Overall, the FWS Recovery Team, as constituted in the early 1980s, just after the Meeteetse ferrets were found, fell far short of its potential to provide essential information and advice to help direct national ferret restoration in a timely, efficient manner. The team at one time or another had members who were knowledgeable about some biological requirements for ferret recovery or could have recruited members who knew more. In addition to providing biological, technical advice to decision makers, the team was also in a position to offer functional organizational and policy process advice to upgrade the ability of working teams, decision makers, and others to work closely and cooperatively. This recovery team had the capacity to function as a high-profile national entity offering advice on a national recovery strategy. Why the FWS failed to direct the team toward these ends remains undocumented.

In 1987, with the FWS's Black-Footed Ferret Recovery Plan about nine years old, the FWS Regional Office contracted Steven Forrest and the FWS Research Center biologist Dean Biggins to co-author a new recovery plan. It is common for the FWS to write its own recovery plans, although it occasionally contracts the task to outsiders when it feels that a recovery team is not needed. The revised plan, which was drafted by late 1987, incorporated much of what was learned from the Meeteetse ferrets using a sound conservation biology perspective. It was approved in 1988. This plan updated progress on ferret recovery to that time and called for new program management as well as other changes. It also encouraged the FWS to take more direct responsibility for ferret recovery than it had over the previous six years and to set a goal to "establish organizational arrangements to accomplish tasks and increase communication" (U.S. Fish and Wildlife Service 1987:29). Unfortunately, the FWS did not act on several of the new plan's recommendations, especially those about improving organization and communication. No significant change in program arrangement, management, or participation resulted.

THE BLACK-FOOTED FERRET ADVISORY TEAM

In 1982, WGF appointed the Black-Footed Ferret Advisory Team (BFAT). This team, which met several times a year, occupied a critical position in the agency's formal program. Circumstances concerning the origin of the team and its basic charge were described by a WGF official (Strickland 1983: 5–6):

> [We] recognized we could not afford to manage this species without considering other people and agencies. To insure decisions made about this ferret population met with agreement from the major land managers in the area, the Game and Fish Department developed an advisory team of representatives from the Bureau of Land Management, the U.S. Forest Service, U.S. Fish and Wildlife Service, Wyoming State Land Board, the landowner whose ranch contained the majority of the habitat for the Meeteetse population, and a representative from the University of Wyoming. The advisory team was created to provide advice and guidance to the Wyoming Game and Fish Department regarding research and management efforts directed at the ferrets.
>
> Initially, the team focused its attention on the ferret population located in the Meeteetse area. Eventually we expect the team will expand its efforts statewide. As efforts are expanded, individuals representing landowner interests may change to include those most directly affected by ferret management. . . .
>
> The Department asked the advisory team to: 1) define objectives for research and management of ferrets in the Meeteetse area; 2) help solicit and review proposals for research projects and advise the Department on issuance of appropriate permits and disbursement of available research funds; 3) help coordinate research efforts; and 4) help locate funding for implementation of a research and management program. . . .
>
> The Department is presently [1983] soliciting funds to support this research program. We hope to have adequate funding to begin this long-term research project by June. We need financial assistance from all those interested in the maintenance and perpetuation of ferrets, including federal agencies, industry, and members of the private conservation community.

It is clear from this that WGF envisioned the team as a means to create a favorable political climate and cooperative image, facilitate agreement on management actions, and represent major land management agencies in the area as well as other groups whose interests might be affected by WGF's actions in ferret management. Thus, the members brought to the team not technical knowledge but political clout. The team lacked national representation; all but one of the initial members were from Wyoming. This created less than an ideal working climate in which to promote national ferret recovery. Nevertheless, the team filled the needs of WGF and was the only advisory team that persisted well into the 1990s.

Although advisory teams are good in principle, BFAT originated or perpetuated many of the problems that beset the program. As a result, its positive contribution to ferret recovery was limited. The advisory team ostensibly served two purposes simultaneously—a technical goal of guiding scientific research and management and a political goal of unifying support and money behind WGF's position. In practice, these were largely incompatible. In such situations, as Garry Brewer and Peter deLeon (1983:185) noted, "when a technical issue enters the political arena, the politician treats it more or less like any other issue, as a possible constraint or opportunity." For example, it was highly improbable that BFAT would have advised WGF to begin captive breeding early and to send ferrets outside the state for this purpose in spite of compelling arguments at the time to do so, in light of WGF's acknowledged preferences to the contrary. Discussion of captive breeding emphasized the possible effects of such action on WGF (especially the lack of a facility and financial resources) and minimized species survival needs (see Carr 1986). Brewer and deLeon observed that the "political process requires consensus, but the very act of exploring options and trying to attain consensus heightens awareness of the many interests and values at stake" (p. 181). It is impossible to achieve agreement and specificity at the same time in such situations.

The advisory team was composed almost exclusively of representatives of government agencies or special interests that had legal or property-rights' authority over the ferrets. This gave the team a decided "power" and "role" orientation (see Harrison 1972, 1975). The work of ferret recovery was nearly always cast in terms of its effects on various organizations (initially, WGF, the FWS Regional Office, the Wyoming State Lands Board, Forest Service, the Bureau of Land Management, the University of Wyoming, and ranchers). The emphasis on authority, domain, and formal representation subordinated task goals (what would best serve ferret recovery) to agency power and control goals (what would best serve the organizations).

BFAT was dominated by decidedly state-centered views. WGF retained veto control over BFAT. The chairman and secretary were WGF employees, and thus the agency significantly influenced meeting agendas, discussions, and records. WGF personnel also often reported to the team. The team met in closed session from time to time, thus precluding open discussion or participation by others, which fostered antagonism and mistrust. Many of the team's recommendations seemed predetermined because the team functioned largely to endorse the advertised preferences of WGF administrators.

Some members of BFAT lacked the necessary scientific and technical knowledge and experience to design a comprehensive research plan to meet the urgent needs of ferret conservation on the local scale and ferret recovery on the national scale, evaluate the research proposals it solicited according to scientific standards, or guide management activities. Few on the team possessed specific or general knowledge about ferret ecology, demographics, or genetics, captive breeding, or management of small populations. Field researchers with first-hand knowledge of ferrets (either from the ongoing Meeteetse studies or the earlier South Dakota studies) were not appointed to BFAT.

BFAT also seemed weak in its administrative capabilities to direct a complex research program, develop a funding base and long-term financial plan, or coordinate research efforts among participants. There was little evidence that team members had explicit knowledge of organizational options or decision processes, such as who should participate, roles for participants, how to structure the program, patterns of leadership, incentive systems, and much more. The team's decisions, as a result, were based on incomplete knowledge of pertinent subjects, and deliberation on both scientific and programmatic aspects of ferret recovery seemed superficial. These limitations were addressed by Robert Finley (1983:34), an observer with the FWS Wildlife Research Center, who commented on BFAT's operations, as well as the FWS's lack of response and the larger implications of the situation:

> The atmosphere for objective research in the Fish and Wildlife Service has deteriorated . . . under the axiom that research exists only for the support of policies and needs of management. It is impossible for Fish and Wildlife Service scientists to plan intelligently even short-term research with any idea of what support will be forthcoming. After dedicated, experienced biologists of the black-footed ferret survey team of the Denver Research Center succeeded in capturing a live ferret near Meeteetse, Wyoming, in late 1981, management officials moved in to set up an interagency committee to plan and fund ferret research. None of the agency representatives appointed to the committee was a qualified research administrator or had any ferret experience. Nearly a year of valuable time has been lost to wrangling over proposals submitted by researchers and usually rejected by the committee. For some reason, the Fish and Wildlife Service has been dragging its feet over funding

and leadership in ferret research ever since the ferret breeding project at the Patuxent Research Center was terminated. Ferret research in Wyoming is being treated as though it were a part of "The New Federalism," i.e., push it off on the states and hope the problem will go away.

I firmly believe that managers should make management decisions, hopefully on the basis of scientific as well as other facts. . . .

It is all too evident that disregard for objectivity is rampant in the prevailing management philosophy. Administrative decisions are accepted as infallible and require no further examination of the natural world. In these times it is more important than ever for wildlife professionals to support those individuals who have the courage to stand up for scientific ethics and objectivity in the face of administrative pressures and abuse. Survival of the Yellowstone grizzly and the black-footed ferret may depend on taking a stand on scientific principles before all the wildlife facts are in.

Additional calls were made for BFAT to be more responsive to the task of ferret recovery. In 1982, the FWS Montana/Wyoming representative suggested that BFAT become a "task force" by having members divide into working groups, research various aspects of ferret recovery, and report back to BFAT for discussion and recommendations. This notion was quickly rejected by WGF (see BFAT minutes, October 26, 1982). In 1984, Michael Bogan (1985:28.2), of the FWS Wildlife Research Center, stated that there was a need

to constitute a new advisory board to direct and monitor ferret research, particularly with the important questions that are fast coming at us, and that that board have as its first charge, the development of plans and priorities for ferret research. The state must realize that it is protecting an animal that has national significance and interest and thus the responsibilities go beyond state boundaries. The federal government must realize the rights and needs of state and private agencies to be involved in ferret research and management. I think we need a more open forum for discussion and a better representation of researchers on the board than we have at present, while maintaining the current representations of land managers and private interests. Furthermore, we need a greater shouldering of responsibility by both the states and federal government for where we are going in ferret research.

Despite widespread recognition of BFAT's scientific and programmatic limitations, the advisory team remained unchanged in structure or operation, with one exception: in late 1984, a member of the NGO conservation community from the Washington, D.C., office of the National Wildlife Federation was appointed to BFAT by WGF. The individual had virtually no contact with the field teams and told the field teams that he did not represent the ISU/Biota research team or its supporters. He quickly and clearly allied himself with WGF.

Advisory teams, despite their worthy aims, can bring out the worst in people. Faulty leadership, too much or too little group cohesiveness, pressures to adhere to group norms, unexamined assumptions, hidden agendas, and various other subtle (or not so subtle) constraints limit group members from exercising critical judgment and from expressing doubts openly when most people in the decision-making group seem to have reached a consensus. Irving Janis (1972) called this phenomenon "groupthink." It is a deterioration of mental efficiency, reality testing, and judgment that results from in-group pressures and brings about premature closure so that the full range of solutions to a problem is never explored.

One of the most blatant examples of groupthink is when organizational leaders express their preferences before asking group members for their advice. One such instance in BFAT deliberations is documented in minutes of the September 17, 1984, meeting. The main issue was if, when, and where to conduct captive breeding. The minutes show that WGF's director was in attendance with several of his senior staff, an unprecedented event. The director began by mentioning that "he would favor locating the facility [to breed ferrets] in Wyoming and emphasized the importance of cooperative funding" (BFAT meeting minutes, September 17; Wyoming Game and Fish 1984:1). After discussion about the roles of advisory teams and individuals and a decision to limit all advice to only narrow technical facts, the director asked BFAT for its advice about captive breeding. Before the advisory team could be heard from, however, another WGF official turned the discussion to the matter of whether ferrets should be captured at all. The question of who would fund the effort was raised again. WGF officials asked a member of the conservation community in attendance, a representative of the National Zoo, if the conservation community would pay for captive breeding in Wyoming. The response was no. After some discussion about WGF's lack of funds, another WGF official "asked what benefit could be derived from the effort" to capture Meeteetse ferrets in 1984. Discussions of natural mortality at Meeteetse and the possibility of the Denver zoo holding ferrets ensued. Another WGF official claimed "that the urgency to captivate [*sic*] ferrets has been over emphasized." The BFAT member from the University of Wyoming moved that the advisory team "not allow removing [black-footed ferrets] from the Meeteetse area this year." The U.S. Forest Service representative seconded the motion, and that was the end of the captive-breeding issue for 1984. Discussion turned to other matters — ferret population estimates and survey guidelines. The "open" part of the meeting then ended and a closed session followed. Discussions in the closed meeting included recognition that the new National Wildlife Federation representative "could not possibly represent the *eastern-based conser-*

vation groups, but that he should attempt to act as a spokesman for their interests" anyway (BFAT meeting minutes, September 17, 1984, emphasis in original). A discussion of media "problems" was followed by adjournment.

Such proceedings were a clear example of groupthink: top officials expressed their preferences and expectations, influenced advisers' discussions, and limited and controlled the final decisions. Discussion was limited to one or two courses of action, resulting in premature closure. Initial preferences (as well as initially rejected options) were never revisited to reassess non-obvious costs and benefits or associated risks and advantages. No outsiders were consulted who might have offered valuable insights that the group had overlooked. Janis (1972) identified these and other decision-making defects as contributing to inadequate problem solving.

For these several reasons, BFAT appeared vague in its deliberations, slow and conservative in decision making, lacking in necessary technical knowledge, and resistant to exploring options for ferret recovery beyond WGF's clearly expressed preferences. The team's membership and stated purpose, "to insure decisions made about this ferret population met with agreement from the major land managers in the area," virtually guaranteed that the team's performance would not keep pace with the heavy demands of ferret recovery.

THE CAPTIVE BREEDING SPECIALIST GROUP (CBSG)

The International Union for the Conservation of Nature and Natural Resources, or IUCN (now the World Conservation Union), was set up in Europe after World War II as an nongovernmental organization committed to conservation of the world's natural resources. It includes a number of specialist groups that consult in various capacities on conservation projects. The CBSG, which is very active internationally, entered the ferret recovery program in late 1985 to provide technical and planning advice to WGF and the FWS. This assistance was funded by the FWS.

A unique set of circumstances made the CBSG's entry into the ferret program possible. By late 1985, the program was in crisis: much of the wild Meeteetse population was dead, the first six captive ferrets were dead or dying in WGF's facility, and professionals in a variety of organizations as well as the press were highly critical of the program's administration. WGF had just captured a second group of six ferrets but still lacked adequate in-house holding facilities, a mix of necessary personnel skills, and financial resources to make captive breeding a reality, and it had rejected the option of sending ferrets to out-of-state facilities. The ferret was rapidly moving toward extinction under the existing program. Help was clearly needed.

The CBSG had some answers. The team was composed of leading authorities from zoos (including the Bronx, National, and Minnesota zoos) and experts from universities and research centers in mustelid breeding, genetics, animal nutrition, and related subjects. The CBSG team leader approached a WGF representative at an international meeting, and later, over the course of several meetings with WGF officials, convinced them to accept assistance from the CBSG. The CBSG offered technical assistance that was absolutely necessary for the captive-breeding portion of the program to succeed. Politically, from WGF's viewpoint, receiving advice from the CBSG helped legitimize its faltering program and declining credibility. However, the CBSG's advice and technical assistance were accepted by WGF within strict limits: when the specialists tried to examine broader captive-breeding and ferret recovery issues, WGF reminded the team that its continued participation was tenuous (Miller et al. 1996).

WGF played up the participation of the CBSG in its press releases, but always made it very clear that WGF, not the CBSG, was in control of the program (e.g., see White 1986). The CBSG went along with this and publicly praised WGF's "vital leadership role." Many CBSG words of support were initially published about WGF's pioneering efforts at captive-breeding ferrets, the "accidental" death of the first six ferrets (which was said to be "an understandable mistake"), WGF's well-qualified staff, and WGF's positive role in ferret conservation. Minutes of the CBSG meeting of October 9–10, 1987, in Laramie, for example, contain a great deal of appeasing language. A discussion of whether to divide the single, tiny population held in Wyoming was introduced with mollifying words about shared concerns among CBSG, the agencies, and others. The CBSG then outlined its argument to split the population, while in response "WGF strongly note[d]" its reasons not to divide it. In the end, it was recorded, "the CBSG accepts the position of WGF that it is preferable to risk the catastrophic loss of the population for the present breeding season in favor of the possible gains for breeding in the 1988 season." This kind of "defusing" rhetoric is essential when new groups enter a relatively closed, hostile environment (Porter 1980). In general, it worked for the CBSG and WGF.

CBSG members were committed to ferret recovery and often traveled to Wyoming, sometimes at their own expense. Some members spent weeks with the captive ferrets. Several major plans were co-authored by team members and WGF personnel (e.g., Ballou and Oakleaf 1987). A symposium held in 1986 was initiated by the CBSG and cosponsored by WGF and others; its proceedings were published in a highly praised book, *Conservation Biology and the Black-Footed Ferret* (Seal et al. 1989). These activities and planning exercises educated many people in the state agency and contributed to the success of the captive-breeding effort. Nevertheless, Miller et al. (1996:100) point out that "though Region 6 [of the FWS] was paying for the advice of the CBSG, decisions continued to be made by Wyoming, which often made for delays. The advice of the CBSG was not binding, and Region 6 did not attempt to assert its own decision-making authority." The team's tenure in the ferret program ended after the 1988 breeding season.

Coordinators

Specialized coordinators, skilled at enhancing information flows for timely, high-quality decision making, can be very helpful in the complex program and policy processes of species recovery. The ferret program had two coordinators, one employed by WGF and the other by the FWS Regional Office. As a basis for examining their performance in the ferret program, we should look first at how organizational designers envision the coordinating role.

The coordinator's role is to integrate the natural, inherent differentiation that emerges among participants in complex and uncertain programs — differences in power, tasks, knowledge holdings, knowledge needs, authority, interests, task orientation, goals, working styles, cognitive and emotional styles, understanding of the nature and urgency of the problem, even language usage and jargon. In programs that involve many organizations and many professional and bureaucratic roles, differentiation may be prodigious. The problem then becomes "how to obtain overall task integration among departments [or groups in a coalition] without reducing the differences that lead to effective subtask performance" (Galbraith 1977:151).

It is the critical job of coordinators to enhance decision making in the face of the many differences that are vital to accomplishing multiple tasks and to joint decision making among interdependent groups. Coordinators, or integrators, operate in three basic ways. First, they are "idea brokers" who stand at the "crossroads of several information streams" and have broad exposure to all functional units of the program from the bottom to the top of hierarchies (Galbraith 1977, p. 153). As a result, they are in a unique position to gather and pass along information. By pulling together information from all over the organization or coalition, they serve the needs of both the whole group and the individuals or functional units within the group. Second, coordinators equalize power differences caused by the necessary task differentiation and they increase trust in joint decision making. Coordinators "create a set of conditions such that power differences due to selective access to information do not diminish the quality of decisions" (p. 149). They can smooth working relationships among people and help manage conflict. Thus they must demonstrate a commitment to superordinate organizational goals rather than personal or subunit goals. In addition, they must be knowledgeable about all facets of the program so that they can help interpret information, options, attitudes, and constraints among all the subunits. Third, coordinators facilitate or manage the decision-making process itself. Jay R. Galbraith pointed out "that merely bringing people together who possess the necessary information to solve a problem does not guarantee that they will use the information" (p. 155). The coordinator's role is "not to make the best decision but to see that the best decision gets made" (p. 156) by helping the group stay open to ideas, encouraging problem-solving behavior, summarizing and integrating information, and detecting when the group is ready to come to a decision.

Coordinators do not supervise or conduct any of the actual work, and they have no formal authority and no staff. Their power comes from their knowledge and integrating skills. Their influence can be enhanced when they take a problem-oriented approach, when the formal information-reporting system includes their work, and when the formal system confers a high status on the role.

A good coordinator requires a special personality. Paul Lawrence and Jay Lorsch (1967) found that successful coordinators do not have a high need for affiliation but can stand between conflicting groups without being absorbed. Galbraith (1977:158) suggested that people who are not dogmatic, who are open-minded, and who are satisfied by working through others make good coordinators, but he noted: "The role requires the individual to behave in ways which remove possible impediments to sharing information and behaving in a problem-solving fashion. Such individuals are difficult to find and training technologies are not yet developed to create them."

THE WGF COORDINATOR

Like every other complex endeavor, the ferret program needed differentiation to be effective, but it also needed integration — a task that fell in part to the WGF and FWS coordinators. The WGF coordinator entered the program fifteen months after it began "to coordinate ongoing research and assist in finding sources of funding for additional work" (Strickland 1983:6). The coordinator was inserted hierarchically into the formal program between WGF's central office and work teams in the field (the ISU/Biota team, the FWS Wildlife Research Center, and other workers). This increased the vertical height of the formal structure, a move that often results in increased communication distortions as data are passed upward and deletions, additions, substitutions, and reinterpretations proliferate. Communication distortions were evident in the ferret program (see the WGF's coordinator's memo of June 15, 1983, to

BFAT and the February and June 1983 WGF ferret newsletters). One example was noted by Steve Forrest (1986:1–2) in a letter to the CBSG leader:

> [The WGF coordinator's previous] memo is clearly in error on this point [winter surveys of ferrets]. The justification is so patently flimsy I cannot help but suspect that the motives for not pursuing the capture option are motivated by something other than concern for the animals' well being. . . . I am extremely upset that this data continues to be cited [by WGF] out of context and without the conditional statement we attached to it.

Little opportunity existed to address problems of communication infidelity. Consequently, errors mounted, distrust increased, and conflict intensified — exactly the opposite of what the coordinator should have achieved.

WGF's ferret coordinator, Dave Belitsky, also performed what organizational designers call "domain defense," as we see in the following letter:

> This letter is a rebuttal of allegations made in a letter to the editor (The Wildlifer, July-Aug. 1983) [Finley 1983] about the interagency committee which plans and funds black-footed ferret research in Wyoming. First of all, I should introduce Wyoming's black-footed ferret research steering committee which is known as the Black-Footed Ferret Advisory Team (BFAT). BFAT membership has been selected to represent private landowners, wildlife management agencies, public land management agencies, and university researchers who would be affected by consequent black-footed ferret management. This involvement of agencies and other interests early in the development of the program is an attempt to avoid the resentment of management action such as that which plagues the grizzly bear program. . . .
>
> Rest assured that BFAT is committed to recover the ferret in Wyoming despite their lack of ferret experience. To expect faster action than has occurred (Remember, the black-footed ferret was considered extinct by many until September 1981) is to believe that endangered species programs can be condensed into "quick and dirty" efforts. Faster action would have resulted in fielding research before needs were identified and ignoring potential negative impacts of research activities on the ferret population.
>
> Finally, I must take issue with drawing parallels between the ferret and grizzly bear programs for the following reasons: 1) Most of the ferret's habitat identified up to now is on private or State of Wyoming land; 2) Very little is known about the ferret's basic biology and habitat requirements; 3) Ferrets, as far as we know, do not cross state lines or national park boundaries; and 4) Even though ferrets are super predators, it is not likely that they could even threaten human life or property. For these reasons, the research/management hierarchy for ferrets is somewhat unique among endangered/threatened species programs. I believe careful comparison with other programs will show that our efforts are on track to recovery. (Belitsky 1984:51)

Communication weaknesses come about for many reasons, not the least of which may be an improperly functioning coordinator. "When problems are complex, individuals may be overwhelmed by the quantity of information," noted Hrebiniak (1978:137). "They may be unable to discriminate between appropriate and unnecessary or invalid data." The WGF coordinator turned preexisting professional arrangements and informal relationships among participants into highly structured ones under the control of the formal program. He also acted as an enforcer of WGF demands rather than an idea broker. He did little to develop information exchange, build trust, or facilitate decision making within the coalition as a whole. Without effective coordinating skills or the cooperation of all organizational participants, the coordinator's performance was problematic. After the last of the ferrets was captured in early 1987 and no more field work was underway, the position was abolished.

Nonetheless, the WGF coordinator served the agency well in several important ways. First, he constituted a WGF presence onsite in Meeteetse, in the region, and in various regional and national meetings — a presence that was both symbolic and substantive. Second, he accumulated knowledge of the ferret situation and passed it along to WGF decision makers, thereby enhancing the realism and confidence of their decisions. Third, he served as chief liaison with the press and the public. These were all important functions for WGF, and regardless of the highly visible intergroup problems, the WGF coordinator was strongly supported by his superiors.

THE FWS COORDINATOR

Because the ferret program came to be dominated by state-level concerns, the FWS Regional Office coordinator played a less visible and more peripheral role than the WGF coordinator. His ostensible role was to coordinate actions to implement the federal recovery plan. This coordinator, Max Schroeder, worked out of Denver, about five hundred miles from Meeteetse, although he did make site visits and maintain communication with other participants. He directed or assisted in several aspects of the field work during the first few years, especially summer work. During its most active period, the first two years of the program, the FWS coordinator had an insignificant role in actually coordinating the program, and eventually the FWS abolished the position.

The coordinators in WGF and FWS actually served "managerial linking" roles, tying "subordinate" workers (regardless of which organization employed them) to "superior" administrators (Galbraith 1977). Those who have linking roles, common in bureaucracies, exercise influence in the decision process as planners, as decision makers themselves, and as resource allocators.

In the ferret program, both coordinators operated in their employing agencies' interests, which hindered their serving the coalition's joint interests. Despite their titles, they did not function as coordinators.

Field Teams

Endangered species recovery usually requires the collection of basic information about the species — populations, habitat, genetics, behavior, and many other important aspects — by field teams. Because this information has direct implications for both management and recovery, field teams often play a major and highly visible operational role. During the first five years of the ferret program, when basic research was being conducted and methods refined, two field teams were active — the ISU/Biota team and the FWS-Wildlife Research team. Toward the end of this period, a few graduate students with the University of Wyoming Cooperative Research Unit were also conducting research; the unit became more active after this period in field surveys, captivity studies on both black-footed ferrets and surrogate species, and other research. Although the FWS team was an important actor in the ferret program, the following description emphasizes the ISU/Biota team because it carried out the bulk of the year-round field work and because, unlike in many other endangered species programs, it represented the major involvement of a nongovernmental organization (NGO).

THE ISU/BIOTA FIELD TEAM

This group played a large role in the ferret program between late 1981 and early 1986. The team physically resided near Meeteetse doing nearly full-time, intensive research from early 1982 through 1985. It facilitated communication and coordination among participants to the extent possible, especially with the local ranching community and FWS field workers, initiated contacts and brought support to the ferret program and the recovery effort from organizations outside the region, generated public support through articles and slide shows, initiated some of the needed management and planning guidelines, and searched for more ferrets and located potential transplant sites over a multistate area. Chief among the field team's contributions was production of a large body of basic scientific knowledge about the wild ferrets (see Casey et al. 1986, Reading and Clark 1990, for bibliographies). The team also generated practical restoration options and introduced and initiated research on a number of important issues, including the setting of standards for reliable field methods, the timing and planning of necessary recovery steps (primarily captive breeding), and the coordination and organization of the program. This group contributed an estimated $600,000 to ferret recovery, mostly in volunteered labor over this period. Its funding of about $200,000 for operations came from nearly a dozen organizations, mostly nonprofits from local to international levels, and several individuals. The operational mode of this team stood in marked contrast to the bureaucratic efforts of both state and federal governments. There was a loose hierarchical structure, informal, joint decision making, decentralized patterns of interaction, and reliance on expertise and judgment of individuals coping directly with the work.

Throughout its tenure in the ferret program, the ISU/Biota team operated without the benefit of any formal connection to the program. Beyond the research permit from WGF, there were no contract agreements or memoranda of understanding that outlined the roles and responsibilities of cooperating parties. Nor were there any recognized legal rights that bound the government to deal with the team (as property ownership bound it to deal with ranchers). Nor was anyone from the team appointed to officially sanctioned advisory teams, coordinating committees, or semipermanent working groups. This precarious relationship to the government, maintained because of existing interdependencies, was finally undone by the crises of 1985.

Until that time, the ISU/Biota team had abided by strictures set early on by WGF and BFAT, including limiting contact with the media and submitting research proposals to BFAT for approval. The team members' assessment at the time was that, as a relatively powerless group, the team probably would not have been able to participate under any other circumstances. But throughout this early period, the team also put constant pressure on the program — by demanding that officials consider larger recovery issues at regional and national levels. As early as December 1981, for instance, the team had developed and distributed a "conservation and recovery plan" that incorporated a national approach to restoration of the ferret; this it submitted to private organizations as a basis for funding and to government agencies as a basis for developing official plans. The team began calling for a captive-breeding component to the program in 1983 and in the autumn of 1983 sent one of its members to the Jersey Wildlife Preservation Trust on Jersey Island (United Kingdom) for a short course on captive breeding. Based on this experience, the team submitted a report exploring recovery options to the agencies for consideration (Richardson et al. 1986; report first released 1983).

The team organized a series of conservation-relevant research projects, including studies of population and habitat, the reliability of techniques for searching for ferrets, signs of the presence of ferrets, and characteristics of ferret-occupied prairie dog colonies, as well as genetic studies, population demographic and genetic models, taxonomic and biogeographic studies, habitat models, and management guidelines. Much of this information was eventually compiled in two monographs (Great Basin Naturalist Memoir 1986, Clark 1989); additional research results were published in peer-reviewed scientific journals beginning in 1982. Team members published a *National Geographic* article and a children's book on ferrets in 1983 and traveled throughout the region presenting public talks about ferrets and the cooperative program to rescue them. Beginning in 1982, the team members also initiated, organized, and wrote (with government personnel in some cases) four Bureau of Land Management technical bulletins on methods for finding black-footed ferrets, identifying translocation sites, reviewing prairie dog literature, and managing the prairie dog ecosystem.

All these activities — initiated by the team as a means of furthering ferret recovery as rapidly and reliably as possible — very likely posed a continuing threat to the legitimacy and control of the program by WGF. In addition, in 1979, Biota Research and Consulting, Inc., had raised questions about federal procedures for awarding contracts for ferret clearance surveys. These and the many differences between the ISU/Biota team and the government agencies described previously led to growing tension.

In May 1985 sylvatic plague was identified in the prairie dogs on which the Meeteetse ferrets depended, and in June preliminary spotlighting surveys revealed fewer ferrets than had been observed at the same time in earlier years. Discussions mounted among the program participants concerning the risk posed by plague and the significance of the low observed ferret numbers. Officials were prompt in responding to the plague threat: a large-scale, joint program was undertaken to "dust" all prairie dog burrows in the ferret-occupied area with a chemical to kill the plague-bearing fleas. This was seen by many, however, as an easily accomplished "techno-fix," good for public relations but of dubious value to the ferrets. Also in June, the ISU/Biota team organized a decision seminar led by an outside expert to explore the ramifications of these developments and management options, and a report was promptly submitted to the FWS Regional Office (Maguire and Clark 1985). Seminar participants included the FWS, ISU/Biota, and university-affiliated biologists, but WGF declined to participate.

In July, the ISU/Biota team, FWS Research Center, and (a few weeks later) WGF personnel began the annual joint spotlighting surveys to count and locate the ferrets. Reports were made daily to FWS and WGF officials. By the end of the survey in August, despite careful and comprehensive coverage to ensure the reliability of the data, only 58 ferrets were found, compared to 129 in 1984. The low numbers led researchers to believe that there were other factors at work besides plague. The ISU/Biota team suggested how this hypothesis might be tested, but WGF officials did not act. Ferret numbers continued to drop, the sense of crisis mounted as both local and national media picked up the story, and yet government officials denied that a crisis existed.

This situation created a dilemma for the ISU/Biota team: should it go along with WGF's assessment, remain quiet, and hope for the best, or should it speak out, aggravate existing conflict, and provoke the agencies into action? Facing increasing criticism from the agencies and frustration with its own powerlessness, the team appealed to its national supporters to investigate the situation. This resulted in increased pressure on both WGF and the FWS in the form of inquiries from national conservation organizations and greater media coverage. Ferrets were finally brought into captivity in September and October, and the disease vector was finally identified as canine distemper. The ISU/Biota team's action was answered by its not-unexpected elimination from the Meeteetse program by WGF a few months later.

The degree to which the team was initially successful in working with the agencies was partly the result of its "participative/collaborative" method of governing itself and of interacting with others. But the ISU/Biota team possessed little power relative to other actors, leaving it highly vulnerable. Its flexible, innovative style of operation and resistance to top-down bureaucratic controls were not well regarded by many agency officials. The team functioned as a "change agent" in a very traditional government setting that did not want to change. The ISU/Biota team was able to accomplish what it did prior to 1986 only because of the particular environment that surrounded ferret recovery efforts, including the organizational setting. The team's loose and informal connection to the program was a serious disadvantage, but it also freed the team to perform many important functions not open to the agencies, functions that not only complemented government activities but also enhanced the scope and depth of the program. According to Rosabeth Moss Kanter (1983), the environmental setting makes the biggest difference in determining the success or failure of innovative ventures, even more so than the people involved. For example, the more a bureaucracy discourages initiative and innovation within its ranks or within the realm of its control, the larger is the potential role for outsiders or individuals to bring about change. The constraints built into the ferret program's structure and operations, in large part, allowed the ISU/Biota team to assume a somewhat innovative role. Much of what the formal program did not supply in terms of problem-solving flexibility, the ISU/Biota team did.

The role of the NGO conservation community in wildlife conservation is sometimes little understood and clearly needs additional definition (Callison 1953, Stahr and Callison 1978, Tober 1989). There is a tendency within the agencies themselves, the media, and the public to rely heavily on agency expertise concerning wildlife issues. This may be, in part, because they hold the legal authority and they are among the best-known groups that deal with wildlife. But in reviewing how the ESA is really implemented, Yaffee (1982:135) noted that NGOs "played the fixer role repeatedly" and that, although both formal and informal means were used by NGOs to aid conservation efforts, formal channels alone were rarely adequate. NGOs helped by championing species, speeding up the process of recovery, and bringing about a higher degree of protection for species than otherwise would have been provided. NGOs provided technical, financial, and professional help and supported and legitimized the roles of professional advocates inside the agencies (Yaffee 1982). James Tober's (1989) study of the role of nonprofits in wildlife policy confirms that they mobilize substantial resources, increase efficiency in resource use, and provide additional organizational settings for a better match between resources and roles. Nonprofits tend to be more flexible, performing tasks that government is prohibited from taking and that for-profits cannot justify. He notes that this is particularly important in international conservation, "where the institutional framework is weak" (p. 196). In addition, nonprofits "mediate between the corporate and government worlds . . . and the public . . . interpreting and translating activities into language meaningful to their constituents" (p. 196). Finally, they "articulat[e] competing values and visions of the future [and] facilitate orderly transitions to those futures" (p. 196).

The ISU/Biota team and its operational style exhibited several weaknesses. First, the team was not intimately connected to its national supporters. As a result, when it needed support and representation in interagency negotiations, it was impossible to raise; the team simply lacked the access and influence to defend itself. Charles Perrow (1970) commented that legitimacy for nonprofit organizations may be an even greater problem than for business or government, that the social mechanisms for assessing legitimacy are not well developed, and that, for the most part, we rely on the "good conscience" of powerful people for direction. No good conscience spoke up effectively for the legitimacy of the ISU/Biota team from leaderships of the larger conservation community, the scientific community, the media, the agencies, or anyone else.

Second, the team was not salaried, nor did it possess any guarantee of funding from year to year. This made the group look like a fly-by-night operation, and it made it all the more difficult to develop a close, long-term working relationship with the agencies, even though its core membership remained the same from 1981 through 1985.

Third, it was impossible for the team to convince anyone in the agencies that it was a nonpartisan player in the perennial state-federal struggle. The team tried not to take sides but to focus on the ferret recovery task itself. Nevertheless, both the state and federal governments came to view the ISU/Biota team as "not on its side" and, by implication, against them.

Fourth, team members varied in their understanding of the extrabiological dimensions of the work and in their ability to deal with the uncertainty, complexity, hostility, and instability of the task environment. Dealing with other major players — all government bureaucracies or large, private landowners with well-defined special interests — took an enormous personal and professional toll on individual team members, especially on volunteer wages for years on end. Individuals disagreed about the sources of conflict and the best ways to manage them productively.

And fifth, as team leader I sought to avoid personal confrontations with agency personnel and thereby reduce conflict, but this left the rest of the team unprotected from the hostile environment. Tensions within the team rose. The team broke up at the end of 1985 at about the same time that the field work ended and the wild ferret population disappeared, although several members continued to work for ferret conservation in other ways.

THE FWS FIELD TEAM

The FWS-Wildlife Research Center field team functioned as a traditional government research unit. Its overall administration changed little and the team leader position remained with the same individual over its years of activity in the ferret program. Initially, the team was most active in the summer and fall but later carried out many wintertime activities. This team's particular expertise was radio telemetry techniques, which proved very important in researching ferret movements, activity patterns, and population dynamics. Unlike the ISU/Biota team, the FWS team had at its disposal trucks, mobile homes and field offices, airplanes, additional equipment, and a considerable budget for salaries of permanent staff and seasonal workers. The team's work significantly increased the base of reliable knowledge about the wild ferrets. The data generated by the FWS team and the ISU/Biota team made up nearly all the information about the Meeteetse ferrets.

The FWS team's base of operations was Fort Collins, Colorado, about four hundred miles south of the ferret population. Bureaucratic constraints limited its flexibility and its activities. On many occasions, the team had to check with superiors before taking on tasks when the need arose in the field. The team was generally conservative and avoided situations that might bring it into greater conflict with WGF. It never publicly commented on the many problems within the ferret program. Like the ISU/Biota team, many of this team's members were poorly equipped to deal with the program's conflict and other difficulties and were subject to personal and professional costs. Nevertheless, the team's participation in the ferret program has persisted to the present (see Miller et al. 1996), providing the only long-term research arm in the entire program. As such, it has served to give continuity and institutional memory to the overall effort.

Conclusions

Intentionally or unintentionally, the advisory teams, coordinators, and field teams lent considerable legitimacy to WGF's formal program and aided functionally in its bureaucratization. The federal recovery team made very limited contributions during this period, but WGF's advisory team and coordinator both had the distinct stamp of agency allegiance, which significantly diminished their utility in developing flexible, cooperative joint action. The federal and state coordinators connected field workers to top administrators to facilitate top-down communication and control. In fact, the misuse of coordinators hindered progress in many ways, not the least of which was to foster mistrust and increase conflict. Except for the CBSG, the advisory teams and coordinators did little during these first five years to institutionalize adequate, efficient, and effective practices. As for the two field teams, their expertise, several research and planning initiatives, and cooperation helped legitimize the formal program. But their job became more difficult as bureaucratic controls tightened; they lost flexibility, professional discretion, and latitude to undertake important tasks. As they learned about ferrets and needed restoration measures, however, they fulfilled their role successfully.

Despite their shortcomings in the ferret program, these programmatic elements can have highly useful roles in restoring endangered species. Special care must be given to their selection and composition, and special knowledge and skills are necessary for good advisory teams, coordinators, or field research teams.

7

Organizational Learning
Institutionalizing Ignorance

Organizations must gather information to fulfill their purposes in society. Relevant information comes not only from an organization's environment but also from the organization itself and its assessment of the appropriateness of its responses to the environment. Organizational learning is the process of using information to adjust those responses. But organizations often do not attend to the task of learning deliberately (Leeuw et al. 1994). Over time a "residual buildup" of policies, rules, biases, and self-interested groups within the organization accumulates — all of which affect the use of information in decision making. Successful learning comes from being cognizant of one's experiences and possessing a useful framework to organize the experience as a basis for insight and improvement. The organizational and individual participants in the ferret program had a wealth of experiences but needed an appropriate, realistic, and functional vehicle to give meaning to those experiences. A number of frameworks are available for this purpose (e.g., Argyris and Schön 1978, Senge 1990).

In this chapter I examine some of the theory of organizational learning and look at what organizations in the ferret program learned from their experiences. I then survey common barriers to learning in order to understand how an organization's behavior can limit its learning potential. Finally, I show how self-blocked learning was institutionalized in the ferret program.

Organizational Learning

Organizational learning differs somewhat from individual learning. The lessons of experience influence an individual's brain and behavioral repertoire, while the lessons of experience influence an organization's structure and culture. An organization is an instrument of society set up to achieve societal purposes; it cannot be reduced to the collection of individuals who constitute it at any given time or to their interactions, behaviors, or decisions. Although individuals, in varying degrees, conform to the organization's structural and procedural requirements and become socialized to the values and cognitive outlooks of its culture, it is these structural and cultural features — organizational maps, memories, and programs, not the individuals — that largely determine how organizations (and the individuals in them) behave. Individuals make the organization's decisions and implement its policies, but it does not follow that when individuals in an organization learn, their organization also necessarily learns. Organizational learning does not occur until fundamental structural and cultural shifts take place that permit improved adaptation, that is, when information is actually used to make the organization's performance more effective. Empirical observation can help determine relatively easily whether organizations learn and how they do it. Ultimately, every organization must develop a system for learning about its own behavior.

Determining what kinds of organizations can best manage endangered species is an urgent issue. Yaffee (1982) noted that some organizational structures are designed for learning, while others are not. Government organizations appear to be poorly designed for quick learning and rapid responses. Lloyd Etheredge and James Short (1983:42) suggested that learning should result in "increased intelligence and sophistication of thought and, linked to it, increased effectiveness of behaviour." To determine if intelligence has increased, Etheredge (1985:66) used three criteria: "(1) growth of *realism,* recognizing the different elements and processes actually operating in the world; (2) growth of *intellectual integration* in which these different elements and processes are integrated with one another in thought; (3) growth of reflective *perspective* about the conduct of the first two processes, the conception of the problem, and the results which the decision maker desires to achieve." He evaluated improvements in effectiveness "by the achievement of different values" (p. 66), that is, by a change in the professed values of the decision maker, in the people that were permitted to help make decisions, and in the kinds of information used in decisions. In short, he judged how open or closed and how democratic decision making became.

According to Chris Argyris and Donald Schön (1978), learning is the process by which organizations detect and correct "errors," defined as mismatches between outcomes and expectations (see also Argyris 1976, 1982). These authors distinguished two kinds of organizational learning. In "single-loop learning," organizations develop skills to scan their environment, set goals, gather better information, manage it, use it in planning, and monitor their own performance in relation to their goals. The entire process is conducted within the context of the organization's central cultural norms and traditions, its understanding of how to do business and the adequacy and reasonableness of its strategies. Single-loop learning is often institutionalized in the form of information management systems, decision-making processes, program evaluation units, and budgets that monitor production efficiency and other indicators of performance. Many organizations become good at changing organizational strategies to meet unchanging norms.

But some "errors" are not easily corrected within that framework. Sometimes the error or conflict challenges the norms themselves. It may appear "as incompatibility of governing values or as incongruity between organizational espoused theory and theory-in-use" — between what groups say they do and what they actually do (Argyris 1982). A program selected to achieve certain goals may be implemented successfully, for instance, yet not be adequate to achieve the goals. It may be that "evaluations precipitate debate on core organizational issues when they not only ask the question 'how well are we doing,' but also, 'does it make sense to do it, even if it is being done well?'" (Leeuw et al. 1994:9). Organizational learning in these cases requires not just a single feedback loop of changing strategies but a double feedback loop that also reexamines the standards by which the organization operates. The process must start with recognizing the unexpected outcomes, acknowledging that they cannot be "corrected" by doing the same thing better, and developing a new and different perspective on the problem. Double-loop learning must institutionalize systems that "review and challenge basic norms, policies, and operating procedures in relation to changes occurring in their environment" (Morgan 1986:89).

LEARNING IN THE FERRET PROGRAM

There is no doubt that single-loop learning took place in the ferret case. The large body of published scientific literature demonstrates that much was learned about the technical aspects of ferret recovery (e.g., Seal et al. 1989, Thorne and Oakleaf 1991, Madson 1995).

Double-loop learning, on the other hand, is harder to demonstrate in the formal ferret program during this period. That mismatches between expectations and outcomes were occurring was obvious. The following quotations, published during and immediately after the crises of 1985, indicate a profound dismay among participants and observers with the program's failure to achieve its objectives.

> At least we can learn from this disaster. Poorly-funded state game departments are not to be trusted with the survival of a species of wildlife. (Bauman 1986:A11)

> It is with the same sadness that I have learned how badly the Wyoming Game & Fish Department has mismanaged their responsibility in recovering what may now be the most endangered mammal in the world, the black-footed ferret.
>
>   Until recently, the ferret was only the most endangered mammal in North America; now we in Wyoming have the dubious distinction of worldwide notoriety. And like a small child, the department's spokesmen are participating in that well-known defense mechanism we see so often used by not a few public servants who have been caught in the web of truth: denial, disinformation, lame excuses, and much finger-pointing at everyone but themselves. (Hampton 1986:A15)

> "We are going to make sure we've learned from this experience so we don't let it happen again." (FWS regional director Galen Buterbaugh, cited in White 1985c:A1,B1)

> While mistakes were made, [WGF's Harry] Harju concedes, were he able to turn back the clock, he said, he would take the same actions, given comparable knowledge. (Zimmerman 1986:2)

> [The ferret case was] a classic example of what can happen when a high-minded philosophy of preservation comes up against the slow workings of bureaucracy, rivalries between public and private agencies, conflicting theories of wildlife management, and mankind's frustrating inability to fathom the mysteries of nature. (Prendergast 1986:36,39)

> [The ferret program was an example] of what can happen when the machinery and dignity of office come to overshadow the purposes the office was created to serve. (May 1986:14)

> "It's absurd," [Steve Forrest] said. "We're going to lose the whole ball game if they're going to play it that way. . . . They [state officials] are living in a dream world if they think those animals have a good chance to survive." (Cited in D. Weinberg 1986:69)

> So much are "experts" learning about the black-footed ferret that the real experts now realize they are dealing with a species virtually unknown to science. . . . What they seem to be learning less rapidly is how to pool resources, communicate, do their stuff before time runs out, and actually rescue

endangered species instead of just keeping them in cages. (Williams 1986: 119)

John Fitzgerald, Defenders of Wildlife's endangered wildlife specialist, said . . . the Fish and Wildlife Service has not given sufficient priority to the ferret situation. "With this being the only population of these animals known, the FWS should have been planning ahead in a worst case sense and budgeting enough to get ahead of this." (Cited in White 1985d:A14)

I suppose Fish and Wildlife Service should have stepped in a year ago when the State agency did not follow recommendations to begin captive breeding that year. Yet there was nothing coming from the Fish and Wildlife Service. (Thuermer 1985:11)

Scientific and organizational reform will not come from within a bureaucracy; it must be imposed from above, by USFWS — which thus far has abnegated its national obligation by not cracking a whip over Wyoming G&F — or by Congress. (Zimmerman 1986:2)

"I don't want this to happen again. When you mix politics and egos and agencies and dollars together with a lot of unknowns, what you are trying to save seems to get lost in the dust." (Steve Forrest, cited in Randall 1986:32)

It is clear from these comments and criticisms that individuals had acquired considerable knowledge about the difficulties in the program. Collectively, they show that people were conscious that appraisals (feedback loops) were needed, and indeed several ideas about the nature of the problems, possible solutions, and cause-and-effect relationships were put forward. They express a general sense that things should have been done differently. There is a general desire to speed up the workings of bureaucracy, manage conflict productively, and achieve the formal goals. There is discouragement that public agencies did not seem to have learned from experiences that had preceded the ferret program and that even a federal agency like the FWS had not foreseen the problems, compensated for the recognized weaknesses, planned and budgeted, and anticipated unknowns more appropriately. There is also a general lack of understanding about why participants were not cooperating effectively, why an "unproven" (in terms of commitment and capability) state agency like WGF was given responsibility for carrying out national policy, and how to keep the machinery of government subservient to the purposes of government. Although many of these comments were fairly simplistic — "politics and egos and agencies and dollars" — some also challenge the basic operating standards and norms of the program.

It is also clear that the organizations involved, and the ferret program specifically, had learned much less than the individuals. We can judge whether the organizational systems in the ferret program learned or not by the same measures used for other programs. Based on empirical observation, did the system demonstrate increased intelligence and increased effectiveness? The recurring symptoms and consistency in behavior over the first few years suggest that the black-footed ferret program did not gain in intelligence or effectiveness beyond certain technical proficiencies and skill in managing political processes and the media. WGF was characterized by "dynamic conservatism" — changing to stay the same (Schön 1971) — in terms of relationships to other organizations, persistent defensiveness, and the obstinacy of bureaucratic controls to deal with highly uncertain and fluid situations. There is little evidence of self-evaluation, scrutiny of the "governing values" by which the program operated, or participative decision processes. There is no evidence that WGF, BFAT, or FWS ever rethought the program's underlying premises about how to conduct business. It is doubtful that double-loop learning took place at the organizational level.

What many individuals learned about the successes and failures of the ferret program was not institutionalized in the appropriate organizations. Unless knowledge is acquired by organizations, it will remain unused because individual knowledge cannot correct organizational errors. The ferret program seems to have been a classic example of what organizational behaviorists call "the implementation gap," whereby an institutional system finds it extremely hard to achieve results in the way it intended (Ascher and Healy 1990).

ORGANIZATIONAL RATIONALITY

Few organizations master double-loop learning (Senge 1990), and few have the ability to encourage and enable the ongoing debate and innovation that drives such learning. One way to understand why this happens is to look at different kinds of organizational "rationality" (Westrum 1986). An organization sees itself as rational when it implements a certain set of actions and procedures that it believes will lead to its effective and efficient operation. Westrum distinguished two general forms of organizational rationality, each of which uses knowledge in different ways that directly affect how the organization learns.

"Calculative rationality" is a strategy by which previously acquired knowledge is used to predict what is likely to happen in the future, and past experience is used to calculate the best future course of action. This experience is codified into cultural doctrines and expressed through the organization's structure, which is set up to react to events in expected ways. Unfortunately, calculatively rational organizations are incapable of coping with surprises and changing environments. The very features that make them highly predictable and efficient simultaneously make them highly vulnerable. Calculatively rational organizations tend to concentrate responsibility for creative thought in particular locations, usually central rather than peripheral parts, even though that is seldom the locus of information and problem-solving ideas. Where centralized thinking dominates, ideas from the periphery are usually seen as a threat, since they indicate that there ought to be structural changes in how the organization operates. The center becomes defensive when confronted with ideas from the periphery, which may account for why WGF and FWS responded the way they did in 1985 to the field teams' information and its implications for ferret restoration. Over time, the center becomes less and less responsive, even pathological. When failure occurs, rather than undertake self-examination (double-loop learning), the organization engages in systematic dishonesty about the nature of the failures (Westrum 1986). "Calculative organizations, therefore, are likely to botch tasks that require rapid information flow, innovation, and critique" (Westrum 1986:10).

In contrast, "generative rationality" is a strategy of proactive, creative problem solving. Generatively rational organizations actively encourage all employees to explore, observe, critique, and produce new ideas — in short, to think. This kind of rationality is critical for the organizational self-evaluation demanded by double-loop learning. Decision-making authority is set at low levels in the organization, and information flows freely within the organization and its subsystems. The organization has the ability to recognize good ideas whenever and wherever they appear and to reward employees for them. If the organization requires restructuring because of these ideas, the system permits it. Thus generatively rational systems are flexible and adaptable. Over time, roles and structures change. Impersonal, constructive, and evaluative feedback permeates the system. This kind of rationality is especially important in keeping organizations operating during times of rapid change, uncertainty, and crisis.

Organizational learning is clearly a function of the structure, procedures, and culture of the organization, rather than the collective knowledge of the organization's people. Learning can also be inhibited by factors within the organization.

Barriers to Organizational Learning

Organizations, especially rigidly bureaucratic ones, sometimes limit their own abilities to learn and adapt (see Roy 1980). Understanding how this happens can provide a basis for making improvements. Gareth Morgan (1986) documented three obstructions to organizational learning. First, bureaucracies impose fragmented patterns of thought, attention, and responsibility on their employees and discourage them from thinking for themselves. Information does not flow freely when hierarchical and horizontal divisions are prominent and rigidly enforced. As a result, subunits may operate with entirely different pictures of what is happening and what needs to be done, and employees may seek different goals and means to achieve them, unaware or uninterested in how these fit into the big picture. These differences foster the development of political alliances that are a barrier to organizational learning. "Highly sophisticated single-loop learning systems may actually serve to keep the organization on the wrong course, since people are unable or not prepared to challenge underlying assumptions. The existence of single-loop learning systems, especially when used as controls over employees, may thus prevent double-loop learning from occurring" (Morgan 1986:90).

The bureaucratic form of the ferret program separated participating groups, limited information flows, and precluded integration and synthesis. In practice, agency officials constrained the roles of the field teams as well as such other agencies as the Bureau of Land Management and the Forest Service (see Reading 1991). Government employees, well socialized to this bureaucratic arrangement, rarely challenged standard operating procedures. Because of these designs, roles, and socialization, learning and adaptation were minimal.

A second major barrier to organizational learning is the nature of bureaucratic accountability, both of employees to managers and of agencies to the public. Holding agency employees responsible for their actions gives them an incentive to engage in various forms of deception to protect themselves (Westrum 1986). This means making excuses ("it was beyond our control"), deflecting responsibility ("the press misrepresented the situation"), obscuring or covering up issues and problems that might place them in an unfavorable light, or telling managers what they think they want to hear. The same deceptions are made by agencies in reporting to the public. No one ever forced accountability on the agencies in the ferret program. Deceptions and misrepresentations occurred, according to Hampton (1986), Bauman (1985, 1986), Skinner (1985), Miller et al. (1996), and others. Excuses were made, and special interests — seldom recognized or acknowledged — were obscured behind scientific complexity or funding scarcity. In one minor example, WGF field personnel reported that there appeared to be quite a few ferrets alive at Meeteetse in the winter of 1985–86 (Miller et al. 1996). To have spoken the truth — that the number was probably fewer than eight — might have confirmed their critics' contention that the wild population was functionally extinct and would have contradicted the agency's bias to maintain wild populations rather than captive ones.

There may be reasons for this kind of behavior. Organizational systems in which accountability fosters defensiveness cannot deal with high levels of uncertainty. There is tremendous pressure for organizations to be on top of things, and this leads them to create overly simplified interpretations of the situations they are dealing with. Critics, bearers of bad news, and whistle-blowers are not appreciated and are often fired or eliminated. Bureaucrats ignore hard problems, hoping that they will go away or that solutions will be found later. Operating styles of the organization are seldom adapted, and double-loop learning seldom occurs.

A third major barrier to organizational learning, according to Morgan (1986), is the difference between what people say and what they actually do — "espoused theory" and "theory-in-use." Employees may try to convince themselves that they have things in hand. They may try to impress outsiders (such as the media or other professionals) that they know what they are doing and that everything is under control. "They also often engage in diversionary behavior, consciously or unconsciously, as when threats to a basic mode of practice lead an individual to deflect blame elsewhere and to tighten up on that practice, intensifying rather than questioning its nature and effects. In such circumstances it becomes increasingly difficult for the manager to confront and deal with the realities of a situation" (pp. 90–91). Groupthink social pressure may reinforce these tendencies, which are difficult or impossible to break. In short, workers may "develop espoused theories that effectively prevent them from understanding and dealing with their problems" (p. 91). Double-loop learning is impossible in such situations because it requires people to bridge the gulf between theory and reality and, in turn, to confront the values and norms embedded in their organization as well as those within themselves.

BLOCKED LEARNING IN GOVERNMENT AGENCIES

Using extensive evidence from a variety of contexts, Etheredge (1985) demonstrated three types of blockages to learning that characterize government performance. First, blockage occurs when agencies adopt similar policies and program management across all circumstances. Second, decision processes in government agencies tend to be closed, relying predominantly on information sources that confirm agency preferences. And third, government agencies consistently exhibit errors in judgment and perception: they underappreciate valuable data, dismiss outsiders' suggestions that they do a reality-check, and often base judgments on wishful thinking. Previous chapters have shown that numerous examples of these problems litter the ferret program's history.

Etheredge (1985:95–122) identified five additional patterns in government behavior that blocked learning. The first key factor was that "earlier appointments [of people to important positions] determined later outcomes" (p. 95). I have argued that both WGF's appointment as lead agency by the FWS in early 1982 and BFAT's membership appointments by WGF later the same year strongly determined how the program functioned.

A second block to learning was that "neither bureaucratically nor personally did anyone accept complete responsibility" (Etheredge 1985:97). Most participants in the ferret program worked for bureaucracies and defined their identities and their activities by their job descriptions. As a result, each individual and subgroup was narrowly responsible, at best, for only a small part of the program. This was recognized by participants and observers: "The key missing element has been individual responsibility. Management and decision-making are too badly scattered for any one person to be — or be held — responsible for the ferrets' fate. 'Bureaucracy doesn't identify excellence, or give it a chance to exist,' [FWS representative Ron] Crete said. 'I honestly believe we have to identify responsibilities, delegate some people and get on with it'" (cited in Zimmerman 1986:8).

A third blockage was that "policy meetings were highly ritualized" (Etheredge 1985:97). In most meetings, such as BFAT, bureaucrats interacted according to traditional roles and past experience and were unable or unwilling to examine contextual, programmatic, political, or even complex scientific issues in ferret conservation. These factors reinforced patterns of collective decision making that lacked intellectual rigor. Etheredge (1985:98) characterized how such groups work: "Beneath the surface of the policy, there was no sense of a common enterprise, not even a common theory about how the operation was to succeed. The personal sophistication of individuals was high, but by any reasonable definition of collective learning, no process ever came together. Collectively, there was no intellectual integrity."

A fourth blockage was that "decision processes [were] designed to affect choices rather than to clarify them" (Etheredge 1985:99). As argued earlier, WGF, through BFAT, did not use comprehensive, systematic methods to guarantee the most thorough surfacing of intelligence or evaluation of options. BFAT seemed aware of WGF's preferences beforehand, so that decision making was more a political process of endorsement and less an intellectual exercise of true problem solving. Certain individuals and organizations were excluded from formal participation on BFAT, not because they were inexperienced or lacked sound judgment, but because their inclusion might have jeopardized the expected political outcomes. WGF and BFAT were not politically neutral participants: in fact, they operated to ensure that their policies and programs would be supported. Learning was not among the agency's goals, but controlling participation, agendas, and outcomes was very important.

A fifth blockage was that "collective learning was inhibited because subordinates were at personal risk if they told the truth" (p. 100) and "bureaucratic assessments were more realistic 'upward' than 'downward' [so that] subordinates were erroneously taken for granted" (Etheredge 1985:104). These two related concepts both have to do with how decision makers understand information from lower echelons. Otherwise skilled bureaucrats were not as adept at utilizing and monitoring subordinates as they were at politicking among themselves. Much information essential for learning was thus underutilized. For example, the knowledge and ability of subordinates seems to have been often overlooked by WGF's State Office and the FWS Regional Office leadership. Several knowledgeable subordinates in the FWS were often bypassed or ignored by superiors. Individuals who spoke up and sought contact with high-level superiors were often penalized. These problems were compounded by a particular type of decision maker at high levels of government. Several bureaucrats seemed at times to be what Etheredge (1985:148) labeled "hardball-politics decision makers," who focused on other bureaucrats and perceived adversaries and who were characterized by "ambition for the self; superficial interpersonal relations; twinship [mirror] images of hardball opponents; weak ethics and disconnected moral restraint; aggressiveness and tactical manipulativeness." Some agency bureaucrats in the ferret program showed limited ability to appreciate or use information from lower ranks.

Each of these patterns of organizational behavior — intrinsic to the organizations themselves, not imposed from without — prevented the ferret program from learning how to improve its performance. It is clear that the same strategies were tried over and over again, with continuing incongruities between the agencies' expectations of how their actions and decisions would affect matters and the actual outcomes and effects. The same strategies were repeated because behaviors and structures had become fixed or institutionalized.

Institutionalizing Self-Blocked Learning in the Ferret Program

The ferret program's structure and operating procedures were rapidly institutionalized, with support from the FWS and other agencies (the Bureau of Land Management, the Forest Service). Once programs are institutionalized they are usually defended at all costs, even when they perform poorly, because they have vested interests in the current definitions of the task they are addressing. Problems are frequently attributed to "outside" events "beyond our control." The response of the National Aeronautic and Space Administration to the Challenger disaster, for instance, according to the Presidential Commission on the Space Shuttle Challenger Accident (1986), was typical: failure was attributed to technical problems, limited resources, and political problems, not to NASA's own flawed decision making or inappropriate program structure. Especially in recent publications, WGF has repeatedly depicted itself as the victim of external circumstances (Madson 1995, Thorne and Oakleaf 1991, Wyoming Game and Fish 1991b). But as Senge (1990) asks, were they "prisoners of the system, or prisoners of their own thinking"? Like most organizations, WGF suffered from a failure to recognize its dilemma — that problems would remain insoluble unless reformulated in broader terms through double-loop learning. The institutionalized structures and operating modes of the ferret program remained a persistent barrier to learning.

By 1985, even WGF belatedly but indirectly acknowledged that its program was not functioning well. In a review of recent developments (Madson 1995: 34) that also seems pertinent to the program's early years, WGF gave an asymmetrical argument suggesting that the agency's only fault has been its "idealism," whereas it has been hampered by "political pressure, internal and external," biological constraints, and shrinking funding. In the years covered by this account, the agency tried to correct these misdiagnosed problems with even more centralized control and policing actions, but since the problem had been misconstrued, the solution did not work. The myriad *organizational* problems that permeated the ferret program were invisible to the agency. "Instead of recognizing a structural source," observed Lasswell (1971a:76) in regard to typical responses to organizational problems, "the trouble may be attributed to irrational opposition or an accelerating rate of change." WGF misattributed the program's weak performance to "having disparate groups involved," selfishness, overcontrol by the federal government, the conflict-oriented press, the misguided ISU/Biota research team, incompetent people, lack of commitment, or other such explanations (e.g., Skinner 1985). Believing that many of the problems were caused by self-aggrandizing individuals, one WGF official concluded that "the lesson in this is to subdue your ego and maintain your concern for the animal. It's not important who gets the credit, but what's done for the animal" (cited in Prendergast 1986:40). Another participant said, "The important thing now is to work together. It's just not constructive to find fault" (cited in Randall 1986:10). Another WGF official claimed that reporters were trying "to ride the ferret's coattails to fame, fortune and escalated professional status" (Skinner 1985:36). A complete list of such statements deflecting attention away from the real, inherent organizational problems would be lengthy. Collectively, these statements illustrate a profound misperception of problems: the ferret program's problems cannot simply be reduced to individual wrongdoing.

The "human relations" understanding of organizations reduces all organizational problems to problems with individual people. But as Perrow (1970:3) noted, "visible organizational problems generally are exemplified by the people in the organization and their relationships with one another" — that is, problems among people are symptoms of underlying organizational problems. In the ferret case, officials' diagnosis of the problem never got beyond the symptoms to a recognition or understanding of the underlying structural and cultural faults.

Etheredge (1985) described five patterns of high-level decision and policy making that limit the effectiveness of organizational learning systems and program performance. First is that decision makers took an organizational perspective rather than a problem perspective. Second is overconfidence. Policy makers "imagined they knew more than they did, and their plans worked more easily in their heads than in reality" (Etheredge 1985:142). Third, emotion came to dominate actions. Fourth, policy making was primarily defensive. These four patterns seemed to characterize the agencies and BFAT quite well during this period. And fifth, participants tended to explain their own behavior by noting their situations and constraints, but described their opponents' behavior by referring to their predispositions and motives. WGF officials, for example, insisted that their actions were influenced by a lack of resources, inadequate data on the ferrets, and harassment by troublesome individuals in other organizations. But they described others' behavior as "selfish," motivated by a drive for "fame, fortune, and escalated professional status." Such comparisons generally portrayed WGF's behavior as appropriate and their opponent's behavior as inappropriate. These patterns or norms, common in bureaucracies, were instrumental in institutionalizing barriers to learning in the ferret program.

Conclusions

Given these numerous entrenched blockages, how can learning and organizational change ever occur in bureaucracies mandated to restore endangered species? If governmental systems could not be reformed in a case as relatively simple as the ferret case, what chances are there to improve implementation nationwide for endangered species or for more difficult goals such as biodiversity conservation or ecosystem management?

Reform will be achieved only if the problems that currently limit performance are understood for what they are and if this knowledge is used as the basis to upgrade the intelligence and performance of organizations. Throughout the ferret program (and in other endangered species programs), there have been calls for participants to stop the accusations, recriminations, faultfinding, and backbiting, with the hope that we can put the conflict behind us and get on with the important work ahead. Such sentiments not only misrepresent the problems but also preclude the critical analyses by which we might pinpoint what went wrong in the past and clarify how changes can improve future programs. This is learning, and we must institutionalize sound learning systems. Observers as well as participants should be encouraged to examine endangered species cases within a systematic, comprehensive, realistic framework, to find fault, and then to correct the mistakes. If people never examine the kinds of problems that plagued the ferret program and learn how to avoid them, participants in future programs will likely repeat the same mistakes, costs (financial and otherwise) will soar, and species losses will accumulate. The public, however, will hear only that there was too much conflict, too little money, too much regulation, or some other external reason. Programmatic problems must be honestly recognized if they are ever to receive remedial attention. The premise of this book is that we can do better, much better than in the ferret case, but before offering ways to improve policy and programs, we need to seek an organized, fundamental explanation for why the program developed as it did.

8

Problem Definition
Analytical Framework, Process, and Outcome

Ferret recovery depended on solving several different "problems." Not all these were recognized, however, and of course anticipating or recognizing problems does not necessarily mean that they can be prevented or solved. How various participants and observers thought about the overall problem of ferret recovery largely determined how they thought about solutions — what factors they considered relevant, how goals were set, what means were used to achieve their goals, and their roles and others' roles in the program. Yet these substantively different standpoints and conceptualizations (or definitions) of the problems and solutions arose from the same set of "facts." Defining problems, obviously, can itself be a problem.

Defining Problems

Contrary to conventional wisdom, problems are not "out there" waiting to be discovered and solved. They do not present themselves to us de novo and in complete form (Latour 1987). "Any given set of conditions that is somehow judged or labeled as being undesirable is not, in itself, a problem or 'the' problem," observed David Dery (1984:25). "Any such set of conditions may, in other words, 'contain' more than one problem, or no problem whatsoever, depending on one's ability to see a way or ways out — that is, to see opportunities for improvement." Rather, problems are *defined* — that is, formulated or constructed — from situations (Simon 1969, 1985). Defining imposes a useful framework on troublesome situations: it suggests the causes and consequences of the "problem," proposes a theory for a solution, and thus emphasizes some aspects of the situation and potential solution and minimizes others (Weiss 1989). Defining a problem in essence configures its solution (Dery 1984). A problem, then, is an opportunity to make an improvement. How a problem is formulated directly affects the range and kinds of solutions proposed and the likelihood that certain solutions will be chosen over others; it determines which groups will have what kinds of power in the process and the likelihood that some solutions will be more successful than others.

Defining problems is difficult for many reasons. Boundary conditions may be unclear, symptoms impossible to separate from root causes, cause-and-effect relationships muddled, or consequences of various actions unpredictable. This gives people considerable latitude in defining problems, depending on their values, assumptions, preferences, personality, relationships with other participants, and other characteristics. Problems are also defined relative to specific organizational and social contexts. Dery (1984:xii) noted that every organization is a "solution to a predefined problem." In the case of the ferret "problem," definitions were clearly socially and organizationally constructed: different problem definitions represented different opportunities for different groups. Brewer and deLeon (1983:2) asked about such situations, "Whose perception or grasp is correct or even 'better'?" They suggested that the best way to avoid having problem definition become a problem is "to be sensitive to the differences [among participants] by including them in a composite, evolving portrait of the problem and what needs to be done to cope with and overcome it" (p. 2).

But not all problem definitions are of equal value in practical terms. An inadequate problem definition can "intensify rather than ease the original problem" (Brewer and deLeon 1983:32). According to Alan Steiss and Gregory Daneke (1980:124), "A plausible but incomplete definition of the problem can be more dangerous than a wrong definition. If the problem cannot be stated specifically, then the analysis has not been of sufficient depth. Even an excellent solution to an apparent problem will not work in practice if it is the solution to a problem that does not exist in fact." Inadequate problem definitions and subsequent program conceptualizations are likely to occur as a result of intense pressure for an immediate response (Wolman 1981). Even when time is available for good problem definition, a weak definition will often be used — the product of political and administrative "satisficing," in which a plausible or convenient formulation of the issue is adopted too rapidly, and adequate knowledge and analysis, or "reality testing" of assumptions and evidence, are simply neglected:

> Too frequently rhetoric is substituted for adequate conceptualization, result-ing in vagueness and a lack of direction throughout the entire formulation and carrying out process. The end result is perceived to be a program which has failed to solve a problem even though no one is quite certain what the problem is. . . .
>
> Policy agendas usually reflect the mobilization of political demands rather than a rational process of evaluating needs, values, and objectives. Thus "problems" frequently appear on the decision-making agenda without having been adequately conceptualized or thought through. (Wolman 1981:436)

Problem definition is widely understood to be the first activity undertaken in problem solving in the policy process, with the expectation that consideration, selection, and implementation of solutions will follow. Problems may be orig-inally defined by a group of people with a grievance, by a community respond-ing to a crisis or catastrophe, by analysts, or by politicians. Several definitions may persist throughout the process. Sometimes they coalesce among several groups of people and later diverge, depending on changing circumstances, values, and outlooks. But Janet Weiss (1989) argues that, in addition to pro-viding an initial analytical framework, problem definition plays other critical roles throughout the policy process. Problem definition may also be a *process* of policy making, a dynamic interplay between mobilizing support, shifting consensus, and taking action. As such an instrument of advocacy, "prob-lem definition redistributes power among participants in the policy process" (p. 114). Problem definition may also be seen as an *outcome* or product of policy making in that it "creates language for talking about problems and non-problems that draws attention to some features of social life at the expense of others, locates responsibility for problems, putting some groups on the defen-sive and others on the offensive, widens and deepens public or elite interest in particular social phenomena, and mobilizes political participation around is-sues or symbols highlighted by the problem definition" (pp. 114–115).

When much reliable knowledge about a problem exists, problem definition must be based on that knowledge. This tends to minimize the diversity of perspectives. But in the face of great uncertainty, there is considerable latitude in defining problems. In the ferret program, the scope of the uncertainty on all fronts greatly affected how participants defined the problem, essentially driv-ing them to assert their particular views early and forcefully and giving them little incentive to consider alternative views.

In 1981, the dominant characteristic of the ferret task environment was uncertainty—the difference between what was known at the time and what would be required to be known to save the ferret. That difference was enormous and pervasive. Scientific and technical uncertainty was high because the only known population consisted of a very small number of animals, the species was nocturnal, secretive, and ground-dwelling and thus difficult to study, and relatively little was known of its biology and ecology. Uncertainty existed in the organizational and policy dimensions of the task as well. It was not exactly clear at the beginning how each organization would behave in the overall ferret coalition. For some, financial resources were not assured, so their longevity in the program was tenuous. Some feared government intervention. Some felt they needed to flex their muscles. The vast ramifications of implementing the Endangered Species Act (ESA), even in this single case, conflicted with the achievement of other societal goals, thus leading to policy uncertainty. For example, ranchers feared that the government might condemn their land or greatly restrict historic land uses, causing significant losses from livestock and oil and gas revenue; government intervention might even force a change in traditional lifestyles. Their fears were heightened when a moratorium on oil and gas leasing was imposed in the Meeteetse area by the Bureau of Land Management within a few months of the ferrets' discovery.

The Dominant Problem Definition

Scores of problematic situations in the ferret program were mentioned in earlier chapters, some major, some minor, some quoted from participants or observers of the program, some drawn from this analysis, some derived from the literature. Altogether, these issues, factors, forces, actions, relationships, causes, effects, and symptoms can be considered the "problem setting," or set of undesirable circumstances from which problems may be defined. They do not constitute a problem definition because in general they do not show cause and effect relationships, do not consider consequences of the undesirable circumstances, and above all do not offer any theories on how to make improvements. But any effort toward solving problems is based on a theory, even if it is implicit, about what caused the problem and what therefore will solve the problem. Some aspects of the problem setting were relevant to some participants or observers but not to others. Some aspects were even nonexistent or invisible to some participants. As a result, each participant offered a somewhat different assessment of the situation and a different definition of the larger "problem" of ferret recovery.

Despite the size and messiness of the problem setting, it is possible to construct one or more useful problem definitions. The operational problem definitions of different participants in the ferret program can be partially re-constructed from the public record of written materials and actions. In the ag-gregate, central tendencies are clear, although details are less distinct. WGF's definition of the problem came to dominate the program even though it was never stated openly, fully, or explicitly. Based on the public record of actions and written materials, WGF's definition of the ferret problem in the first few years of the program seems to have included the following points:

- that ferrets were the property of the state and therefore WGF had authority and control over their destiny
- that ferrets should not leave the state and therefore the national recovery program should be centered in Wyoming under WGF
- that WGF was the agency mandated to manage the state's wildlife and therefore the new ferret program should be subsumed under existing orga-nizational structures, operating procedures, and historical precedents
- that WGF had the necessary and sufficient ability to lead a national recovery program and therefore all other participants should fall in line behind WGF without criticism or questioning
- that considerable financial resources in addition to the state's contribution would be required to save the ferret and therefore other actors should pro-vide financial and other resources as needed by WGF
- that ferrets had always persisted at Meeteetse and therefore there was no urgency to change traditional management
- that too little was known about the population to justify manipulating it
- that captive breeding was a risky and untried technology and therefore should be avoided or postponed
- that the program was conceived not as a management or recovery program but as a research program and therefore it was considered a success simply because data were being collected

In practice, this definition restricted the scope of relevant investigation and opportunity so as to "accommodate available resources and policy instru-ments, interests, constraints, prevailing values, and other commitments" to WGF's own interests and abilities (Dery 1984:xii). "Viewed as inquiry sys-tems," Dery continued, "organizations are designed to ask certain questions to the exclusion of others. Organizations simultaneously collect and suppress data. Underlying premises—those premises that problem redefinition would seek to challenge—govern what actions an organization takes, as well as the realm of conceivably relevant information and knowledge" (p. xii–xiii).

There seemed to be four underlying elements upon which WGF's problem definition was built, and which governed its actions and precluded redefinition.

STATES'-RIGHTS IDEOLOGY

This viewpoint was at the core of WGF's culture. It figured prominently in the agency's relationships with all other participants and had paramount consequences for how all aspects of the ferret program were structured and carried out.

The power and roles of the states relative to the federal government is a major issue that dates from the founding of the nation and has been manifest throughout American history. Its most profound expression, of course, was the Civil War — the War Between the States — but even that bloody conflict did not resolve the divisive, inherent paradox of a nation composed of states. The issue is less about rights (except when the term is used as a code word for opposition to certain federal policies) than about power. Harold Lasswell and Myres McDougal (1992) recognized power as having two components, authority (formal power) and control (effective power). Authority without control is "pretended power," control without authority is "naked power." By handing the lead to WGF, the FWS set up a situation in which the federal agency retained authority but abandoned control, while at the same time WGF developed strong control with very little authority to direct a national program.

Yaffee (1982) noted that the federal role in wildlife management has grown throughout the twentieth century and that the 1973 Endangered Species Act "was framed in a time when strong federal regulation was considered to be appropriate policy" (p. 57). Yet historic questions of wildlife ownership and jurisdiction are still debated between state and federal governments (Bean 1983). In the 1980s and 1990s, "new federalism," the Sagebrush Rebellion, and concern about "unfunded mandates" were among the pressures swinging the debate toward increased state power and responsibility. The states'-rights claim in wildlife management has been widespread. For example, John Ernst (1991:106) noted that "because states traditionally have controlled taking [of wildlife] through sport hunting and trapping seasons, they often view the federal endangered species program as a usurpation of their authority." It has even been suggested that few acts of Congress have caused more friction between two levels of government than the ESA's intrusion of the federal government into management of a state's resident wildlife (Smith 1977).

In the ferret case, this doctrine asserted that WGF had both authority and control over all wildlife within the state and thus governed who would be in charge of the program, which participants could participate in the program, and which were trespassing, so to speak. In short, the states'-rights premise set the stage for the distribution and use of power among actors. It figured into

WGF's identity and defined the agency's expectations and demands for the entire program. Other wildlife "turf wars" between WGF and FWS were playing themselves out at the time. For example, grizzly bear management in the Yellowstone region had a long history of domain disputes during the decade preceding the ferret's rediscovery.

WGF manifested its states'-rights position from the beginning of the black-footed ferret program in 1981 to the present. Thorne and Oakleaf (1991:245–246) described the premises under which the department developed its ferret program:

> Wyoming Statute 23–1–103 declares that all wildlife in Wyoming is the property of the State. It is the policy of the State to provide an adequate and flexible system for control, propagation, management, protection and regulation of wildlife in Wyoming.
>
> The Wyoming Game and Fish Department (WGFD), under the direction of the Game and Fish Commission, is responsible for fulfillment of this mandate. Implicit in this mandate is prevention of extinction of any wildlife species by managing populations at secure levels for the benefit of the public. . . .
>
> Successful development of an endangered species programme ultimately depends upon a good working arrangement between FWS, which should have a broad policy perspective and authority, and state agencies, such as WGFD, which have the physical facilities and personnel to see that endangered species policies and programmes are executed.

According to WGF's view, the federal government would remain in the distant background with its "broad policy perspective and authority." Part of the federal role, as the state seems to have perceived it, was to provide financial support to WGF for personnel and physical facilities (owned and operated by the state) for ferret-related work. In short, WGF would run the show, the federal government would pay for it, and all other participants would be subordinate to this arrangement. WGF tolerated the presence of other players only as long as they provided key information, money, or legitimacy, and did not pose too much of a problem for WGF. Needless to say, this basic assumption of state authority, ownership of wildlife, and control was not a good basis for a cooperative partnership to restore ferrets nationally. It is not surprising that it became a major problem in implementing federal endangered species policy.

BUREAUCRATIC MANAGEMENT ORTHODOXY

The second underlying premise of WGF's problem definition was the orthodoxy of bureaucratic management. Bureaucratic management assumes certain power relationships, which, in this case, closely corresponded to WGF's states'-rights views. Like most natural resource programs, the ferret program was initially defined and shaped within bureaucratic agencies. Only a very limited range of structural and operational options was thus deemed plausible, namely, those that maintained or enhanced agency power and constituted the program along bureaucratic lines. Significant negative consequences resulted for how participants interrelated, how decisions were made, how resources were allocated, and how work was performed:

> The die was cast when USFWS gave the state of Wyoming control of the program without making them accountable for their actions. At the time [1981–1982] questions were raised, and issues of program control and agency conservatism have followed ferrets since the beginning. The problems are not personality differences, but rather organizational. Even if there is progress toward recovery, failure to attend to issues of policy design and implementation will reduce efficiency and effectiveness of the program. (Miller 1992:8)

> There were several reasons behind these strained interagency relations. First, and probably most important, were historic relations between agencies and actors involved in the BFF [black-footed ferret] reintroduction program in Wyoming. Ultimate control of the ferret recovery program probably lies at the heart of this problem, but several other issues are also important. . . . Suffice it to say that general mistrust and suspicion prevailed among several key participants and agencies. (Reading 1991:4)

There are numerous examples from other programs of government bureaucracy getting in the way of species restoration (see Clark et al. 1994). One is the effort to save the California condor in the 1980s:

> Overall, we believe that one of the most important conclusions to be drawn from the battles of 1985–1986 is that endangered species bureaucracies are really no different from any other bureaucracies. They follow the same immutable law of short-term self-interest, and this goal tends to dominate all others. The tragedy of endangered species bureaucracies is that in pursuing this goal they can force the species they are charged with protecting to serve bureaucracy rather than the reverse. . . .
> Government agencies very definitely need to be watched closely to ensure that they fulfill their obligations. (Snyder and Snyder 1989:259–261)

This collective experience confirms that government bureaucracies operate in self-serving ways. Frequently, scientific or technical issues are invoked to legitimate or justify — rather than inform — bureaucratic decisions (Majone 1989). Indeed, considerable resources may be devoted to collecting data to construct such explanations (Sabatier 1978). The ferret case does not seem unique; bureaucratic management dominates many programs.

Extensive research on the structure and functioning of bureaucracies can help us understand how the ferret bureaucracy worked. In general, bureaucratic organizations have not stood up well to the rigorous examinations of sociologists, psychologists, and political scientists (J. Wilson 1989). Edward Giblin (1978) noted that traditional management approaches developed in bureaucracies simply do not work in many instances and are especially faulty in complex and uncertain tasks. Yet the increasing role of government bureaucracies in wildlife conservation has serious consequences for the future of biodiversity conservation (Langenau 1982, Jackson 1986).

Elliott Jaques (1980:439–440) concluded that many societies, including our own, "are being subverted by the inadequacies of their bureaucratic systems. . . . By and large our bureaucratic institutions are abysmally organized. They are tailor-made for trouble." Boyd Littrell (1980) noted that our institutions, especially public ones, are becoming increasingly bureaucratic, that this fact poses a significant dilemma in a democracy, and that in bureaucracies "there is less extensive participation than some might hope and that bureaucracy serves as a tool for maintaining power in relatively few hands" (p. 270). Perrow (1979:6) agreed with the two main charges against bureaucracies: first, that they are "inflexible, inefficient, and in a time of rapid change, uncreative and unresponsive" (the social engineering criticism), and second, that they "stifle the spontaneity, freedom, and self-realization of their employees" (the human relations criticism). But he thought that the biggest danger in bureaucracy is "how it inevitably concentrates those forces [social resources] in the hands of a few who are prone to use them for ends we do not approve of, for ends we are generally not aware of, and more frightening still, for ends we are led to accept because we are not in a position to conceive alternative ones" (p. 7).

Problems lie not just with bureaucratic structures but also with the individual bureaucrats who staff such organizations. For example, John Baden (1980:38) noted that the staffs of our land and resource management agencies tend to be well-meaning and competent in the technical sense, but that this "is by no means sufficient to insure quality management. There are, unfortunately, many examples of perverse institutional structures generating suboptimal results." Despite their dedication, bureaucrats face numerous institutional constraints (Hoben 1980).

Certain personality types are drawn to and work well within large bureaucracies. Moreover, working in bureaucracies has profound effects on individuals. "The nature of bureaucracy and its impact upon the personalities of its members demands serious rethinking. . . . We must restructure bureaucracies in such a way that individuals can develop and sustain meaningful human relationships within and without the organizational context" (Williams et al.

1980:403). Bureaucrats perform the role of leaders in many programs, and bureaucracies tend to select leaders that possess not only technical competence but also considerable political skills (Hancock 1980; cf. Etheredge's (1985) descriptions of "hard-ball politicians"). Such individuals are especially skilled at establishing and maintaining favorable power relations for themselves and for the bureaucracy that employs them. The results in terms of task orientation and achievement are often disappointing.

Bureaucrats may resist outside intervention in their activities even when it can be reasonably demonstrated that intervention will benefit the public and the bureaucrat. Judith Gruber (1987) examined bureaucrats' behavior across several different policy arenas and their resistance to democratic governance either through direct citizen participation or elected officials. "Bureaucrats resist [democratic] control," she concluded, "because they enjoy autonomy, because their lives are easier if they are their own masters, and because they feel that they know best" (p. 87). Gruber identified how this happens. First, the bureaucratic working environment does not raise democratic norms that might guide workers' behavior. Second, bureaucrats are insulated from democratic life. They are public officials, yet they have not undergone the "socializing ritual of the electoral process" (p. 101). They assert that they are concerned only with

> administrative matters, technical services, substantive programs and job satisfactions or dissatisfactions — not with political issues or the search to implement democratic norms. . . .
>
> A self-image of technician or administrator can, of course, be useful for preserving one's autonomy vis-à-vis political leaders. If what one does is not political, then politicians have no business intervening. The obvious expedience of this posture for bureaucrats invites scrutiny and, perhaps, disbelief. But I do not think that this apolitical persona is contrived, a ruse elaborately designed to protect bureaucratic turf. . . . The myth has become genuine belief. (Gruber 1987:102–104)

Moreover, bureaucrats rarely communicate with political leaders or the public and have little contact outside the agency; when they need advice, they ask other bureaucrats.

Third, bureaucrats tend to "redefine" norms to serve their own needs. Specifically, they redefine policy making as something outside their realm, thus rendering them immune to democratic control. They redefine democratic control as responsiveness to individuals or interest groups, thus proving that they are indeed under democratic control. They redefine elected leaders as politicians too self-interested to serve the public interest, thus giving bureaucrats a mandate for "guarding the public weal against the designs of politicians" (p. 115). A corollary is that they redefine the public as incapable of deciding what is best for the public interest, thus forcing them to save the public from itself. And they redefine the work of their own agencies as exempt from democratic control. Gruber (1987:92) concluded that, "overall, these interviews paint a challenging picture for those concerned with democratic control of bureaucracy. The bureaucrats not only describe themselves as being relatively free from such control, they also do not perceive much of a need for it."

Bureaucratic management orthodoxy and its built-in views about people and power relations were not a good basis for a cooperative effort to restore ferrets. Like the previous premise of states'-rights views, it came to be a major problem in implementing federal endangered species policy.

SCIENTIFIC CONSERVATISM

WGF's program was based on a number of convergent assumptions about science and its use in management: that ferrets always had and always would persist at Meeteetse, that management action must be based on more data than were available initially, that both onsite management and captive breeding were too risky, and that even if a problem developed, there would be advance warning and time to respond accordingly.

WGF dismissed arguments made by the ISU/Biota and FWS research teams that the Meeteetse ferrets were at great risk of extinction from stochastic factors alone. Based on field work at Meeteetse, conservation biology theory, simulation modeling, museum and historic research, and extensive field searches in other regions, researchers argued that the population's survival to date was no guarantee that it would persist indefinitely. Many remnant populations probably survived the massive poisoning campaigns of earlier decades but died out one by one as a result of chance events in demographic, genetic, or environmental factors. Renewed efforts to find additional populations after the Meeteetse find turned up no ferrets. Indeed, no new ferrets have been found since 1981. In spite of the evidence, WGF was adamant that the Meeteetse ferrets were "safe" and that no special management attention was required. Events proved the agency wrong.

WGF seems to have envisioned the program at the beginning as a research project to collect data on which to base future management. BFAT was established early on primarily to guide research and find funding for it. Despite the calls for science, however, the agency often "simply dismissed the . . . research" (D. Weinberg 1986:63), and BFAT delayed research while it reviewed proposals. Moreover, exactly what kind of data were needed for what ends, and what constituted adequacy, were never defined. Michael Soulé (1986) has argued that "the call for more research . . . is often abused when it is used as an excuse to delay action" (p. 7) and "the risks of non-action may be greater than the risks of inappropriate action" (p. 6). Conservation, which was certainly the prime goal of the ferret program, should not have been retarded because of scientific uncertainty.

The agencies were also conscious of the high risks involved in the situation and averse to taking any action that could jeopardize either the continuance of the tiny population or their own public image. The uncertainty of the situation did not indicate clearly what action should be taken. The urge to establish some certainty in terms of scientific knowledge, funding, power relations among the organizational players, as well as other areas, was understandable. But there were also risks in delaying action, as demonstrated in 1985.

Positivistic science tends to be a conservative institution. The professional norms in science are to advance and test all hypotheses and base all claims on objective data, analyzed according to statistical rules. Yaffee (1982) noted that science has been successful since the 1960s in defining the endangered species problem as a technical issue (as opposed to an issue of conflicting social values, such as economics versus species preservation). This has led to decades of building up technical rules by which decisions are made concerning endangered species, such as the solely biological criteria for listing under the Endangered Species Act and the usual technical solutions of limiting take, protecting habitat, and captive breeding. Like most recovery efforts since passage of the act, the ferret program was thus largely cast as a scientific problem. Even though ferret protection had widespread social, economic, and political implications, the language of ferret recovery remained fundamentally scientific and technical. Scientific conservatism satisfied the scientific norms of both the wildlife biologists and the managers who were trained in the same tradition. In addition, defining the problem as scientific and then promoting science as the means of solving it were a way of building power for that community of people.

WGF's use of science was extremely conservative and largely avoided key recovery issues. For example, a list of "steps in an effective endangered species management programme" promulgated by Thorne and Oakleaf (1991:249) demonstrates this cautious devotion to scientific method:

> 1. Conduct adequate inventories throughout the historical range of the species
>   A. Use rigid sampling scheme to ensure that the best habitat is surveyed first
>   B. If no populations are located, aggressively test a null hypothesis that the species is extinct

2. Evaluate the probability of extinction for each known population separately and the probability of extinction for the species (all populations combined)

3. Complete adequate planning for recovery and update as the recovery programme progresses.

It is not until step 4, "*if* it is determined that the species is truly threatened with extinction" (p. 249; emphasis added), that the program may move to establish a captive population ("without affecting wild populations"); develop captive-breeding techniques; locate, rank, and "provide adequate management" for reintroduction sites; develop translocation techniques; and finally establish and manage new populations. This simplistic invocation of science distorts the importance of science when it is applied to appropriate inquiries. The plan is acontextual and unrealistic. It ignores the pressing realities of endangered species needs; it would be so time-consuming that any endangered species to which it were applied would probably become extinct before its completion. It also does not account for the momentum of people and resources ready to respond to the fortuitous discovery of ferrets. The inappropriateness of this approach to species recovery is clear. Employed more appropriately as a tool to achieve ferret conservation and recovery, science should have been used to tackle hard scientific questions using state-of-the-art concepts and techniques and rigorous experimentation, especially to optimize captive breeding and reintroduction procedures. Science should have been used to improve insight and judgment.

Scientific conservatism, in this case, colluded with bureaucratic conservatism to defer measures both to protect the Meeteetse ferret population and to restore the species. The agencies could claim that they were indeed doing something by adopting the time-honored approach of conducting requisite science. This stance enabled them to avoid the risks associated with taking action. It provides some insight into why the state balked at removing animals as early as 1984 for captive breeding:

> Translocation, however, was simply not a viable option in 1984 owing to the lack of national effort on Steps 1, 3 and 4C [identifying sites for reintroductions]. Early recommendations to start breeding the ferrets in captivity focused only on development of the necessary techniques (Steps 4A), while continuing to ignore all the other steps in the programme, which should have been carried out on a national scale. This lack of logic was not an effective approach to administrators of government agencies species [*sic*] beset by demands that far exceeded available funding. (Thorne and Oakleaf 1991:250)

SCARCE RESOURCES

WGF claimed that the paucity of information about ferret biology and ecology prevented the agency from taking any early management action, that field data were unreliable, and that captive-breeding technologies were untried and risky. It asserted, too, that lack of facilities, staff, and money limited its ability to carry out the program that had been handed to it.

In the broadest terms, resources in the ferret program included information, scientific and otherwise, on which the program would be built; people who had the knowledge and skill to gather data and carry out actions to save ferrets; organizations that, with proper design and management, had the power and facilities to carry out needed work; and financial resources. The single most important "resource" in the task environment, however, was the tiny ferret population itself. Control over it was extremely useful to agency bureaucrats as political leverage on other participants and as a magnet and justification for money. The agency that controlled access to the ferrets significantly influenced deployment of all other participants' resources. Any organization that wanted to help save them had to operate through the formal state program and under its controls. WGF controlled access to the ferrets via its research-permitting process, for example, as well as law enforcement, influence with other organizations, and influence with the media. This put the agency in a critical position of power to legitimate or delegitimate other actors. As WGF officials acknowledged, the agency possessed few other resources (see Strickland 1983), and so it used this power to garner dollars, information, facilities, personnel, and more control. To this day, it has been largely successful in pursuing that strategy.

Reading and Miller (1994), for example, describe continuing efforts by WGF to control others. In 1988 plans were made to extend the captive-breeding program beyond the boundaries of the state. "WGF was able to extend its control over those out-of-state facilities," according to these authors, "by refusing to sign the FWS recovery plan unless a WGF representative was named chair of the committee that coordinated the captive breeding program between institutions. Participating institutions were also forced to sign agreements giving WGF ultimate control over protocols and animals in their facilities and were excluded from the federal money that funded the Wyoming breeding center" (p. 85, citations in original omitted). In addition, the numbers of ferrets sent to each out-of-state facility were too small to conduct comparative studies, and thus WGF retained control of research. During reintroductions that began in 1991, the agency also restricted research in ways that compromised methods and experimental design, and it limited communications with local ranchers, resulting in delays, distrust, poor agency relations, and poor monitoring of released ferrets. Because WGF controlled the ferrets, the reintroduction in Montana was also delayed. "WGF requested the delay ostensibly because more animals were needed for the captive breeding program, for the Wyoming reintroduction program, and for research. Yet all the captive facilities approached or exceeded capacity at that time, suggesting that WGF may have had other motives" (p. 86).

The "lack of resources" claimed by WGF may actually be attributed to four factors. First was the agency's refusal of assistance. Several organizations with considerable resources indicated a willingness to aid ferret recovery but either were rebuffed by WGF or, after witnessing the state of affairs in Wyoming, channeled their resources to other endangered species programs. Had the ferret program been truly national in scope, participatory in format, and rational in its approach, resources would probably have been readily available.

Second was the waste of resources. Individual knowledge and skills were not put to best use, organizations were not structured or managed in ways that integrated people, knowledge, and other resources, and funds were not allocated optimally. Some tasks, such as searching new areas for ferrets, were unnecessarily repeated, and in some cases the most costly option among several was chosen, such as the duplication of captive-breeding facilities and personnel in Wyoming. Outside professional skills were sometimes ignored. Collectively, this waste of resources reduced the program's efficiency significantly.

Third was the major inflation of costs caused by delays and lack of contingency planning. It would have been much cheaper to increase the captive population from, say, twenty-five ferrets rather than seven, which might have been possible if captive breeding had been initiated in 1984, for instance. (Of the eighteen ferrets that formed the nucleus of the captive-breeding population in 1987, only seven actually contributed genes to succeeding generations.) Similarly, Miller et al. (1996) indicated that later reintroductions of ferrets were less efficient and less effective, and thus more costly, because of WGF's failure to use pre-release research results and to conduct post-release monitoring. Numerous case studies have shown that species recovery costs are ultimately much higher when remedial action is delayed until the species has dropped to extremely low numbers because restoration takes so much longer and more intensive management techniques are required (Clark et al. 1994).

Fourth was that financial resources were indeed limited. FWS budgets had been reduced over the few years preceding the ferret discovery, and certain programs had been scheduled to be phased out until the ferrets were found. The discovery of ferrets gave new life and more resources to certain FWS programs. WGF also projected large deficits in its immediate future. Its efforts to establish a "wildlife trust fund" had been foiled over previous years by ranching and agricultural opposition. Finding ferrets represented a much needed symbol of wildlife conservation that was valuable to the agency for attracting money. The ISU/Biota team, with no guaranteed annual budget and no reserve funds for research, also lacked adequate finances. The ferret find permitted them to lobby for funds from conservation and research organizations. Although ferrets attracted resources for government and NGOs alike, it was highly uncertain how much would be available and for how long. Lack of resources, especially dollars, constrains many programs, and numerous calls have been made to reinvigorate national efforts to restore species, especially with increased funding (Dingell 1991; Murphy 1991). More commitment from the public and elected officials as well as better use of funds by government would make greater resources available for the protection of biological diversity.

From the beginning, WGF called for all other participants to turn over their financial resources for reallocation and redistribution. Later, FWS largely paid for construction of a captive-breeding facility for WGF and funded staff to operate it, although the federal agency reserved considerable funds for its own operation, too, particularly the FWS Denver Wildlife Research Center. Other federal agencies, such as the Bureau of Land Management, also allocated money to WGF or its contractees (for example, University of Wyoming researchers) for specific tasks. The ISU/Biota team did not turn over its funds to WGF because its grantors did not permit any transfer or change in the use of the funds, especially to support state governments. Even though WGF never obtained a pot of money directly under its exclusive control, it acquired and directed substantial financial resources. The ferret program in its formative years, in fact, was significantly better funded than most programs. It is estimated that at least three million dollars (or its equivalent in volunteered labor) went into the recovery effort over the first five years.

Thus, although the resources available to the ferret program were not unlimited, they were much greater than WGF suggested. The premise that the program was constrained by a lack of funds was largely a consequence of the other three premises that underlay WGF's problem definition. Resource paucity was caused largely by WGF's insistence that the ferrets were its property and that, if ferret recovery were to occur, it would be in Wyoming under its control. This meant that many people and organizations interested in supporting ferret recovery were forced either to funnel their talent, information, and dollars to WGF or not to contribute at all. This was wasteful because facilities to raise ferrets, which existed elsewhere but could not be used, had to be duplicated in Wyoming with public and private monies, for example. The overcontrol of the program and the conflict it brought conveyed to some potential participants that it was not worth their time to contribute. Once potential funders witnessed how strictly WGF forced its views on the program, some simply reallocated their money to other needy endangered species where the likelihood of useful participation and success was greater. Finally,

WGF's scientific conservatism caused numerous delays. The agency assumed the ferrets would always be around, giving them plenty of time to collect data prior to taking management action. Total costs would have been much lower if the urgency had been recognized, contingency planning had been in place, and recovery actions had been taken much earlier than they were. In short, WGF's problem definition and program management severely limited the resources available to the program. It is not surprising that such a situation came to be a major problem in implementing federal endangered species policy.

Critiquing the Dominant Problem Definition

Weiss (1989:117) provided an extremely valuable discussion of criteria by which to evaluate problem definitions:

> What is a good problem definition? . . . The answer lies in how definitions perform as overture [analytical framework], process, and outcome. As overture, Quade (1975) suggests evaluative criteria such as whether the definition considers the whole problem, whether it implies alternatives that have realistic promise of improved outcomes, whether it permits systematic analysis of alternatives, whether it is clear about the objectives to be achieved, whether it focuses attention on a manageable set of factors, and whether the definition is meaningful to decision makers. As process, quite different evaluative criteria emerge: which actors are mobilized to participate in decision making and which are excluded, which actors are placed on the offensive or defensive, which institutions are legitimized and strengthened and which are not, which groups become more credible and powerful, which decisions are made openly in the legislative arena and which are left to bureaucratic discretion. As outcome, yet another criterion becomes paramount: which political values are moved forward and which are moved backward.

The dominant problem definition throughout the ferret program, that of WGF, had many consequences for the coalition of interests involved and for the ferrets themselves.

PROBLEM DEFINITION AS ANALYTICAL FRAMEWORK

Development of feasible solutions stems directly from the analytical power of a good problem definition. The dominant definition of the ferret problem was analytically weak on several counts. First, it did not articulate the whole problem. It failed to consider the history and development of the ferret situation, analyze the causal and conditioning factors, or project trends in the situation. Only certain kinds of information were permitted to be introduced to the problem-solving arena. For instance, historical trend data (over the last hundred years) would have helped characterize mortality factors, population behavior, and habitat relationships. Neither decision analysis nor population viability assessment, two techniques that would have been extremely useful in highlighting risk factors, were considered. What was known from zoo captive-breeding experiences was not brought to bear on the ferret case in its early years.

Second, consideration of the context of the problem seemed to be very limited, focusing largely on the reactions and representation of other agencies. The dominant problem definition failed to recognize the complete range of local, regional, and national interests, the inherent interdependencies among the participants, or the professional roles and contributions of the field teams. The high potential for conflict, for intelligence failures, or for delays and short-sightedness in decision making was ignored.

Third, the dominant problem definition did not clarify what goals were being sought. It was not until the FWS recovery plan of 1987 that formal federal goals were spelled out. The unanimous goal of "saving ferrets" did not say how, when, and where the coalition would save ferrets. Rather, it allowed all participants to read into this phrase whatever they wished — whatever their operating goals suggested. Lack of common goals reduced the program to reacting to incoming information rather than fitting information, decisions, and changing circumstances to an overall plan or goal. There are reasons for vagueness, of course, not the least of which is that it makes evaluation more difficult and accountability nearly impossible. Lack of goals made the program less manageable in its day-to-day operations and gave little guidance to decision making and organizing for action.

Fourth, the dominant definition did not permit a systematic exploration of alternative solutions. It was founded on unexamined assumptions and proceeded along well-worn routes in terms of procedures, participation, strategies, and, naturally, outcomes. The opportunity for a model program was lost at the very beginning.

WGF seems to have revised its problem definition after late 1985, when the wild ferrets nearly all died, some captive animals also died, and no new ferrets had been found in the wild. For example, in evaluating extinction risk using data and analysis provided by the ISU/Biota and FWS field teams, WGF concluded that its "new" analysis showed that it was highly unlikely that any unknown wild ferret populations remained and that captive breeding was therefore mandatory. "This perspective has formed the foundation of Wyoming Game and Fish Department (WGFD) management and planning for the ferrets *since 1986*" (Thorne and Oakleaf 1991:245; emphasis added). This conclusion was new to WGF even though the data, analyses, and similar conclusions had been put forward by others years earlier. Although captive breeding had not initially been a significant part of WGF's problem definition, it rapidly became institutionalized once funds and facilities provided by outside sources and circumstances left no other acceptable options.

There is evidence of the weak role of problem definitions in other endangered species cases, but it is largely implicit in observations like those of Snyder and Snyder (1989) and others. Few authors except Yaffee (1982, 1994a, 1994b) have explicitly talked about how endangered species problems and contexts were defined. But it is probable that narrowly bounding such problem definitions to emphasize short-term advantage to a bureaucracy and to meet other possibly competitive interests is a common feature. One reason for this is, again, the large amount of uncertainty present in endangered species programs. Not analyzing problems rigorously may permit administrators to assume that everything is under control and that any uncertainty will be dealt with adequately in the future. Another explanation may simply be that agency administrators, biologists, and managers do not know how to analyze and define problems to serve particular ends, to explore a variety of solutions, or to organize themselves productively for action. Combining uncertainty with ignorance about options will surely produce problem definitions that incompletely capture context and therefore reality. Instead, traditional frames of reference in biology and bureaucracy will be employed, leading to the "bureaucratic conservatism" and other problems discussed by Yaffee (1982).

PROBLEM DEFINITION AS PROCESS

The ferret case illustrates very well that the act of defining problems is a part of the social construction of reality, the heart of the policy-making process. By defining ferret recovery as a states'-rights issue, as a bureaucratic control issue, as a conservative science issue, and as a scarce resources issue, WGF was able to manage perceptions, public opinion, legitimacy, other participants, information, money, and decision making for many years. Part of the process of defining problems is promoting a given "package of ideas" about the problem, finding subscribers, and building and nurturing networks and coalitions of like-minded people and groups. This build-up of support for one definition over another—which Weiss (1989:114) said helps organize "the thinking and values of a diverse set of potential allies"—is capable of shifting organizational inclinations and redistributing power among participants.

The primary focus here is participation. The public record shows that WGF limited participation and input from other groups except to accommodate and conform to other agencies' needs. This strategy bolstered the legitimacy and authority (and thus the power and opportunities for control) of government and undermined NGOs. WGF branded NGOs as "fringe" elements, elitists, interlopers, troublemakers, demagogues, insubordinates, and—most damning of all—"eastern conservationists." The agency denied the legitimacy of their participation, and it denied the numerous talents, contributions, and resources they might have brought to the program. The many decisions and actions of exclusion must be seen as a function of the agency's problem definition, as an integral part of the *process* of defining ferret recovery.

PROBLEM DEFINITION AS OUTCOME

Problem definitions are also the results or products of the policy-making process. Weiss (1989) identified four outcomes of problem definition—language, responsibility, awareness, and mobilization—and two simple criteria by which to evaluate them: Which political values were moved forward or backward? Which measures of success were used and which consigned "to the scrapheap of the irrelevant" (p. 98)?

The language created to articulate problem definitions sanctions and legitimates certain values, positions, programs, or people and denigrates others. As such, language becomes a concrete outcome of problem definition. WGF's persistent emphasis on the word *control,* for instance, led to the perception that control was indeed a major concern, even a major goal of the program, and a major measure of its success. Implicit in this argument was the notion that only government looks after the "public good," thus reinforcing the values of governmental authority but weakening the value of nongovernmental, citizen, and professional input.

Another noteworthy example of the role of language as an outcome of policy making is the use of the word *ecosystem* in reference to the Yellowstone region where the Meeteetse ferrets resided. The term has been adopted and promoted by environmentalists (with varied scientific backing), but it has been deliberately avoided by government agencies, particularly the Forest Service, presumably to avoid its implications of certain kinds of management regimes (Clark and Minta 1994).

Another real outcome of problem definition is the assignment of responsibility and the tallying up of costs and benefits. In the program's first few years, WGF largely took credit for developing what the agency considered a successful program to save ferrets from extinction, and it minimized, edited, or ignored the role of various "fixer" groups such as the Captive Breeding Specialist Group. This definition cast government in a good light and put the burden of proof on the outside groups, thus further reinforcing divisions between groups. But when problems arose, the agency blamed external causes beyond WGF control.

The language used by the agency set the stage for how the costs and benefits of the program would be viewed by the public. Focusing on benefits, specifically the increase in ferrets in the captive-breeding program, this language minimized or precluded examination of the program's real costs. Reading and Miller (1994:91) noted that "these [ferret] numbers are certainly a source of pride and represent the culmination of tremendous human effort on behalf of the species. Yet the numbers alone are deceiving because they do not account for inefficient utilization of resources, costs to recovery in terms of genetic diversity lost, opportunity costs lost, losses in public support for the program, future success, or many other facets of the recovery program that are essential if the program is to ultimately reach the objective of species recovery." Even today, the costs of the ferret program have never been counted against the benefits, nor are they likely ever to be scrutinized under the dominant problem definition.

As an allocation of responsibility, the dominant problem definition is simple, convenient, and optimistic. It is the legacy of a long tradition of imbalance in weighing the social, economic, and environmental costs and benefits of natural resource "use." Any shift in responsibility resulting from alternative problem definitions might understandably be resisted by many government administrators.

A third outcome of problem definition is the awareness brought to certain issues and whether they are perceived as problems. Weiss (1989:116) noted that problem definition relies on "a package of concepts, symbols, and theories" that its proponents tout to stimulate interest. For example, by defining the ferret restoration challenge as not urgent, WGF perhaps bought time to consolidate available resources, clarify authority relationships, and avoid mistakes that might have been made in haste and under pressure. WGF prevailed in focusing attention on the single variable of the number of ferrets as a measure of the success of its program. But it failed to use the eleventh-hour rescue of ferrets to thrust into public awareness the value of protecting all endangered species, possibly because such a move would have brought the agency into conflict with strong economic interests in the state (livestock and agriculture).

Over the years, various aspects of the ferret program have drawn the attention of other groups. The Sierra Club Legal Defense Fund, for instance, pursued legal implications of WGF/FWS management of the program. And for many ranchers throughout the West, the ferret is only one in a growing list of endangered species whose legal protection and management may increasingly conflict with traditional ranching activities.

Problem definitions also mobilize people to action and coalesce interest groups by articulating and linking previously unrelated issues, ideologies, and values. Weiss (1989:116–117) noted that while some groups are "energized" and "empowered" by particular problem definitions, others may be "silenced." The dominant definition of the ferret program called for mobilization of government along traditional bureaucratic lines in terms of organizing a program, garnering resources, determining patterns of participation, arranging supportive alliances, setting agendas and schedules, and directing and controlling activities. This definition put WGF at the center and in control of the entire effort through defederalization of the program. Thus, as an agent of mobilization, the dominant problem definition promoted states' rights and bureaucratic management orthodoxy.

Analysis of the dominant definition of the ferret problem reveals the complex workings of public policy processes and the roles played not only by biological imperatives but also by organizational and political forces in endangered species programs. As Weiss (1989:117) observed, "the intellectual and symbolic contributions of problem definition tend to blur into the array of political and institutional forces that also bear on policymaking and policy outcomes." As conceptual framework, the dominant definition of the ferret problem was analytically weak. As process, it was exclusive and polarizing. But as outcome, it was extremely powerful in maintaining the conservative status quo politically and bureaucratically and in further concentrating power and legitimacy in state government. Even the crises of 1985 and 1986, the consequent fault-finding, and the resulting changes in program focus were not sufficient to catalyze a significant redefinition of the problem or to question the validity of the underlying premises.

What accounts for this triumph? First, it is intuitively simple and conforms to human tendencies to think in terms of local, short-term, and self-serving scales. All its various elements reinforce one another to form a strong, coherent "package of ideas." At face value, it appears valid and requires no special knowledge or critical thinking. Second, the strength of certain political symbols in Wyoming (and the region) — states' rights, individual and property rights, and scorn for the federal government, environmentalists, and easterners — provided a highly favorable medium for WGF's definition. Even agricultural and livestock interests that had battled WGF over other issues sided with its definition of the ferret recovery problem rather than permit any influences from outside the state's borders. Preexisting ties and alliances (for example, with the University of Wyoming Cooperative Research Unit) were invigorated by this definition. Conservation biologists or conservationists, who might have offered the strongest alternative problem definition, were relatively few and isolated in Wyoming. Moreover, some environmental organizations in the state have broad overlap of membership and leadership with WGF. Efforts by the ISU/Biota team to heighten awareness and enlist support from regional and national conservation groups met with little success. Some groups had other, higher priorities than ferrets, some believed a state-run program was not worth their involvement, some feared that antagonizing the agencies over ferrets would put their other wildlife programs at risk, some were co-opted by WGF, and still others failed to see the fundamental dynamic at play, the enormous stakes, or the opportunities for improvement.

In addition to the currency and local appeal of the political symbolism of WGF's problem definition and the distribution and organization of its advocates, WGF had a natural advantage simply in being a government agency. Despite widespread questioning of governmental authority, purposes, and mechanisms, government still provides an authority signal recognized in no other entity. Government remains the manager of wildlife. To my knowledge, no investigative reporters knowledgeable about complex policy and organizational processes covered the ferret program, and so, outside of a few pointed questions in times of crises, the media uncritically passed along WGF views to the public. These seem to be the main reasons why the WGF definition came to prominence and why it has remained there.

An Alternative Problem Definition

Existing organizational arrangements, historical momentum, value perspectives, and political interests greatly restrict the range of problem definitions that receive serious consideration. Yet throughout the entire ferret program, an alternative problem definition has existed with varying degrees of visibility. Many features of this definition were expressed by participants and observers since the early years of the program. But, as Weiss (1989:114) pointed out, "problem definitions must accommodate political realities, but they also help to create those realities," and they can "carve new channels in institutional arrangements." Several elements of both the dominant and alternative problem definitions helped shift thinking, information flows, management actions, agency relations, and many other institutional arrangements surrounding endangered species issues in general and ferrets in particular. Given time, interest from new communities (or flagging attention from old interest groups), shifting political winds, or changes in the ferret situation itself, the dominant definition may undergo redefinition or give way to alternative definitions that may provide better analytical frameworks and serve a larger number of citizens. Among the features of an alternative problem definition might be the following:

- that the ferrets belonged to the American people and therefore the FWS — a federal agency — had the authority, control, and therefore collective custodial responsibility for them
- that many resources (money as well as expertise and facilities) already existed nationwide to contribute to ferret recovery and therefore these assets should have been used wherever they were located
- that the FWS was the agency mandated to manage national recovery of endangered species and therefore the new ferret program should have been led by that agency in cooperation with the states and other interested parties
- that the ferret situation was characterized by enormous uncertainty and complexity and therefore the most suitable organizational response was flexible, participatory, generative, problem-oriented, and open
- that the ferrets' existence was extremely precarious and therefore conservation and restoration measures should have been swift, deliberate, responsible, and state-of-the-art as a matter of principle and practice
- that the serendipitous rediscovery of ferrets in 1981 offered a unique opportunity to develop a model recovery program and therefore this chance should have been seized immediately
- that the experience, concepts, and techniques for recovering endangered species were already available and therefore the ferret program should have capitalized on this knowledge from the beginning
- that the ferret program was primarily a conservation and recovery program, not a research program, and therefore knowledge about ferrets available in 1981 was sufficient to proceed with such programs as disease monitoring, captive breeding, and dividing the single Meeteetse population

The primary features of this definition are its national conservation scope, inclusive participation, task orientation, collective resources, and grounding in reliable knowledge. All these contribute to the definition's analytical advantages. Its focus on recovery goals rather than research goals, its leadership by a federal rather than state agency, and its encouragement of practice-based learning would have opened up a wider range of feasible alternatives. This greater specificity would have been more useful to decision makers. Its attention to the situation's uncertainty and complexity would have lent more realism and manageability to day-to-day affairs. With national resources at hand, the program could have proceeded more quickly. The rare opportunity to develop a model program might have fostered a flexible and generative pattern of learning throughout the program. Simply by bringing in more people's ideas, this definition would have been likely to do a better job of considering the whole problem — social, economic, political, organizational, as well as scientific dimensions.

This definition also provides a better map of the problem universe. Rather than limit input and participation to a small number of other agencies and special interest groups, it considers national interests and capabilities. Although it does not necessarily obviate bureaucratic domination, the collective resource base and national scope would have promoted better accountability and cooperation and more open decision making. Fewer decisions might have been left to bureaucratic discretion. Yet it does not violate any agency's legal mandates. It would have brought a wider array of scientists, conservationists, and the national public into the program. Equalizing power among participants would have promoted greater creativity, focus on the goals, and even ongoing self-appraisal. Understanding of the uncertainty and complexity of the program would have led to a more flexible, interdependent, and less defensive organizational structure.

Finally, the alternative problem definition creates language that emphasizes cooperation rather than control, recovery rather than research, national rather than state interests, urgency rather than delay, active management rather than avoidance. It might have drawn attention to issues of national endangered species recovery, not just local focus on single species. It might also have mobilized those interested in promoting the common interest over special interests, and it would have shared risks, rewards, and responsibilities among coalition participants.

Any change in the direction of the ferret program will depend on whether the black-footed ferret can ever generate enough interest — whether a new problem definition and the values it espouses can ever matter to enough people — to build a consensus of advocates and to create a new order of awareness, language, responsibility, and action. Only when a problem definition "span[s] institutional arenas" to "find common ground" does it prevail (Weiss 1989:114).

Conclusions

One reason that problems are often poorly defined is limitations or "boundedness" of human rationality and objectivity (March 1978). Conventional mental activity is often insufficient to embrace the uncertainty and complexity set loose by an anomalous event such as the discovery of the small Meeteetse ferret population. Conventional viewpoints, it would seem, misled some participants at first into believing that ferret recovery would be a straightforward task, both biologically and bureaucratically, and that traditional approaches would be adequate. WGF personnel housed the first six captive ferrets together, under the assumption that all would be safe because they had all come from the same population. The disastrous results of this perception provide a clear example of bounded rationality. Although participants behaved rationally according to their own assessments, their rationality was itself narrowly bounded. People tend to create simplified models of the world; their behavior then is rational with respect to the model but not to reality (Simon 1957). Walter Lippmann (1922) described this discrepancy in a book chapter entitled "The World Outside and the Pictures in Our Heads."

The urge to simplify problems is commonplace. Complexity is difficult to comprehend, and most people — including the wildlife biologists and agency managers usually assigned to endangered species programs — are trained to think selectively, narrowly, and linearly about problems. In trying to make complex problems manageable, most people resort to ignoring certain parts and emphasizing others, but "such simplifications often succeed only in creating an illusion of understanding that in turn misinforms and further complicates the problem at hand" (Brewer 1984, personal communication).

To counter the pervasive problem of bounded rationality, however, interdisciplinary problem-solving methods have evolved to guide the focus of attention in tackling complex problems (Lasswell 1971a, Brewer and deLeon 1983, Brunner 1987). These integrated concepts, described in the next chapter, minimize the simplifications and distortions of individual subjective analyses of complex situations. These methods help individuals and groups identify and sort through a problem setting to extract or create useful problem definitions.

PART II

Reconstructing Endangered Species Recovery

Collectively, we have gained enough experience with endangered species recovery in the last few decades across many cases, contexts, and continents to realize not only that fundamental changes are needed but also that improvements are indeed possible. The ferret case study provides a great deal of insight into how endangered species policy and programs are actually organized and operated, and what their outcomes and effects are. It offers numerous opportunities to pinpoint where the difficulties lie and suggest how to correct them. The practical question is, How can we reconstruct the recovery process to make it more successful?

The idea of reconstruction is useful in that it is a positive, active approach to designing and refining successful recovery programs. A reconstructive approach first takes apart the elements of the problematic situation to understand them and gain insight, and then reassembles them in new ways that eliminate obstructions and counterproductive activities (Sullivan 1995). Its objective is "to bring about fundamental changes in prevailing institutions" (Lasswell and McDougal 1992:363). The idea of reconstruction is based on applying practical reason (developed from John Dewey's pragmatism and Aristotle's practical philosophy) to problematic situations, while acknowledging that none of the participants can pretend to be strictly objective. In Part II, I reframe the recovery process within its public policy context and suggest some new principles and practices more consistent with that framework.

Many appraisals and recommendations for improving the performance of the recovery process have been published recently. Cook and Dixon (1991) looked at improving recovery plans, as did Tear et al. (1995). Beatley (1994) appraised habitat conservation planning. Eisner et al. (1995) promoted scientifically sound ESA policy, the National Research Council (1995) reviewed the use of science, and the Ecological Society (1995) also recommended improving the role of science in the process. Miller et al. (1994) described a model for improving programs. O'Laughlin and Cook (1995) and Defenders of Wildlife (1995) suggested new directions for the ESA. Backhouse and Clark (1995) came up with eight practice-based lessons to improve implementation. Beedy (1995) offered ten ways and the *Endangered Species Bulletin* (Anonymous 1995a) added more ways to make the ESA work better. The New York Academy of Sciences (1995) examined the policy process, while the Administrative Conference of the United States (1995) proposed ways to improve decision making. Clark (Forthcoming) recommended ways to improve problem orientation, appraisal mechanisms, and practice-based learning. There have been many additional proposals for improving the performance of the endangered species recovery process.

These appraisals, mostly conventional in scope, tend to address technical issues, such as Beedy's (1995) recommendation to eliminate critical habitat designations and assess "take" (legal killing) at a population level and Defenders of Wildlife's (1995) recommendation to expand the roles both of science and of the states in recovery efforts. Nearly all recommendations concluded that more money is needed. These kinds of recommendations are certainly helpful, but there is widespread recognition that scientific, legal, and regulatory tinkering will not result in more successful programs. Even the National Research Council (1995:3), after asserting that "the overall conclusion is that ESA is based on sound scientific principles," emphasized that sound science alone will not prevent many species extinctions.

We must refocus our attention away from conventional, predominantly technical views and look instead at what Westrum (1994) so aptly called "the human envelope" of species recovery. The human envelope is the network of people and organizations that protects endangered species — scientists, managers, recovery teams, agencies, landowners, NGOs, conservationists, and recreational users of wildlife from hunters to bird watchers. If the human envelope is not handled well, in Westrum's words, "the species will not be handled well" (p. 329), and if the human envelope fails, the recovery process will also fail. We need to ensure the efficacy of endangered species' human envelope. We need to devise a more functional understanding of the very process of people and organizations interacting in the recovery task. From this we must reconstruct a set of principles and practices that are clear, consensual, and workable. The alternative problem definition of the ferret situation described in chapter 8 suggested a way of reconceptualizing endangered species recovery in general. It pointed to some of the problems as well as the opportunities inherent in the process by which policies are formulated and implemented.

Part II offers a framework for comprehending the dimensions of the human envelope and an analytical method of discovering what kind of change is needed. It also offers some concrete suggestions for improving the constituent organizations and professionals — improvements that must be made in addition to continual gains on technical, scientific fronts, such as field assessments, population viability assessments, and adaptive management. The next three chapters do not offer any guaranteed fixes for what is wrong in current principles and practices used in ESA implementation, nor are they tied specifically to problems of the ferret program. Instead, they describe more reflective, policy-oriented — and thus more realistic, practical, and corrigible — approaches with a much better chance of success.

The reasons for focusing on the behavior of organizations and professionals within the context of the public policy process may not be obvious. The conventional view holds that *extrinsic* factors are the major causes of programmatic failures. The belief is that if programs simply had more funding, more detailed or longer-term scientific research, less outside interference, less scrutiny by the media, and more detailed legal specifications, they would work better. This is true in part, but it does not address fundamental weaknesses within the system itself, which will undermine even the most lavishly funded and meticulously researched programs (Schlesinger 1968). By contrast, the functional view suggests that the human system of individuals, organizations, and policies that make up the species restoration process has *intrinsic* behavioral properties that largely determine if a recovery effort will be successful or not. These variables may be invisible to some participants, but in fact they can be perceived, analyzed, and manipulated to achieve desired outcomes — in this case, to improve the performance of the recovery program. Just as killing predators will not increase the number of deer when the limiting factor is disease, neither will external forces such as increased funding improve programs when the limiting factor is organizational problems internal to the system.

The sheer complexity of endangered species problems tells us there is no single, straightforward, technocratic recipe for successful implementation of the Endangered Species Act that can be followed in every case. But despite the unique content and context of each case — species, ecological setting, threatening processes, scientific details, individual and organizational involvement, or public controversy — there are useful ways of understanding the human envelope that promise improved performance in all cases. We must be clear about what we want to accomplish, we must specify the myriad, difficult constraints on current restoration policy and programs, and we must build new, practicable processes.

9

Species Recovery as Policy Process
Shifting the Perspective

Shifting focus to the human envelope of species recovery is a big step toward opening up constructive new avenues to tackle problems. Reconstructing the recovery process around a policy-oriented approach — as we might call the focus on the human envelope — can help guard against oversimplifying problems, ignoring contexts, and demonizing opponents. It can facilitate the flow of information within and between groups and help assure that science is well used. It can help foster a culture of learning in both individuals and organizations. Knowing about the policy process opens up many opportunities to improve decision and policy making.

A practical model of the human envelope already exists to guide participants in fathoming its complexities, avoiding the kinds of problems that plagued the ferret case, and constructing practical solutions. It can be used to understand any conceivable human interaction and identify, describe, and account for the details of any problem (Lasswell and McDougal 1992). The approach taken here to reconstructing the endangered species recovery process, the policy-oriented approach, rests directly on the inclusive model of the policy process and problem solving. This method has been applied to natural resource management (Ascher and Healy 1990), defense (Brewer and Shubik 1979), energy (Brunner 1980), space (Brunner 1992), global climate change (Brunner 1991a, 1996), risk assessment (Fischhoff et al. 1984), and social service policy and programmatic problems (Brewer and Kakalik 1979, Brunner 1986).

One of the challenges in species conservation has always been how to address unbounded policy problems, including ESA implementation, when our intellectual, organizational, and analytical resources are bounded. We can meet the challenge by elaborating how we conceptualize problems, map out relevant factors, understand the causal factors and what is likely to happen to them, and deal with alternatives. The science-based approach to recovery, which calls for more science alone, has been one of the standard ways of dealing with extinction problems. Although science offers a useful framework and starting point for understanding species needs (Fri 1995), it does not address the human factors that in most cases are to blame for development of the problem. "Science's success in framing and answering questions within the scientific realm is indisputable; but for many other problems that fall outside the bounds scientists delineate the rational bias, tight discipline, and quantitative procedures erected to support the scientific edifice provide little help" (Brewer and deLeon 1983:3). Another traditional means of handling recovery problems has been the agency-based approach, which called for giving the agencies more authority and money, and in some cases turning recovery efforts over to state agencies. But this has not led to meeting the goal either. The alternative, policy-oriented approach incorporates the best features of both the science-based and the agency-based approaches, but goes far beyond either one by relying on the social process model and allied concepts of problem solving. Many valuable conceptual and applied tools already exist but remain largely unknown and unused by wildlife biologists, management agency administrators, and nongovernmental conservationists (see Brewer and deLeon 1983, Ascher 1986).

Although my focus in this book is on ESA implementation, I am also concerned with improving the entire ESA policy-making process. Toward this aim, in this chapter I reframe the work of endangered species recovery as a policy process problem to make practical intervention options apparent.

The Workings of the Policy Process

The policy process is the interaction of people as they try to solve problems, find meaning, and forge a workable society for themselves. In the words of the political scientist Harold Lasswell (1936), it is the process that determines who gets what, when, and how. People tend to behave in interactions in ways that they *feel* will leave them better off than if they behaved in other ways (Lasswell 1971a). Participants in the process—whether organized in groups or acting as individuals, whether elites or rank-and-file workers — are decidedly unequal: seldom is there a level playing field, and some participants have more to play with than others and make larger contributions to outcomes.

Policy is not simply the set of prescriptions offered by government or other groups, as it is often conceived. Real policy evolves over time in a given context as participants interact. Tober (1989) called policy an abstraction, "a pattern of behavior rather than separate discrete acts" (p. 142). Similarly, Samuel Dana and Sally Fairfax (1980:xiii) emphasized that policy emerges from "a series of negotiated settlements resulting from the interaction among competing interest groups, among competing regions, and among agencies competing for the support, interest, and attention of the public." But the aggregative nature of policy means that there are no guarantees that policy will meet the needs of society as a whole. Yet the myriad groups involved, the different challenges they face, their efforts to work with or against one another, and their limitations in dealing with complex issues — in short, the policy process — determines how wildlife is managed and how natural resources are used, and thus it must be heeded (Ascher and Healy 1990).

Policy, then, involves many nonrational and subjective elements as the limits of experience, knowledge, and organizational capabilities are reached, as identities, expectations, and demands come to play, and as personal, disciplinary, educational, epistemological, organizational, and parochial biases and ideological allegiances are acted upon. The interplay of these variables is often subtle and "invisible" to many participants, who may insist that they are neutral and objective, or that they are acting in the public interest. Narrowly constructed views of self and situation can be deeply entrenched in an individual's identity and an organization's culture. If these perspectives become the basis for demands, strategies, and actions, then serious problems are likely to develop in the form of inadequate problem-solving, poorly designed programs, or conflict. The policy-oriented approach, on the other hand, appreciates the actual difficulty of the work to be done on all fronts and guards against narrowness and blind spots. It increases the visibility of relevant events concerning a problem and its context.

All policy derives from the network of participants, wherein some have formal roles prescribed by statute while others are involved because of their special expertise, the power they represent, their long-standing association with formal organizations, or the impacts of the policy on them. Influence over the process is a function of the changing strategic positions of participants, which in turn is influenced by many factors. All participants in species recovery work are part of ongoing policy processes, whether they see themselves as such or not. Not even scientists are outside this value-laden social process. Participants who use a comprehensive model of this process to guide their understanding and participation are at a decided advantage. Recovery programs staffed by such people are likely to be more successful than programs that lack such knowledge and skills.

Traditionally, federal and state governments have monopolized or dominated endangered species recovery, resulting in single-agency and single-problem definition domination. Such domination often results, both conceptually and administratively, in the exclusion of other important matters. As Yaffee (1982) noted, many people and organizations capable of improving implementation — such as small expert teams, nongovernmental organizations, knowledgeable citizens, and those who will be affected by policies — are often excluded from administrative networks, and it is often impossible to get them a formal role in these processes. This kind of policy process serves the few at the expense of the many. Building a greater range of expertise, resources, and flexibility into programs and ensuring that they cannot be stifled or designed out in midstream would avoid many common problems. Individuals in such a coalition must be not only policy oriented but also highly task oriented. Substantive knowledge used in the process — in the case of species conservation, such knowledge consists of biology and related social science fields — must be fully complemented by knowledge of how the policy process itself works and how to participate in it effectively. It is not easy to find that kind of talent. It will not suffice simply to assign mid-level biologists or bureaucrats to organize and manage recovery programs. Leaders, managers, and other participants in recovery programs must learn how to carry out these special "policy process" tasks at the same time they undertake the technical tasks of species restoration. That is what it means to be a policy-oriented professional.

It is helpful to view the policy process as having a life cycle, in which problems emerge, are defined and dealt with through strategic statements and tactical means, and eventually are solved, stabilized, or worsened. Brewer and deLeon (1983) described six phases in the process (derived from Lasswell's [1971a] seven decision-making functions): initiation, estimation, selection, implementation, evaluation, and termination. These are defined in table 1. Understanding the flow in any social process can enable scientific observers, decision makers, or participants to locate themselves comprehensively and realistically in the overall process and thus improve the performance, power, and participation of planners, managers, researchers, and others involved in conservation. In addition, it enables participants to guard against common weaknesses that occur in each of the six phases (Ascher and Healy 1990; table 1). How, though, are participants to learn these skills?

Table 1. The life cycle of the policy process and recommendations for each phase (after Ascher and Healy 1990).

1. *Initiation (recognition of a problem; creative thinking about it; preliminary assessments of concepts and claims)*

    Avoid simplistic problem definitions with a single objective.

    Don't let a single organization dominate.

    Don't assume that the program will benefit everyone.

    Don't discount long-term consequences.

    Balance local and central (usually government) participation.

2. *Estimation (scientific study of the problem, likely impacts, and outcomes; normative assessments; development of outlines of a programmatic response)*

    Bring in diverse experts right away and minimize their biases.

    Don't let expert opinions overrule preferences of those affected by decisions.

    Don't exaggerate the expected benefits or discount the possible costs.

    Don't focus only on easily measured or easily understood data; ask the hard questions.

3. *Selection (focused debate on the issues; formulation and authorization of a program to solve the problem)*

    Coordinate governmental decision making, especially when there are stronger and weaker agencies.

    Don't allow agency rivalries to block achievement of the program's goals.

    Don't overcontrol participants or beneficiaries.

4. *Implementation (development and application of a specific program)*

    Avoid "benefit leakage," the extension of programs beyond their original targets to the point of wasting resources.

    Make sure government management agencies do not succumb to the natural selfishness of the private sector.

    Avoid intelligence failures and delays.

    Ensure adequate coordination and appraisal.

    Insist on appropriate organizational arrangements.

5. *Evaluation (comparison of expected and actual performance of the program; reconciliation of the differences)*

    Ensure that decision makers and managers are sensitive to criticism.

    Learn explicitly and systematically from experience (strive to understand the complexity of causes and effects, consider long time spans and changing contexts, and conduct adequate follow-up).

6. *Termination (discontinuing or revising programs)*

    Consider the effects of termination and deal fairly with people affected by it.

    Anticipate and manage antitermination coalitions.

    Realize that any program termination may be perceived as a program failure.

A Method for Learning about the Policy Process

Several decades ago, Harold Lasswell and his colleagues developed an integrated set of concepts and propositions to identify, define, and solve problems in the policy process (Lasswell 1955, 1956, 1965, 1970, 1971a, Lasswell and Kaplan 1950, Lasswell and McDougal 1992). Lasswell, founder of the modern policy-analytic movement, labeled this set of conceptual tools the "policy sciences." Lasswell and McDougal (1992:xxi–xxii) described the origins of the policy sciences (see also deLeon 1988):

> What we sought was a framework of theory and procedures that would, whatever the community, both facilitate the clear postulation of basic community goals and provide a map, with categories of empirical reference, appropriately comprehensive in potential reach and capable of being made as precise as needed, for the systematic, contextual examination of the many significant variables affecting authoritative decision, and rational appraisal of the aggregate value consequences of alternatives in decision. The values that we recommended for postulation were of course those that are today commonly described as the values of human dignity.

The overriding goal postulated by the policy sciences is "the realization of human dignity or a commonwealth of democracy" — a goal that should be kept in mind by all participants as they analyze policy problems and devise solutions.

DESCRIPTION AND BENEFITS OF THE POLICY SCIENCES APPROACH

These conceptual tools, which include working models of decision and social processes as well as a procedure to orient rationally and comprehensively to problems, were designed to broaden the role of logic and empirical inquiry into issues, alternatives, and outcomes (Tribe 1973). This framework helps people escape the confines of thought and action often imposed by narrow professional disciplinary biases and partisan perspectives. It provides methods to look at the policy process as a whole. In using the policy sciences, "the challenge is not how to generate all the answers before the questions are asked in a specific case, but rather how to organize the . . . inquiry. . . . The approach is not to specify ahead of time that particular factors or issues are most important, but rather to ensure that the right questions are raised and the right problems addressed. The consequent need for a multi-disciplinary perspective on the social process precludes seeking answers in single disciplines. The importance of the policy making process itself precludes a narrow technical focus on the substantive issue alone" (Ascher 1989, personal communication).

The policy sciences' holistic approach focuses on the social process, that is, the interactions of the participants, and it recognizes their perspectives, roles, strategies, and values. The policy sciences' problem-solving tools are specifically designed to address both technical and value-laden issues simultaneously. Under such circumstances, "ideology, ethics, politics, economics, and other considerations are involved. Policy is determined by the complex resolution of all the relevant factors, of which rational analysis is but one" (Brewer and deLeon 1983:182).

With a distinct frame of reference and epistemology of practice, the policy sciences are a powerful problem-solving heuristic (Brunner 1982). Policy scientists consistently draw on a broad range of knowledge areas and relevant disciplines to solve problems — including philosophy, history, economics, political science, law, sociology, psychology, and the biological and physical sciences. But the policy sciences' framework has more than academic relevance. It was designed to help bring about practical solutions to any kind of policy problem. Most important, it offers sound models for thought and action and it alerts people to the many kinds of problems that can appear in any problem-solving endeavor:

> Most preventable policy mistakes stem from a failure to ask the right questions or to appreciate the answers: typically, some critical part of the context is misconstrued or it is overlooked altogether. In either case, the mistake becomes apparent only in retrospect — after commitments have been made and the results turn out to differ from those expected. For a variety of reasons such mistakes cannot be entirely avoided, but they can be minimized through the systematic use of adequate conceptual tools. Such tools are designed to help you perceive more of the relevant context, and to help you understand the details within that context more reliably. (Brunner 1987, personal communication)

Through the questions that they provoke about a problem setting, the policy sciences provide a way to figure out what is "missing" from the policy process in terms of rationality, practical politics, and morality, and how to "fill in the blanks" (Brunner 1996, personal communication). These conceptual tools recognize the practical limits of people's objectivity and rationality that result from limited analytical tools, cognitive abilities, and time and resources, and they can be used to guide the course of inquiry. Brunner (1987:1) asserts that learning to apply the policy science framework "pay[s] off in practical results — more reliable estimates of when, where, and how to intervene effectively, under time and other resource constraints." If conservationists, administrators, and managers could gain reliable knowledge in wildlife science and biology as encouraged by Romesburg (1981, 1991) and, at the same time, gain reliable knowledge of the decision and social processes that use their technical knowledge, then they could greatly enhance their performance.

In solving any complex problem, the distinctive outlook of the policy sciences calls for three interactive and simultaneous activities: *problem orientation,* which demands that any problem be understood in its entirety, *contextual analysis,* which helps make sense of an often bewildering array of potential information that relates to the problem, and *synthesis of methods,* not just multidisciplinary but interdisciplinary approaches to collecting and analyzing information and effecting changes (Lasswell 1971a, Brewer and deLeon 1983, Brunner 1987). How this outlook might benefit wildlife biologists, conservation biologists, and natural resource managers was described by Clark (1992, 1993) and others.

PROBLEM ORIENTATION

Lasswell and his colleagues outlined a distinctive method of "orienting" to problems rationally and comprehensively, responding appropriately to their complexity, and understanding them usefully. He described five procedurally rational tasks that are essential in problem solving: clarification of goals, description of trends, analysis of conditioning and causal factors, projection of future developments, and invention, evaluation and selection of policy alternatives (Lasswell 1971a, Lasswell and McDougal 1992). Table 2 provides a brief list of questions that can guide participants in orienting to a problem.

These five tasks can serve as guides to content (that is, to the significant variables), by reminding people what questions are worth asking about any problem, and as guides to procedure, by recommending that people perform the tasks in an orderly manner (Lasswell 1971a). In examining any problem, every detail must be understood within its context; the five-part agenda allows the context to emerge. Brunner (1992, personal communication) noted that many problem-solving efforts fail because people rush to make explanations, projections, or evaluations without first considering goals and trends.

Another approach is to ask the following questions in problem orientation (Brunner 1996, personal communication): What outcomes do we prefer? What are the problems—discrepancies between goals and actual or anticipated states of affairs—with respect to achieving these goals? What alternatives are available to participants and others to solve the problem? Would each alternative contribute toward solving the problems? Did each alternative work when tried in the past on relevant occasions? Why, or under what conditions, does it work satisfactorily or not work? This procedure must be reiterated to refine and supplement consideration of goals, alternatives, and evaluation.

Table 2. Intellectual tasks of decision making or problem solving (from Willard and Norchi 1993:587).

---

1. *Goal clarification.* This task refers to the processes through which individuals or groups seek to understand what their preferences are in relation to a particular problem. When this task is performed by a group, and the problem under consideration is the way in which the group plans to organize itself, the group is engaged in determining its basic policies. These are the policies to which individuals commit themselves for the communities of which they are members.

2. *Trend analysis.* This task involves a description of history in terms of what past decisions have produced, in relation to clarified and specified goals. Where are we now in relation to fundamental preferences?

3. *Factor analysis.* This task involves an identification and assessment of the predispositional and environmental factors that have affected past decisions. What are the factors and their interrelationships which may affect future decisions?

4. *Future analysis.* This task involves anticipating the likely course of future decisions. What is the likely impact of future decisions on the achievement of fundamental preferences and basic community policies?

5. *Invention of alternatives.* If one does not like what is predicted for the future, if it is not compatible with clarified goals, what can one do about it? What are the alternatives in the management of authoritative decision for doing things differently?

Endangered species restoration needs comprehensive and early problem orientation. No program should begin tackling the "solution" to a problem without understanding first the nature and scope of that problem. A call for better problem orientation is not a call for endless studies — which are often used to delay action and avoid responsibility and accountability — but a call for practical intellectual rigor.

CONTEXTUAL ANALYSIS

Problems do not exist in a vacuum, and so creating a map of a problem's context is essential to understanding the problem at hand. Table 3 lists the basic features of the context and questions to ask about each of these. People — individuals and groups — whose interests are advanced or harmed by alternatives or solutions to the problem will help define the boundaries of action that will be technically feasible and politically justifiable. It is vital to understand their perspectives; it is on the basis of their identities and expectations that people make demands or claims on society through the policy process. Participants use whatever resources they have to compete or cooperate in the process

Table 3. Questions to address when examining a particular problem in context (from Willard and Norchi 1993:590).

---

1. *Participants.* Who is participating? Individuals and/or groups? Who would you like to see participate?

2. *Perspectives.* What are the perspectives of those who are participating? Of those you would like to see participate? What would you like their perspectives to be? Perspectives include:
   • Demands, or what participants or potential participants want, in terms of values and institutions
   • Expectations, or the matter-of-fact assumptions of participants about the past and future
   • Identifications, or on whose behalf are demands made?

3. *Situations.* In what situations do participants interact? In what situations would you like to see them participate?

4. *Base values.* What assets or resources do participants use in their efforts to achieve their goals? All values, including authority, can be used as bases of power. What assets or resources would you like to see participants use to achieve their goals?

5. *Strategies.* What strategies do participants employ in their efforts to achieve their goals? Strategies can be considered in terms of diplomatic, ideological, economic, and military instruments. What strategies would you like to see used by participants in pursuit of their goals?

6. *Outcomes.* What outcomes are achieved in the ongoing, continuous flow of interaction among participants? Outcomes can be considered in terms of changes in the distribution of values. Who is indulged in terms of which values? Who is deprived in terms of which values? Outcomes also refer to the ways in which values are shaped and shared. The particular ways in which values are shaped and shared are called practices or institutions. Practices are specialized to the shaping and sharing of specific values. How are practices changing? How would you like to see practices change? What is your preferred distribution of values?

---

to make sure their demands are met. These assets include more than just power and money: the policy sciences recognize eight fundamental value categories — power, wealth, enlightenment, skill, well-being, affection, respect, and rectitude. For example, a group may use its knowledge or skill to support its demands for respect. The situation in which participants interact is also a key feature of the context in terms of geography, crises, organizations, and resources. The strategies used by participants to achieve their goals may be either persuasive or coercive. The outcomes of these interactions will indulge some people's demands for certain values and deprive others — that is, some people will get their way while others will not. Policy process interactions will also have certain effects in terms of new practices adopted or old ones rejected. All these interactions of social process need to be mapped to illuminate the context of a problem. The brevity of this list belies the amount of time and effort required to explore these topics fully and realistically.

The list does not supply answers, of course; it only "provides a guide to the explorations that are necessary" in the social process (Lasswell 1971a:39). Each problem setting requires it own contextual map, and experienced interpretation and judgment are essential on the part of mapmakers, be they participants or analysts. Any participant or analyst in the endangered species recovery arena should also seek to clarify his or her own standpoint in terms of perspective (identity and expectations), values, strategies, and preferred outcomes. Many factors, interrelated within the whole, must be dealt with simultaneously, but contexts do not break down easily for analysis because of their complexity. To understand and analyze the whole problem requires returning repeatedly to the five tasks outlined in problem orientation.

SYNTHESIS OF METHOD

As the policy sciences are employed to explore problems and solutions, they must rely on and integrate varied kinds of data brought to a case, make different kinds of information meaningful to varied audiences, and organize, manage, store, and present information in problem-focused, practical ways. This can be an extremely difficult job: "The policy sciences have rather special data requirements. As compared with the physical sciences, they have more data of varying degrees of quality; less agreement and hence less certainty about which data to collect; a greater need to keep data in simple, easily reconfigured formats; and more complex problems in the communication of analyses, results, and recommendations" (Brewer 1975:458). Taking a problem-oriented, contextual approach to species recovery forces integration and synthesis of knowledge, whereas disciplinary, epistemological, organizational, or parochial standpoints result in data that may be incomplete, fragmentary, or useless to some participants. Without a means to synthesize knowledge for practical action, species recovery is less likely.

Three Tools to Improve Policy Processes

There are no sure-fire antidotes to deeply rooted policy problems. But three methods may be employed directly in the service of species recovery efforts as well as many other problems. They can help generate more practicable improvements, patterns of more useful and less divisive decision making, and more responsive, corrigible, and creative programs. They are extremely helpful in improving participants' knowledge of decision and social processes and their ability to participate effectively. They have successfully addressed policy process problems in other contexts and in a few endangered species cases.

APPRAISALS IN THE POLICY PROCESS

Appraisal plays a crucial role in the policy process as a necessary preliminary to learning and improvement. Appraisal is especially important in a democracy: citizens often have minor roles in initiating or constructing policy and programs, but there is a continual need for honest, comprehensive, independent evaluation of programs and policies. Citizens must help establish the conditions under which effective appraisal can take place as well as offering alternative solutions to recognized problems.

The central issue of appraisal is the assignment of responsibility and accountability for outcomes, both successes and failures and at both organizational and individual levels (Lasswell and McDougal 1992). There must be some consensus on what behavior serves the common interest and what serves special interests. This task is easier when the goals are clear. A strategy for locating responsibility should include several objectives. Did implementation conform to the policy aims? Was authority abused? Were previous appraisals made and were results widely accessible? (Secrecy is harmful to trust and credibility.) Were resources used efficiently? Were people treated respectfully? Was a sense of fairness shown? Was recognition given to people deserving commendation? Was appraisal incorruptibly carried out? The appraisal mechanism must be suited to the task to give a realistic appraisal of performance. Appraisals should be independent, free from coercive pressure by official bodies or unofficial interests. Simple in-house review is rarely adequate; outside review is essential. Ideally, appraisal should be an ongoing part of all existing programs and decision functions, although in reality it seldom is.

Appraisal can be a problem in big organizations. It may be difficult to determine at what point bureaucratic malfunctioning becomes unacceptable. How many complaints about poor performance or malfunction are needed? Lasswell and McDougal (1992:1,255–1,257) listed some indices of bureaucratic poor performance: "official hesitation" (excessive deferrals and referrals), "red tape," "absence of originality," "callousness," "resistance to proposed innovation," "omissions of opportunity to be helpful," "pseudo-enlightenment," "self-attention," "sycophancy," "empire building," and "cut-throatism." Under these conditions, unless the appraisal function is independently embodied, it is likely to get lost in the bureaucratic fog of self-promotion, manipulations, and public relations.

The performance of organizational systems and their policy impacts can be measured in various ways. Brewer and deLeon (1983), for example, described four general criteria used in policy and program evaluation: *Effectiveness* is the actual output compared to the planned output over a certain period. *Efficiency* is the ratio of inputs to outputs, and it sometimes focuses on the transformation process, or progress. One prominent measure of efficiency is dollars per unit return. *Equity* is the criterion that measures whether "similarly situated people [are] treated equally" (Brewer and deLeon 1983:337). The equity measure indicates the presence of productive cooperation or disruptive competition or coercion. *Adequacy* is the measure of whether the program or policy decided upon was in fact capable of solving the problem as defined. Brewer and deLeon (1983:112) commented on the extraordinary difficulty of setting appraisal standards, a task that should be done early in the policy-making process: "A most striking realization is that there are no answers whose truth can be proved and whose efficacy can be confidently foretold. Rather, one hopes that analysis will enhance understanding of problems and create opportunities to exploit many perspectives of them by using diverse criteria to represent the hopes and expectations of those whose lives will be touched by pending decisions" (p. 112).

In appraising the first few years of the Wyoming ferret program, were appropriate decision-making mechanisms to secure wild ferret populations established in a reasonable time frame? Were ferrets restored efficiently with regard to money and time? Was the state-run program sufficient to meet established goals of fully restoring the black-footed ferret nationwide? Was participation democratic? Were ferrets afforded the same protective measures as species of similar status? Similar questions can be asked on a larger scale. What have been the outcomes and effects of the ESA and its programs? Have ESA resources been well spent or have agency budgets simply been maximized? Are species of similar status treated equally? Are the ESA and its programs *sufficient* to restore species?

One way to improve evaluation is to conduct net assessment, that is, to integrate and evaluate information collected from all parts of the program (field teams, working groups, top-level decision makers, etc.). Each unit would submit regular written assessments of how well its part of the program is functioning — how information is flowing, how decisions are made, whether targets are being met, how its part contributes to the whole. These assessments would be widely circulated, and if problems are identified, they can be discussed openly and honestly and every effort can be made to correct them regardless of where they are. The core decision group (such as the agency in charge or the recovery team) would make the overall net assessment to keep the program on course, and its assessments would be made public.

The policy process, as it has been revealed through the workings of the black-footed ferret case as well as other cases, may be difficult to fathom because of its complexity, its many nonrational determinants, and its many inherent, nonmanipulable components. It is incumbent on us, however, to try to understand these processes and reform them for the better. Is there a design to avoid the problems in the first place?

DECISION SEMINARS

Endangered species recovery efforts may include recovery teams, project teams, working groups, field teams, coordinating groups, government agencies, special interest groups, conservation organizations, and some core decision group that oversees and manages the program. There are many different ways such a diverse assemblage can organize itself to achieve effective decision making in clarifying and achieving its common goals (Litwak and Hylton 1962). One particularly effective problem-solving group is the decision seminar, which was designed to encourage specialists and decision makers to integrate their knowledge to address complex problems (Lasswell 1960, Brewer 1975). Widely used in other situations (see review by Brewer 1975), the decision seminar holds much promise for improving species recovery efforts. It offers a significant advantage over conventional means of decision making by employing strategies to sharpen insights into the problem at hand, explore possible solutions, assign institutional responsibility, and manage data. The format is specifically designed to overcome the limitations of individual problem solving by organizing and directing a group's attention to key issues. It uses the policy sciences' problem orientation, contextual mapping, and multiple methods to gain insight into community problems, clarify community goals, and generate alternative policies. In addition to analysis and instruction in decision-making procedures, the seminar is used — as its name indicates — for making actual decisions about policy (Brewer 1975, Willard and Norchi 1993).

The decision seminar differs from conventional decision mechanisms or settings in seven ways, according to Brewer (1975). First, all government and nongovernment interests are considered, and the process by which decisions are made is explicitly and continuously studied. Three central questions are asked: "Who is currently making choices about the problem under consideration? How are these choices made? And under what circumstances might they be improved?" (p. 442). Second, ten to fifteen concerned and willing analysts participate in the seminar and contribute intellectual skills and outlooks on the problem. Continuity and commitment by them are absolutely essential. The seminar is also open to outsiders, however. Third, an explicit problem-solving orientation is used. Participants contribute written and oral assessments of the goals of all relevant individuals and groups involved. They analyze the context of the problem and determine its past trends, factors affecting those trends, probable future outcomes, and options available to meet the problem. Schedules are set to focus attention on the problem. Fourth, participants make independent assessments of the problem and its possible outcomes. These independent judgments are compared, common views discussed, and discrepancies considered. New information may change judgments. Fifth, all relevant methods of analysis are used. They may encompass a broad array of techniques and knowledge areas, and new methods are encouraged at all turns. All methods are continually examined and improved. Sixth, all the above steps are directed at making decisions, so the seminar's activities are aimed at on-the-ground applications. Actual responsibilities for all phases of the work are assigned. And seventh, participants' analyses and activities are documented and used throughout to recall information and stimulate imagination in problem solving. This becomes the group's "institutional memory."

The "construction, orientation, attitude, and style of the participants" (Brewer 1975:443) constitute the unique characteristic of the decision seminar. Seminar participants are few in number, committed to active involvement, and ready to explore successive iterations of problem definitions and solutions, over months or years if necessary.

For decision seminars to be successful, they must demonstrate certain features: they must appreciate reality, the whole context of the problem must be comprehensively treated, the approach must be interdisciplinary, major time commitments are necessary, and seminar participants should have access to decision makers. (Decision makers may themselves be part of decision seminars.) The strategy must include several components. Seminar participants and decision makers must have a similar understanding of the problem context and its scales of time, space, and complexity. The seminar must identify and define the problem so that solutions are both scientifically manageable and relevant. Participants must map the "problem space" relative to affected groups and existing institutional capabilities. This reveals institutional overlaps, omissions, and contradictions and gives a picture of how many institutions are in fact responsible. Once the context has been mapped, participant groups identified, problems defined, and existing institutions assessed, institutional responsibilities must be matched to the problem sets. This reveals inadequacies or overlaps in existing policies and programs and needs for new ones. The seminar must continually refine these analyses. The next step is to distinguish among relatively hard data (quantitative), soft data (which tend to be less precise and less reliable), and even softer (for example, symbolic) data.

Finally, the seminar must develop systems to manage vast amounts of data and render them usable by seminar participants.

There are potential problems in the use of decision seminars, although their structure and functioning seek to avoid such problems. These include discontinuity of core participation, institutional rigidity, indirect decision access, insufficient attention to a problem's context, and financial problems. But of course all these problems are common to conventional programs, too.

Institutionalizing this approach in endangered species recovery will require commitment from federal and state governments, conservation organizations, and other participants. This commitment is worthwhile given the benefits that decision seminars could bring to species conservation. Decision seminars could be tried in prototyping exercises.

PROTOTYPES

A prototype is a small-scale project to implement a trial change in a social or policy system, such as changing people's assumptions about how they should interact or who should share what kinds of power. It goes beyond the notion of a simple pilot project in that its primary goal is to gain information about relevant factors. It is a way of improving institutional practices as well as scientific knowledge, especially in complex, uncertain situations with a high potential for conflict (Lasswell 1963, Brewer and deLeon 1983). Prototypes have been widely and practically employed in many different settings (Lasswell 1971b), including improving endangered species recovery (Clark et al. 1995a, 1995b).

The key feature of prototyping is its "provisional, improvising, exploratory approach to a context" (Lasswell and McDougal 1992:895). Because of the amount of uncertainty, originality, and spontaneity in social systems, the researchers or initiators of prototyping projects cannot predict at the outset whether the strategies they select to change a system will be the most suitable. Therefore, part of what they must do is adapt their methods throughout the course of the project. However, the project should not be modified too quickly or too often. It must be granted an adequate trial period to develop some support, legitimacy, and "power" before being evaluated in relation to what had existed originally or to some other modification. Prototypes must also guard against political control, a challenge they face because they deal with institutional practices in the power arena. A prototype lost to "the requirements of the powerful" becomes merely a political manipulation.

Prototyping is a technique that builds corrigibility into every application (Lasswell 1971b). Because it is not a simple "cookbook" approach to intervening in the policy process, it permits continued learning and creativity to take place: even though its objectives are explicit, ambiguities remain that must be worked out over the life of the prototyping effort. It establishes a process to detect and correct errors, and thus it is a way to accumulate successes and weed out failures (Brunner 1995, personal communication). If found to be valuable, a prototype can be repeated, improved, and incorporated into existing policy and institutional practices. Ultimately, the aim of a prototypical approach is to learn through self-observation, insight, and understanding to devise better strategic and tactical programs. It has been suggested that this ability to learn — rather than the achievement of specific policies — is what indicates rationality in policy making (Majone 1989).

Prototyping is an answer to the need for innovation, creativity, and new initiatives in the decision setting of endangered species conservation. One significant advantage is that it can be applied almost immediately to any of the hundreds of endangered species recovery programs now under way or planned. It need not wait until top administrators decide it is worth trying. Innovation and improvements are most likely to come from the bottom up, where real policy is made and where the benefits will pay off in practical terms. Every recovery program can develop its own systematic approach to learning and improvement through prototyping and report its results to all those concerned with conserving biological diversity.

Prototyping was used in the recovery program for the endangered Australian eastern barred bandicoot, a medium-sized marsupial (Clark et al. 1995a, 1995b). After decades of conventional efforts to restore this species, field surveys in November 1991 turned up so few animals as to precipitate a crisis: acknowledgment of failure. In a two-day review, key participants located several major problems in the program's organization and operations. Based largely on the report of this review meeting, Backhouse et al. (1994) identified five weaknesses: lack of reliable knowledge, inadequate definition of the problem, lack of leadership, absence of comprehensive management, and lack of ongoing evaluation:

> To their credit, many participants in the bandicoot recovery effort recognized the program's inability to recover the species and were therefore eager for critical self-analysis and ideas for improvement. Thus the atmosphere was conducive to the 1991 program review. Following that review, a major reorganization took place. In early 1992, a decision group was set up, a strategic planner was assigned, and four working groups were established. The new recovery program sought to establish reporting lines directly between senior decision makers and the field staff, regardless of agency allegiance. Although several problems remained, significant improvements resulted during 1992. The year began with about 109 bandicoots declining toward extinction; the

year ended with more than 250 bandicoots in reintroduced wild, semiwild, and captive populations. (Backhouse et al. 1994:262)

Prototypical changes made to the program included more responsive decision making that brought senior managers closer to the program. The working groups were "given the authority, guidance, and resources to develop and meet their own targets using their professional expertise." And the strategic planner's setting of goals, targets, timelines, and responsibilities "helped put the program on a more objective footing" (p. 263). Once a prototypical reorganization took place, the program began to turn around. Backhouse et al. noted, however, that these changes were made possible largely because of coincidental reassignments in senior management in the state agency in 1992 and 1993. Moreover, not all the problems identified in 1991 were addressed by the reorganization, and additional changes were made. Nevertheless, such prototyping elements as team building, cooperative decision making, renewed field work, and appraisal can be transferred from this project to other endangered species efforts. Participants in the bandicoot program concluded that prototyping did work and answered their need for innovation, creativity, and new initiatives in endangered species recovery.

These tools—appraisals, decision seminars, and prototyping—have been around for decades yet are little used in species restoration efforts, despite their proven benefits in establishing new patterns of human interaction. In real contexts, there are interests rooted deeply in the status quo that resist change and improvement.

Perils and Words of Caution

Despite these and many other approaches to improving decision making in the policy process, several authors have warned about the intractability of problems in policy making. These barriers should be kept in mind by those seeking to improve endangered species conservation. One such problem is the gargantuan complexity of relationships among the participants, the values at play, and their dynamics through time. Not only might it be impossible to configure improvements practically in real world contexts, but there is currently no societal institution in control of the endangered species recovery process. The U.S. Fish and Wildlife Service is as close to such a institution as currently exists. Yaffee's (1982) study of the FWS Endangered Species Office suggested the need for building better policies and programs for endangered species recovery, with the conclusion that "clear objectives and performance standards are helpful but not sufficient to ensure effective control after a bill becomes a law" (p. 160). He noted that only two kinds of statutory mechanisms are available to affect the quality of implementation: redistributing resources and modifying processes. Both, however, have limited value in creating successful programs because the agencies have so many opportunities for administrative "redefinition" of the law. The only opportunity open to a policy or program designer is to alter the strategic positions of participants. Yaffee concluded that significant improvements in policy are difficult or impossible because the policy designer "must not only specify the directions of the game clearly, but pick the mix of actors, rules, and initial power allocations to achieve the desired outcome — all with only a small part of the system's resources under his or her control" (p. 161). He recommended using periodic review boards, public participation, and mechanisms for including many groups outside the normal agency network. But since his book's publication in 1982, virtually none of his recommendations has been used or institutionalized by the FWS (Yaffee 1992, personal communication). He concluded that improving ESA implementation may be impossible:

> While we like to think that there are scientific or technical reasons for making policy choices, often there are not. While science can and should inform choice, rarely can it do so definitively. Most policy choices involve fundamental questions of social value — issues for which technicians have only one voice among many. The central issues of the endangered species case — determining what is ethical behavior and what is valuable to protect at what cost — require individual and group assessments of what is moral and what is valued. Economics and biology only help us slightly in making these choices. (p. 162)

Another barrier to policy improvements, according to Lloyd Etheredge (1985), is an inappropriate focus on trying to correct obvious failings in technical, rational analysis. Four common explanations for program failure are that "it lacked multiple advocacy," "it lacked good institutional memory," it was "poorly organized to provide reliable forecasts," and "it was insular and the decision makers exhibited a 'groupthink' syndrome" (p. 106). But Etheredge argues that these explanations do not hold up to closer examination: all four focus on improving rational decision making under the assumption that decision making is rational, which it obviously is not (see Simon 1957, Brewer and deLeon 1983, Brunner 1991b). "Rationality has little to do with policy, one way or the other, and maximum technical rationality would not change a great deal" (p. 202). He argued that correcting shortcomings in rationality — "failed analytical brilliance, poor design of bureaucracies, inadvertent flaws in decision-making processes, or simple cognitive errors" — would help, but would not provide the degree of improved performance expected (p. ix).

Etheredge believed the fundamental problem to be the motivations of decision makers themselves. To achieve any improvement, we must first appreciate the weaknesses and vulnerabilities in existing agencies at the most basic level. He concluded that improvements are theoretically possible in the executive branch of government, in Congress, in the press, and in universities, but are extraordinarily difficult in practice within the agencies. If this view is accurate, few solutions, simple or complex, are likely to make much headway in improving program performance.

These are formidable barriers to improving policy in any complex decision-making and policy-making arena, and their relevance to the business of endangered species restoration should be considered. Describing these barriers does not mean they are insurmountable, but that efforts toward improvement must be calculated to be effective and that we can expect progress to be incremental. This requires individuals and groups to know as much as possible about policy processes before taking action.

Conclusions

Numerous recovery plans in recent years have acknowledged the "socio-economic" or "political" roots of species endangerment yet have failed to come to terms with these issues. The grizzly bear plan (U.S. Fish and Wildlife Service 1993), for instance, claims that endangerment of the species "is largely a result of social belief systems in the American West" (p. 28) and calls for a "management system that seeks to integrate all biological, social, valuational, and institutional forces" (p. 29). Yet nearly all of the 181-page document is devoted to biology, with specific objectives being to identify population goals, provide a population monitoring approach, identify limiting factors and measures needed to remove these, and establish recovered populations (p. 15). Increasing rationality and technical detail and dismissing the human dimensions out of ignorance, fear, or bias cannot lead to program successes. As Weiss (1989:117) pointed out, "Difficult to measure and understand is not the same as unimportant."

Focusing on the human envelope of species recovery and understanding the workings of the public policy process are a necessary first step in making the process more open, more participatory, more self-aware, more comprehensive, and more competent. The policy sciences are a convincingly comprehensive approach — offering both the conceptual paradigm and the necessary techniques — to help people understand and participate more effectively in the policy process. The three-part effort of problem orientation, contextual analysis, and synthesis of methods is firmly grounded in practical problem solving and intellectual rigor. Taking a policy-oriented approach to problem solving in our collective efforts offers perhaps our best hope of reconstructing the ESA implementation process. The techniques described in this chapter are just three among several very useful ways to develop problem-solving and decision-making skills and achieve substantive outcomes.

Nevertheless, achieving a better ESA implementation process remains highly problematic. At least three tasks are evident. The first is to appraise the goals and record of ESA policy implementation. The second is to explore the kinds of participants, rules, and relations needed to achieve successful implementation. Many of the organizations that can improve implementation (such as NGOs and small, expert teams outside government) are not now participants in the conventional implementation network. The third task is to realize that any new ESA policy prescription will probably be forced to operate with limited resources in a dynamic context. All three tasks will be difficult to carry out given the many factors that conspire to resist change.

New Organizational Arrangements
Processing Information for Effectiveness

A growing number of people are becoming aware of the paramount importance of organizations in endangered species conservation. Noting "significant shortcomings in traditional approaches to wildlife management and administration," Kellert (1996:202) attributed many problems to "questionable bureaucratic and organizational structures, . . . strong historic allegiances and traditional ideologies and . . . an inability or unwillingness to consider all relevant wildlife values in formulating and implementing policy." Brewer (1992:15) stressed that "environmental problems are urgent, and conventional institutional arrangements to understand and deal with them appear inadequate or lacking." And Lowry and Carpenter (1984:4) concluded that a "wealth of anecdotal evidence suggested that efforts around the world to ensure the sustainable exploitation of natural systems are suffering from governmental disorganization and mismanagement." Similar recognition has come from Stanley-Price (1989), Campbell (1980), Casey et al. (1990), and Culbert and Blair (1989).

Despite growing awareness of the importance of organizations, however, there is resistance to using knowledge and experience from organizational designers and consultants to aid species conservation. Claiming that their projects and species are unique, some biologists and managers do not allow that the organization and management literature, with its analytical case histories, theory, and experience, could be of practical value to their situations. Those who have studied organizations would point out the fallacy of that argument: extensive research on many different kinds of organizations facing different challenges has revealed common problems, patterns, and concerns (Hrebiniak 1978).

But as Kellert (1996:180) has succinctly shown, "The challenge of making government agencies perform effectively and efficiently constitutes a difficult goal indeed." However, just as there are means to understand the policy process and improve it, there are also ways to understand organizational systems and processes that provide leverage points to intervene and change them. The challenge is clear and urgent: we must determine what kind of organization can best manage endangered species.

Reconstructing Organizations

Organizations are the locus for programmatic improvements for several reasons. First, to understand why organizations behave as they do, we must take into account the collective situation in which individuals carry out their work (Katz and Kahn 1978). Second, the success or failure of programs is largely dependent upon the type of organization carrying out the program (Clarke and McCool 1985). And third, the organization itself is the only unit where permanent change is possible (Galbraith 1977, Hrebiniak 1978, Tichy 1983).

DESIGNING ORGANIZATIONS FOR SPECIES RECOVERY

All organizations share certain common properties: they must take in information about their environment, process it, and respond strategically and tactically. Of the many models describing the workings of organizations, "information-processing" models are particularly useful in demonstrating how to align tasks, task environments, and outcomes (e.g., Galbraith 1977, Tushman and Nadler 1978, Westrum 1986). These models generally view organizations as composed of people and groups sharing a common purpose, dividing labor, coordinating activities via an information-based decision system, and carrying out work through various programs. Richard Daft (1983:8) says that "organizations are social entities that are goal-directed, deliberately structured activity systems with an identifiable boundary. . . . Organizations have a technology—they use knowledge to perform work activities." James Fesler (1980:18) notes that "an organization . . . is both a policy-program-decision-*making* set of processes and a policy-program-decision-*executing* set of processes, and they intertwine." Program effectiveness is a function of matching the organization's information-processing capabilities with the information-processing requirements of the work to be accomplished. These requirements include not just the knowledge content of the effort but also the accessibility and usability of the intelligence—its complexity, diversity, and stability, the hostility present in the task environment, and, above all, the degree of uncertainty.

Uncertainty increases the amount of information that needs to be processed by organizations in order to reach their goals (Galbraith 1977). If what needs to be known to complete a task is already known, then the work can be planned and decisions made in advance. If it is not, however, then more intelligence will need to be gathered and processed as the work progresses to keep decision making up to date for resource allocation, schedules, and priorities. The information-processing mechanisms of the organization must be able to collect and disseminate information and make decisions to guide the organization's interdependent efforts, resolve conflicts, and complete tasks at specified performance standards.

The essence of organizational design is to find and apply structural and operational arrangements that permit effective information processing (Galbraith 1977). Not all organizations are equally good at this key task. Program designers must understand the information-processing needs created by the characteristics of the task environment and design the program in response. To the extent that a program's information-processing requirements change over time, the task of program design and management is continuous. A program that must address much uncertainty in a hostile situation needs to be structured quite differently from a program that carries out routine tasks with little uncertainty, low stakes, and well-established standard operating procedures. If the situation is highly uncertain, complex, unstable, diverse, and hostile, then the organizational system needed is "organic;" if all five of these characteristics are low, then a "mechanistic" structure is needed.

In organic organizations, tasks, positions, and people are better integrated toward the common enterprise (Burns and Stalker 1981). There is a network structure of control and authority, and communication tends to be more lateral than vertical along a hierarchy. Knowledge and experience are recognized throughout the organization, and commitment is more highly valued than loyalty or obedience. At the other end of the continuum are mechanistic organizations, which tend to have more specialized tasks and positions, with an emphasis on the technical means by which tasks are completed. They are more centralized and internally focused, and their hierarchical structure provides governance from the top down and loyalty and obedience from workers (Burns and Stalker 1981).

Compared to most wildlife management work, endangered species restoration generally indicates a need for organic structures. There may be enormous uncertainty in the biological systems under consideration. The National Research Council's Committee on the Application of Ecological Theory to Environmental Problems (1986), for instance, listed five sources of uncertainty in ecological systems — complex relationships between species and their environments, unpredictable natural variability, probabilistic rather than deterministic behavior of populations, errors of estimations and measurement, and basic lack of knowledge. Comparable uncertainty also exists in organizational systems. For instance, the organization's relationship to its markets or competing businesses may be uncertain. Or changing societal values as expressed by legal mandates or special interest lobbying may cause unpredictable swings in an agency's operating environment. Uncertainties are further complicated by differences among individuals in organizations in such factors as motivation, commitment, personality, communication skills, tolerance for ambiguity, capacity to handle stress, and need for recognition.

Three steps are involved in designing an appropriate organization or program. Assessing the task environment is the first step. The second is to understand what kind of organization would best meet all the conditions of the task environment and to decide whether that ideal organization would be compatible with the structures and cultures of existing parent organizations or agencies. After considering alternatives and tradeoffs, the third step is to make appropriate design changes to correct any limitations or perceived pitfalls (Lorsch 1977). Managers who do not know the range of organizational alternatives must rely on tradition and intuition.

THE INFLUENCE OF ORGANIZATIONAL CULTURES

The central determinant of the character of every organization, program, or team is its culture. Culture is a set of values and cognitive perspectives that is largely shared by members. It conveys the feeling or pervasive way of life that dominates an organization's programs and teams (Harrison 1972). "An organization's ideology affects the behavior of its people, its ability to effectively meet their needs and demands, and the way it copes with the external environment" (Harrison 1972:119) — including how it understands and processes information. If the organization's culture is well matched to the work to be done, it will aid information processing and job completion; if it is not, it will hinder the work. But the importance of culture's effect on the quality of work is often unrecognized or unappreciated, especially in government agencies (Peters and Waterman 1982). Improvements in business and industry in the last few decades have resulted from research into the structure, management, and culture of programs, and many guidelines from these studies can be directly applied to improved recovery programs.

Individuals join certain organizations because they tend to share the values and views of that organization. If they do not, they must become socialized to them if they are to remain on the job. Some people become highly socialized to organizational cultures, others less so. Those who are very highly socialized to the culture are often considered "company men," especially if a culture is power- or role-oriented. Much of the conflict between and within organizations is the result of cultural differences.

The concept of organizational culture and its controlling influence on individual performance has been described by many researchers. Harrison (1972) sets out the several vital roles that culture plays. It provides the values and goals toward which effort is directed and by which the organization evaluates its success and worth. It prescribes relationships between individuals and the overall effort, a form of social contract that shapes expectations. Culture also guides how behavior should be controlled in the organization and identifies which controls are legitimate. In addition, it identifies characteristics and behaviors of members to be "valued or vilified," thus setting the reward or punishment systems. The organization's culture tells members how to treat one another and people in other organizations — "competitively or collaboratively, honestly or dishonestly, closely or distantly" (p. 120). It also establishes guidelines and methods for dealing with the external environment — "aggressive exploitation, responsible negotiation, proactive exploration" (p. 120).

There are four main cultural orientations — task, power, role, or person cultures (Harrison 1972) — and they affect the selection, processing, and use of information. A person-oriented culture, which is quite rare, puts the welfare of its workers above all other considerations. A power-oriented culture tries to dominate its environment and vanquish all opposition. A role-oriented culture has extensive rules and regulations governing strictly defined roles and is concerned with its legitimacy, hierarchy, status, and symbols of rank. These last two often typify bureaucracies. Excessive reliance on power and roles by some agencies may increase internal efficiency but does so at the expense of external effectiveness, successfully meeting novel tasks. Such bureaucracies have a tendency to place procedural correctness before task completion. Finally, a task-oriented culture rewards achievement of the primary goal. Task-oriented organizations evaluate their actions in terms of task accomplishment and then shape their structure and operations to meet the task's requirements. This kind of "contingency approach" is highly adaptable and stands in marked contrast to the fixed rules and roles of agencies that are frequently in charge of recovery programs. Because of their high risks, high stakes, urgency, and uncertainties, species recovery programs must be strongly task-oriented. Task-oriented groups process information more effectively and efficiently and thus learn and change rapidly as circumstances require.

ORGANIZATIONAL LEARNING TO IMPROVE
INFORMATION PROCESSING

Organizations succeed to the extent that they can get, process, and act on information concerning the task to be done, the operating environment, and the organization itself. The task of adapting to these dynamic, constantly changing demands principally involves organizational learning. An organization that processes information well is an organization that learns well.

A number of organizational designers have suggested ways to upgrade the responsiveness of organizational learning systems. Morgan (1986:91–95) summarized four general principles for good organizational learning: (1) "Encourage and value an openness and reflectivity that accepts error and uncertainty as an inevitable feature of life in complex and changing environments." (2) "Encourage an approach to the analysis and solution of complex problems that recognizes the importance of exploring different viewpoints. . . . This is best facilitated by managerial philosophies that recognize the importance of probing the various dimensions of a situation, and allow constructive conflict and debate between advocates of competing perspectives. In this way issues can be fully explored, and perhaps redefined so that they can be approached and resolved in new ways. This kind of inquiry helps an organization absorb and deal with the uncertainty of its environment rather than trying to avoid or eliminate it." (3) "Avoid imposing structures of action upon organized settings. . . . When goals and objectives have a predetermined character they tend to provide a framework for single-loop learning but discourage double-loop learning. . . . More double-loop learning can be generated by encouraging a 'bottom-up' or participative approach to the planning process." (4) "Make interventions and create organizational structures and processes that help implement the above principles."

Janis's (1972) ideas for remedying groupthink in decision-making groups would certainly enhance the learning capabilities of organizations. The group should assign and reinforce critical evaluator roles. The group should avoid stating preferred outcomes in advance and should seek strict impartiality in its deliberations. Outside groups should be tapped for expertise. Group members should seek outside advice individually, and the group should invite outside experts to group meetings and actually listen to them. At least one group member should play the devil's advocate to support contrary views, criticize assertions, and point out discrepancies. The group should thoroughly scrutinize all feedback channels both within and outside the organization for useful signs about the appropriateness of their decisions and choices. The group should divide into subgroups to discuss issues again and then reconvene. And "second-chance" meetings should be held to give voice to any remaining doubts.

Westrum (1986) provided several principles for developing "generative" rationality within organizations. All members of the organization should be encouraged to pay attention to the system's overall goals and problems. Those whose work is interdependent should be linked for cooperation in problem solving. All parts of the organization — high or low, central or peripheral — should be scanned for solutions and contributions. This may require formal exercises to generate, transmit, and acknowledge new ideas. Creativity and critical thought by all personnel should be welcomed and rewarded. This effort can be facilitated by not structuring the organization too rigidly. Finally, the organization must examine its mistakes honestly and deal with them as system problems rather than people problems. The organization can best repair problems when its people are willing to open themselves to "dispassionate and impersonal" criticism.

The myriad ideas covered here to improve organizational learning can be boiled down to a single notion, best expressed by Morgan (1986:91): "In essence, a new philosophy of management is required, to root the process of organizing in a process of open-ended inquiry. . . . The whole process of learning to learn hinges on an ability to remain open to changes occurring in the environment, and on an ability to challenge operating assumptions in a most fundamental way." This single new approach could prove to be a powerful agent for change within current wildlife management bureaucracies without posing the threat of structural or operational changes. These alternatives can help organizations, whatever their information-processing capabilities, to respond more effectively to the task environment of species restoration.

High-Performance Teams as an Improvement

The high-performance team is one alternative to current operations. It is a practical design that promises the responsive learning system, task-oriented culture, and organic structure that is needed. Task forces and project teams to address endangered species problems can be installed either within organizations or, better yet, as parallel organizations (described later) both to manage the task and to guide and advise the organizations involved (Westrum 1994,

Clark and Cragun 1994). Task forces are temporary teams focused on short-term problems, while project teams are more permanent groups focused on long-term or continuing problems. In both, team building is required to bring about a climate of cooperative problem solving with extensive communication among team members, high morale, and a focus on successful task completion. Although managerial work in these teams is demanding — requiring skill in staffing, leadership, communications, planning, organizing, decision making, and handling and using information (Brinckloe and Coughlin 1977) — professionals find it easier to exercise generative rationality and creative problem solving within such high-performance teams, skills that they can then take back to their organizations.

Every species recovery effort includes not only people directly involved in the effort but also a larger network of influential people and organizations (Westrum and Samaha 1984). The team's major challenge centers on the dynamics of group members who have to work together effectively in day-to-day decision making and on-the-ground action. At the network level, where different organizations and agencies are represented, responsibility is more diffuse, even though several agencies may be required by law to participate. The major task is networking to maintain cooperation and commitment to the program among the many individuals and organizations. Information flows are more difficult to coordinate than within the intensive recovery team situation itself, but, on the other hand, ample resources are usually present and available within the larger network.

STAFFING THE HIGH-PERFORMANCE TEAM

Ideally, teams should consist of professionals with long formal training and experience. Members should be mature, well socialized, and dedicated to high standards of ethics and performance. They should have broad knowledge and the ability to work without supervision or extensive rules and regulations. They should be selected for their problem-solving ability and willingness to deal with the risky and ambiguous situations presented by species recovery.

A key consideration is individual willingness to work as part of the interdisciplinary team. Because professionals are trained to make independent decisions, they may not be accustomed to having their judgment questioned by those from other disciplines. The ability to operate effectively in a group context is not a universal trait and demands prior experience and skills. The stress of working in high-risk situations may inhibit the requisite mental flexibility. The data used may be ambiguous and confusing. For example, determining the fates of a few reintroduced animals may be impossible, yet the success of the effort requires it. Two dangerous responses to this situation might be "Let's wait for complete information" and "Let's pretend that the information we have is sufficient." Effective team members must be willing to deal honestly with such incongruities and pitfalls. Others may respond to minor failures by engaging in fault finding or personal criticism, which lead to tensions that might seriously disrupt group functioning. Equally ineffective, however, is the team member who is unwilling to question team actions in spite of personal doubts. Intellectual conflict is normal and can be constructive in a team, but it must be handled professionally.

COGNITIVE AND EMOTIONAL CHARACTERISTICS

Two important traits of high-performance team members are the ability to make decisions fast and to base decisions on all available information. Species restoration may require rapid decision making, since the external situation may change rapidly: the population, for example, may experience a rapid die-off, and rescue of remaining individuals would be possible only by quick decisions. Oral communication, absence of personalized fault finding, and a willingness to examine any and all alternatives are essential parts of rapid decision systems. If the group's ability to act and react is quick relative to the environment's rate of change, it can stay on top of the situation. A good model is the famous and successful project team called "Skunk Works" at Lockheed (Westrum 1991). The success of the Lockheed team in producing superior military aircraft in record time, under budget, with few staff has led to the application of the name "skunk works" (originally from Al Capp's comic strip *Li'l Abner*) to many small, lean, innovative, productive teams in research and development laboratories. Such teams foster creativity and invention — even in the face of official resistance — through close communication, congeniality, intense work, excellent leadership, and mutual respect, trust, and confidence.

A second requirement is the maximum use of the entire group's cognitive skills. This kind of generative rationality can enhance the human resources available for decision making (Westrum 1986). The ability to generate insights and the willingness to place one's observations in front of the group are essential. Otherwise, the dominant intellectual or political members of the group become the filter through which all communications pass, and such an underutilization of the group's total brain power must be avoided. While leadership is important, excessive control by leaders may result in the stifling of some members' contributions. Communication practices that facilitate high creativity, such as emotional supportiveness, brainstorming, and nonpersonally directed evaluation of ideas, are helpful (Stein 1975). They can aid in spotting problems and formulating hypotheses. Donald Schön's (1983) idea of "reflective practice," described in the next chapter, can help develop these self-aware, cognitive skills. Solutions to problems must be rapidly generated, sifted, and implemented. The team needs to have a heavy flow of useful ideas and to maximize the entry points for new ideas and perceptions from both the inside and the outside. The major danger is that the group will engage in groupthink, channeling and stereotyping the group's decision making to satisfy the urge to maintain group cohesion. Openness, flexibility, and a willingness to admit biases are essential in coping with the uncertainties of the recovery process.

Just as the high-performance team requires certain mental features, it also demands particular emotional traits. Restoration is a risky and uncertain business fraught with dangers — the probability of rapid changes in field conditions, the inability to foresee consequences of the team's actions, the high risk of partial or complete failure, and the politicized context. The anxiety, emotional rigidity, and defensiveness brought on by these problems can lead the team to adhere to ineffective policies in the face of contrary evidence or to show unwillingness to admit mistakes or failures. The more politicized the context, the more likely it is that team members will take refuge in denial or faultfinding.

One key to team effectiveness in handling emotions is to build internal support. There must be a strong, mutually supportive atmosphere within the team, including recognition that team members are highly competent but can and do make occasional mistakes. Just as the team takes collective credit for success, it also takes collective responsibility for mistakes, and it must be understood that an individual's making a mistake will not result in withdrawal of the group's support. When failure occurs, it must not be denied but investigated, since it may reflect systemic problems that could be changed to avoid future mistakes. Mistakes are an occasion for learning. Mutual respect is thus a requisite for effective team functioning. It aids in rapid repair of system defects. Indeed, it is the glue that holds the team together in the face of adversity. But respect may be difficult to achieve if the team is assembled from persons unfamiliar with each other. Different training, different cognitive models, and different coping styles may lead to suspicion, faultfinding, and scapegoating. The interdependence of team members needs to be emphasized so that heterogeneity is seen as a group strength.

LEADERSHIP OF HIGH-PERFORMANCE TEAMS

A willingness to reexamine failures objectively and to learn from them is likely to develop only if the team is protected from outside interference. It is the leader who must act as a buffer, supporting the group even in the face of adversity and criticism. The leader sets the focus of a high-performance team and needs to have the respect of team members. This usually means that the leader must have excellent technical skills to be able to help team members with technical problems (G. Weinberg 1986). But specific leadership skills are also necessary: the willingness to be objective and fair and to take responsibility for the overall mission. Being right is not a substitute for being effective.

To function well, a high-performance team must be future-oriented and resist rationalizing its past failures. Failures are a constant hazard that must be squarely faced, effectively grieved, and then left behind as new solutions are developed. Forward movement is particularly difficult when the environment is politicized. One resolution to this problem is for the group to maintain maximum openness inside but present a solid front to the outside — although the danger here is that the group might take its image of confidence too seriously and fail to consider its problems dispassionately. On the other hand, group success may also present problems, making the group's high performance seem like magic. Inexperienced individuals may find this degree of success destabilizing (Wambaugh 1984): there may be a tendency toward external overconfidence accompanied by inner doubt, leading to bragging and anxiety. Risky operations, by their very nature, will provide a mixed crop of successes and failures. In an uncertain environment, only some sources of variability are under team control. Thus, it must be emphasized that success is only partly explained by group skill. Similarly, failure may result only partly from group mistakes. The role of the leader is especially important here in providing a steadying influence and explaining the team to itself. The leader must maintain a realistic assessment of the degree of control the team has and keep its expectations within reasonable limits.

Another important part of the leader's role is managing conflict, which, in species restoration, is likely to be high and constant. Conflict is the natural result of inherent and necessary differences, but it must be skillfully managed to produce ideas and solutions and not degenerate into personality issues and scapegoating. Conflicts that are mild when the group is starting out may become serious in the face of imminent failure or political pressure from outside. Leaders who provide for effective conflict resolution can free the team from preoccupation with its own problems (Brown 1983).

One criterion for assessing functioning is that a healthy group spends most of its energies solving external problems rather than internal ones. Neurotic groups spend most of their energies on internal structuring, conflict, and fault-finding. In neurotic groups, minor failures trigger increased group conflict; in healthy ones, they are a signal that something needs attention. Leaders can do a great deal to focus the group either on solving problems or on studying its own internal performance.

Another important task of leadership is managing relations within the network—the organizational context of the high-performance team. The best teamwork in the world will be useless if authorities decide to terminate the effort or take conflicting actions. Thus, explaining the team's operations and getting cooperation from outside agencies and the public is a necessary task for the leader. The goal is to get commitment and resources from outsiders, and the key ability is to provide links to these outside sources of power, influence, knowledge, and money. Probably the most important contact is with the agency or other organization that funded and initiated the effort (Litwak and Hylton 1962). If it feels the team is not carrying out or is exceeding its directive, it may withdraw support. Regular reports on progress are critical but may need to be supplemented with visits and presentations in person. Wildlife professionals may pride themselves on being apolitical, but political skills are absolutely essential in maintaining support for their projects. Other sources of power are also important. Federal and state regulators, wildlife organizations, industry, universities, landowners, and private individuals may feel that their interests are threatened by a species restoration effort. Again, the leader's function as public relations arm and apologist may be absolutely essential for the project's success. In some cases, compromises — or what Mary Parker Follett (1970) called "integrations of divergent objectives" — may be necessary for the project's continuance.

Reconstructing Bureaucracies

Conceptualizing organizations as information-processing entities helps focus attention on the organization's capacity to learn and adapt to the task environment. High-performance teams constitute one useful design for any kind of organization either inside or outside bureaucracies. But it is not necessary to get rid of bureaucracies altogether. Suggested here are three mutually reinforcing alternatives for countering the bureaucratic weaknesses of the agencies.

DEBUREAUCRATIZING RECOVERY EFFORTS

Government agencies can be debureaucratized in several ways, although two major obstacles must be overcome. The first is their dynamic conservatism, widely recognized by people outside government. Most agencies suffer from the "institutionalization of solutions, which carries with it the institutionalization of problem definition" (Dery 1984:84). "It sometimes appears," noted Hrebiniak (1978:239), "that organizations are really collections of well-oiled techniques, in search of problems to which to apply them. It seems that organizations occasionally succumb to a massive means-ends inversion. They are less interested in seeking and solving new problems than they are in using existing methods to solve only 'appropriate' problems, that is, problems that fit their methods." Failure to recognize dilemmas is another major organizational obstacle to improvement, according to Daniel Katz and Robert Kahn (1978). Many organizations remain dedicated to institutionalized norms and practices even when problems are insoluble under those terms of reference. David Dery (1984) also concluded that when new programs are implemented by old bureaucracies, innovation is lost to program execution. Dilemmas and the mismatches they create between expectations and outcomes call for double-loop learning and reformation of fundamental perspectives. But bureaucracies tend to resist changes that threaten their social system — culture, existing special interests, and established problem frames.

There are three possible targets of change within organizations: individuals, groups or subunits, and the structure of the overall organization (Katz and Kahn 1978). But the three do not respond equally well to efforts to debureaucratize. Trying to change individuals by giving them new information, training programs, counseling, and psychotherapy has proven an ineffective method of debureaucratization. The attempt to debureaucratize by changing groups of workers or managers assumes that peer groups can be instrumental in organizational change. Modest success has been achieved at this level using ad hoc peer groups, organizational groups of "families," and sensitivity training groups, combined with survey feedbacks, extensive counseling, and coaching to debureaucratize. But direct manipulation of structure is the most powerful tool for achieving enduring systemic change (Katz and Kahn 1978). The target variables here are the authority structure (or the distribution of power and participation in decision making), the reward/incentive structure, and the division of labor (or job enlargement and enrichment).

Donald Warwick (1975) proposed principles for change in public bureaucracies and stressed that debureaucratization must begin *within* the organization. Employees must understand that agency hierarchy and rules are problems for themselves as well as for others; then and only then will commitment to change be made. All significant internal constituencies must be involved in order to foster a sense of the problem. This must be followed by a careful, collective diagnosis of the problem and broad-based discussion on concrete alternatives for change. Support for debureaucratization must be sought in key controllers, allies, and constituencies external to the agency. Finally, a strong coordinating body, including at least two senior appointees as well as representatives of other key groups in the organization (secretarial and clerical staff and professionals) must be appointed.

This approach has yet to be tried in the management agencies that currently dominate implementation of endangered species policy. But if practitioners can envision the great potential gains, then "the enormous inertia of established structures and, related to it, the many and varied needs served by hierarchy and rules" just might be overcome (Warwick 1975:215). If these changes could be brought about, society could be satisfied that responsible governmental agencies were giving endangered species recovery their best efforts.

James Q. Wilson (1989) made several suggestions to improve bureaucratic organizations. His hope was that debureaucratizing government would revitalize it. Government bureaucracy, said Wilson, needs to mimic some of the best parts of the private sector — a bias for action, small staffs, and a high level of trust. At the individual level this will require energy, pride in output, and initiative, and at the organizational level it will require capable leadership, a clear and strong sense of mission, talented employees who believe they are part of something special, and exacting performance standards. Regardless of the difficulty in effecting change, the ideal is worth considering in practical ways.

Change requires, first, agreement (or at least a similar outlook) on what constitutes the core tasks for all parties to tackle. Organizational leaders must effectively use the incentives at their disposal to support people. Certain constraints must be acknowledged: neither professionals nor bureaucracies are neutral, professional peer groups set certain standards, and there are many real demands on workers. All tasks not key to the mission should be subordinated or even ignored. To meet the core mission, leaders must establish and authorize special teams or task units. There is no place for domain- or status-conscious participants. But there are difficulties: Wilson (1989) points out that leaders may face challenges to their right to define the organization's mission as well as the tasks that are appropriate to the mission.

Second, people in both government and NGOs must negotiate with their political superiors to find workable agreements about key constraints. This kind of agreement potentially removes considerable uncertainty in program responses. But getting political approval may simply be impossible. The support of politicians and high-level bureaucrats is unreliable given the dynamic nature of problems and politics.

Third, people both in and out of government must possess authority and control over resources commensurate to the shared task. "In general, authority should be placed at the lowest level at which all essential elements of information are available" (p. 372). The key goal in managing authority and resources is not to over- or undercentralize. In endangered species conservation, this means that field teams, recovery teams, and other "parallel" units should possess considerable authority and resources, and this in turn means that members should be carefully recruited from the best talent and experience available. This suggestion contrasts with existing bureaucratic arrangements by which current employees are reassigned from other units or tasks with little consideration given to their overall knowledge, skills, or likely contribution to the task.

Fourth, people and organizations must be judged by the results, even though these are not always clear and are often in dispute. Wilson suggested that one way to accomplish this is to shift the burden of appraisal away from professional evaluators (if any exist in endangered species policy) and self-serving bureaucrats to the clients and customers and let them "vote." Clients and customers of the output of public policy, including the public, universities, NGOs, and professionals, should have access to several different suppliers of services. Government should be just one of several potential suppliers; universities, nongovernmental organizations, or even private business — separately or in combination with government — could also provide this service. A key question is whether the species restoration service will really be supplied by the market, although current evidence suggests that it will.

Fifth, people and organizations should seek to keep the number, size, and authority of bureaucracies as small as possible. Government bureaucracies, like all organizations, seek stability through standard operating procedures and will change them only in response to external demands. This means that government bureaucracies need careful scrutiny by outside monitors as they work on endangered species conservation.

According to Wilson (1989:375), many organizational and policy problems "are much greater in government bureaucracies because government itself is the institutionalization of confusion (arising out of the need to moderate competing demands); of red tape (arising out the need to satisfy demands that cannot be moderated); and of avoided responsibility (arising out of the desire to retain power by minimizing criticism)." We can expect the problems of government bureaucracy to go away only to the extent that people assume responsibility for public works, whether it is species conservation or any other societal problem.

ADDING PARALLEL ORGANIZATIONS

One structural means to change bureaucracies is the use of a parallel organization. Warwick (1975) pointed out that it is unlikely that the problems of bureaucracies can be removed by replacing them with organizations that are more task oriented and more qualified to handle the demands of the uncertain task environment. Bureaucracies already control the network of authority relationships, patterns of participation, and legitimizing processes, and it is unlikely they will let other types of organizations move to the forefront of species conservation. But replacement or reorganization is not necessary to effect better programs. The addition of a parallel organization can make existing bureaucracies more responsive both to their external environment (including the task, other agencies, and the public) and to their internal environment and their own people.

A parallel organization is simply a second and different mechanism for involving people in the same organizational tasks by grouping them temporarily in different ways, setting up new decision-making channels, and changing information flows. As Rosabeth Moss Kanter (1983) explained, the existing hierarchy takes care of routine tasks, while the parallel organization adds a new problem-solving mechanism. "The main task function of the parallel organization is the continued reexamination of routines; exploration of new options; and development of new tools, procedures, and approaches — that is, the institutionalization of change" (Kanter 1983: 204–205). Parallel organizations are "flexible, but formal problem-solving and governance organizations that serve to supplement bureaucracy and exist side by side with it, not to replace it. . . . [They are] an attempt to institutionalize a set of externally and internally responsive, participatory, problem-solving structures alongside the conventional line organization that carries out routine tasks" (Stein and Kanter 1980:371–372). The parallel organization thus provides an alternative or supporting management option to those that already exist by offering a more appropriate fit between the demands of a complex and uncertain situation and the agencies' capabilities (Cohen 1971). Stein and Kanter (1980) summarized their experience with parallel organizations, demonstrating the successful and efficient use of these organic structures within more mechanistic bureaucracies.

A parallel organization might include professionals, managers, bureaucrats, and technicians — on egalitarian terms — who are committed to working closely together over long periods on difficult organizational problems. They have support and recognition from their parent units or organizations, access to resources, and opportunities for growth and learning. Given the opportunity and the power, participants generally feel a sense of community and take pride in serving the parent organizations or coalition. If empowered by the parent groups to make decisions and take action, they can do so. Kanter found that by maintaining the parallel structure's flexibility and readiness, organizations can anticipate and prepare for change. At the same time, participants in the parallel organization are energized by their experience of community spirit and teamwork and the significance of their work. However, administrators must insure that parallel organizations are not taken over by bureaucratic values and procedures. "The idea behind having a second, or parallel, organization alongside routine operations only makes explicit what is already implicit in an integrative, innovating company: the capacity to work together cooperatively regardless of field or level to tackle the unknown, the uncertain. In a formal, explicit parallel organization, this is not left to happenstance but is guided — managed — to get the best results for both the company and the people involved" (Kanter 1983:359).

A parallel organization is not a specific program to solve a localized problem but a way to manage innovation, participation, and change so that the organization and its employees remain adaptive. Temporary problem-solving teams, special programs, standing committees, and research-and-development efforts may form under the auspices of the parallel organization to respond to the changing needs of the organizations involved.

Although traditional recovery teams have shown some features of parallel organizations, they do not go far enough. The FWS could use the parallel organization alternative to constitute strong, task-oriented endangered species recovery, advisory, and work teams.

GETTING COMMUNITIES INVOLVED

Limited staffs and budgets, uneven interest, hierarchical structures, and heavy work loads are chronic problems and will likely grow worse in the future for the agencies involved in the ESA policy process. One solution, proposed by Mark Poffenberger (1990), to offset severe agency constraints is to enfranchise community groups, including the nongovernmental conservation community, universities, and local citizens. These groups, collectively or individually, can complement agency responsibility and work demands. Such empowerment has sweeping implications for ESA policy and procedures — indeed for many power, authority, and domain relationships that have been in place for years. "Empowering local groups requires agencies to give up some of their authority," noted Poffenberger (p. 102); "this demands a strong political commitment to the devolution of power on the part of the bureaucracy." A word of caution, however: this is not a recommendation to turn endangered species recovery over to local groups. The participation of federal, state, and local governments and input from scientific, conservation, and community groups is the only way to provide for the necessary shared responsibility, representation, and solid deliberation of all issues, perspectives, and strategies.

The agencies need to initiate prototypical changes in their programs to respond to species conservation needs. A series of community-involvement prototypes could serve as good learning experiences at low cost in terms of dollars or risk to the species. They would help eliminate overly centralized planning, relax rigid responses to different local and regional situations, increase political support, delegate some management authority, and institutionalize effective programs into mainstream management systems. The premise is that enhanced communication, participative structures, and shared responsibility are necessary to improve management and to help both agency staffs and communities better understand the actual problems and solutions (Poffenberger 1990; see also Clark et al. 1989a, Miller et al. 1996).

Poffenberger described a three-stage process to bring about agency improvements (see also Korten 1980). In the first diagnostic research phase, the agency learns to accept its past errors, involve the community in the planning process, and incorporate local knowledge (both ecological and socioeconomic) in both planning and implementation. Agency staffs work with communities to understand what issues generate conflict between them, to create new approaches to gathering information about the problem, its context, and its solutions, and to generate better methods of communicating. In the second stage, the agency sets up pilot projects to learn to use the new procedures for cooperative participation, planning, and implementation, integrates these into its broader structure and operations, and makes local adjustments (depending on human and financial resources). Third, the agency expands and institutionalizes the new concepts and procedures for participatory management, with particular attention to coordinating the management transition temporally and spatially and to creating a learning mechanism within the agency.

Successful agency change can be driven by individuals within an agency, although insiders are often alerted to problems and the need to change by people outside the agencies. Change may come from policy decisions of high-ranking administrators, who by the stroke of a pen can affect hiring practices, reward systems, or standard operating procedures but may do little to change staff attitudes or develop better implementation methods (Poffenberger 1990). In contrast, "learning-based change"—from the top down and from the bottom up—is more likely to be lasting because it depends on discussions and examinations by a working group representing different perspectives of agency and community problems and needs.

Several kinds of people are needed for learning-based agency change to be successful. First are facilitators, who catalyze, accelerate, and systematize change in agencies that are open to change. Facilitators are sensitive to the agency's historic objectives, the problems at hand, and policy and procedural issues. They carry out extensive discussions with both agency staffs and nongovernmental groups and identify key agency staff who also see the need for change, people whom Yaffee (1982) called "internal advocates." Second are key insiders, who develop a coalition for change within the agency and formally represent the change process to the community. Their loyalty to the organization, knowledge of its operations, and the respect of their colleagues are valuable assets in integrating new ideas into existing structures and practices.

Key insiders may include senior officials and mid-level managers. Third are outside resource people or "fixers," to use Yaffee's term, who help define problems and develop solutions. These include academics and researchers, private-sector professionals, NGOs, and other nongovernmental practitioners.

Poffenberger promoted the model of working groups to bring about change in resource management. Working groups foster sympathetic interactions and constructive dialogue so that the community and the agency *enable* each other to develop new management capabilities. Like parallel organizations or decision seminars, working groups are long-standing, candid, problem-solving groups that bring together a wide range of expertise, perspectives, and data. Meetings are regular and agendas clear, membership is based on individual interest and ability to contribute and not on agency representation, programmatic decisions are based on group discussion and consensus, and flexibility is maintained to synchronize field activities with agency planning, budgeting, and procedures.

As a center of learning, the working group develops new paradigms and processes for partnership in management. Working groups can begin by sending out research teams to study the interactions of the agency and the community and diagnose the sources of conflict between them. Involving field staff in meetings helps the two-way flow of information. Conversely, bringing senior members into the field is another group learning technique that encourages discussion of relevant social, economic, political, and organizational issues. Diffusing this new learning through the agency and the community is a major task that must overcome skepticism and resistance from both sides, facilitate political acceptance, remove organizational and procedural barriers, include all levels and functions, establish training programs, institutionalize management authority, and identify community organizers. Poffenberger pointed out that although there are many successful pilot projects, few ever develop into successful national programs, and that this final stage of implementing change demands special attention and timing. Agency change is a long-term process that requires continuity and stability in staffing and leadership, funding, and political support. As Stephen Kellert (1996:178) noted, "Support for endangered species conservation will emerge when people believe this effort enhances the prospects of a more materially, emotionally, and spiritually worthwhile life for themselves, their families, and communities."

Conclusions

"Is there hope?" asked Warwick (1975:205), of changing public bureaucracies. He concluded, in part, that any "reorganization plan pegged only to considerations of rationality is doomed to failure." Without some change in the cultures and learning abilities of bureaucracies as well as in their structure and functioning, endangered species programs in the future will merely replay the weaknesses evident in the ferret program. The task of recovery must be seen as "enveloped," as it were, by a larger societal setting, and the organizations and professionals that undertake recovery must be able to create some meaning out of that milieu. There must be systems in place for learning about the recovery task and its human envelope and responding appropriately.

The information-processing model of organizations is particularly useful for elucidating the human envelope of species recovery because it stresses the constant interaction of task, organization, and environment. Keeping participants' attention focused on the constantly changing relationships among these opens a wide variety of options for reconstructing the recovery process. In this chapter I have offered some guiding principles for debureaucratizing public agencies and developing a learning culture within organizations. There are increasing pressures — but also opportunities — for agencies to embrace new ways of framing their work.

The working environments of our natural resource management bureaucracies have grown more complex and problematic in recent years, and resource needs to meet endangered species problems are acute. But this reality also brings opportunities for the agencies to forge new, productive working relationships with the NGO sector, especially nonprofits, to meet the challenges. High-performance teams are one particularly powerful alternative to meet the growing needs. Set up within bureaucracies or as parallel structures and fostered by both agencies and NGOs, they can begin tackling problems on any scale and then build on their experience. Knowledge of organizations and public policy is needed for these or any other improvements, because "while policies are written in words on paper, they exist only in the form of the individuals, organizations, and agencies that implement them and the nature of the information, resources, authority, and incentives that flow between these actors" (Yaffee 1982:9).

Explicit design and management of endangered species restoration programs may significantly improve the current situation. But it is clear that changes in organizations will first require changes in individuals. Not only must people make every effort to reframe endangered species recovery as a policy process problem and strive to reconstruct organizations that will facilitate their efforts, but they must educate themselves thoroughly on the best ways to carry out their professional practices.

Civic Professionalism
Meeting Society's Needs

Individual professionals are indispensable in the endangered species recovery process. Their knowledge and skill are instrumental in improving program performance. A professional, in this context, is someone with specialized training who participates in a community with standards of practice and
shows a commitment to public service. But there are problems that afflict
professionals in general (Schön 1983, Brunner and Ascher 1992), in the endangered species field (Clark et al. 1994), and in the ferret case (Miller et al.
1996). These problems include myopic overspecialization, loss of integrity, a
weak civic ethic, self-interest, and blindness to their role in democratic society.
An individual professional's perspective and strategy are molded and constrained by conventional experience, education, established policy prescriptions, and organizational structures, cultures, and practices. Thus the relationships among larger policy processes, organizational systems, and individual
professional performance are indeed intricate. In this complex setting, the
good professional must blend knowledge, skill, integrity, interdependence,
civic responsibility, leadership, and learning into a mode of operation that
contributes to communal standards of problem solving in a responsible way.

In this chapter I look at how individual professionals might change the
way they understand and use their expert knowledge and skill for more effective participation in endangered species restoration and natural resource
management.

Professionalism: Part of the Problem or Part of the Solution?

Professionalism is currently undergoing dramatic reorganization in all sectors of society. Such changes as the redistribution of decision authority in the United States (from federal to state), for example, greatly affect the roles of professionals and put them under increasing stress. In contemporary natural resource fields, the ideals of skill, integrity, and public responsibility are coming into direct conflict with the imperatives of the bureaucratic organizations that train and employ professionals. Even some of these bureaucracies are now becoming aware of the problems that face their professionals. The concept of professionalism is an old one, but the current organization and education of professionals is relatively new. Just a few decades ago, there were no professionals serving endangered species, biodiversity, or ecosystem conservation; university training and agency jobs for these specialties did not exist. In these fields, as in others, the principles and practices adopted by professionals are determined by their education and understanding as well as the settings in which they practice.

CONVENTIONAL PROFESSIONALISM

Schön (1983, 1987) described changing concepts of professionalism and the dichotomy between science and application (or between rigor and relevance, as he put it). The conventional mode of professional practice, which characterizes nearly all the professions and dominated most of the ferret restoration program, is based on "technical rationality." Technical rationality is a model of professional knowledge and its use based on positivist philosophy (Schön 1983). Theory, or research, is distinguished from application, or practice. Professional practice consists of the mastery of a specialized field of knowledge (which is systematic, rigorous, empirically testable, and usually scientific) and the application of theory and technique to particular kinds of problems. Technical rationality rests on certain assumptions about science, rationality, and politics (Brunner 1996). The purpose of science is understood to be the discovery and use of universal laws to predict the consequences of changes in systems. Its predictive power and the resulting reduction of uncertainty thus make science the basis on which to build political consensus and make policy decisions. This philosophy has given rise to the outlook that professionals are "objective" and "neutral" in their dealings with society, but this view is more self-serving than real (Brunner and Ascher 1992). This mode of professional practice has been institutionalized in the professions, their societies, and the universities that have trained practitioners for over a century. It also dominates the agencies in natural resource management. Professionals' reluctance to engage in deliberative, democratic discourse has led the public to perceive them as no more than technicians, often unable to justify their activities morally or politically (Sullivan 1995).

Positivism, the philosophical underpinning of technical rationality, has three basic tenets: a conviction that empirical science is the only source of positive knowledge about the world, an intention to obviate mysticism and superstition, and a program of extending scientific knowledge to human society. Positivism assumes a fixed relationship between means and ends and resolves problems by manipulating the means rather than questioning how the ends were derived, what the scope of the problem might be, or in what setting the problem developed. But, as discussed in chapter 8, problems are the products of imposing frameworks of human value on reality, and this relationship between subjective human frames of reference and problem settings is underappreciated by technical rationalists. Problem solving is always subjective.

Over the last forty years, it has become apparent that, as a device for solving society's problems, technical rationality is not sufficient. In real-world professional practice, problematic situations are too complex, uncertain, and instable, too idiosyncratic, and too beset by clashes of values, interests, and goals to submit to purely technical solutions. The limits of technical rationality are quickly reached in such "indeterminate zones of practice" (Schön 1987:6). Professionals working in such situations and using the approaches of technical rationality face a dilemma: should they cling to practices that are technically rigorous and accepted by their professions but ineffectual in resolving important problems? Or, should they employ more artful, craftlike methods that may make real contributions to clearing up the mess but may not be well grounded in science? Many are fearful of leaving the high, hard ground of science and entering the swampy lowlands of everyday practice. Some practitioners respond to this dilemma by devising various strategies that enable them to cling to technical rationality, however inefficient it may be for solving problems. They develop selective inattention to data outside their realm of expertise, or they mold or redefine situations to fit their knowledge base or available techniques, or they simply label data outside their normal frame of reference as irrelevant junk or politics and ignore it.

These severely bounded approaches are not effective in solving society's many growing problems. The record of endangered species recovery over the last twenty or more years is just one example. Society relies heavily on the specialized knowledge of professionals to define and solve all kinds of societal problems. But public confidence in the abilities of conventional professionals to overcome them erodes when professionals ignore value conflicts that virtually paralyze society, when they breach public faith in their moral standards, or when they fail to perform as expected (Schön 1987). As a result, conventional professionalism is coming under severe scrutiny.

The loss of public confidence hinges on the question of professional knowledge. Does professional competence consist only of applying standardized rules, techniques, and approaches, or is there another dimension, seldom acknowledged, of "professional artistry" that can help restore relevance to the professions? This new way of understanding and working respects intuition, creativity, and nontraditional approaches to achieve desired results. It is not constrained by the blinders of positivism and reinforced by conventional professional norms, university systems premised on technical rationality, or the cultures of natural resource management agencies. Many professionals, while not abandoning rationality, have come to adopt a new mode of practice that has much greater relevancy in solving society's problems.

CIVIC PROFESSIONALISM

This new model of professional practice, which Sullivan (1995) labeled civic professionalism to stress its commitment to public service, is based on nonpositivistic assumptions about the world and, in turn, gives professionals different identities, expectations, and guides to practice. Science is seen not as a means of discovering truths and predicting consequences of events, but as a means of providing "freedom through insight" by bringing more factors more reliably into the decision-making process (Brunner 1996). Science provides a rational approach to testing, evaluating, and adapting alternative policy solutions in the face of uncertainty and ambiguity. Scientists, like other policy participants, must establish their credibility through their experience and their performance of these tasks. Technical competence needs to fit hand in hand with civic responsibility. Civic professionalism requires a reorientation of professional life to bring it into better accord with the profession's deepest aims and potentials, and it requires a greater awareness of self and the social context of problem solving. This ideal can be achieved only if participants are able to develop a stable consensus about their common interest and understand that both professionals and citizens will be best served by shared standards of excellence and reciprocity (Sullivan 1995). Building consensus, developing leadership, and establishing a habit of participation will require changes in identities, expectations, and demands for both groups. Also required will be changes in professional education and in working arrangements.

Several authors have described what this new model of civic professionalism will entail. Schön (1983, 1987) offered a new way for professionals to think about tough practice situations, a way of incorporating more intuition and creativity in an artful application of professional knowledge. He called this new mode of professional practice "reflection-in-action." Professionals are increasingly faced with unexpected outcomes of their professional practice and problems that seem intractable because of their uncertainty, uniqueness, or value clashes. They reflect in action when they respond to these particularly difficult problems not only by following standard rules of inquiry but also by inventing new rules — essentially reframing the problem until it can be solved. Means and ends are redefined interactively, and new theory is created. In this way, problem solving can proceed even in the face of enormous obstacles.

The legitimacy of reflection-in-action is rarely recognized, except through the success achieved by its skilled practitioners, which is commonly attributed to experience, talent, mystique, intuition, wisdom, good luck, artistry, or the like. Schön, however, argued that there is no mystery in this kind of problem-solving success. He says that all professionals reflect on their activities, while they are under way or after the fact. But some people also consistently and insightfully reflect on their premises, asking themselves not only how they can solve a problem but also how they have been thinking about it. This kind of reflection can increase the efficacy and success of professionals across many different situations of daily practice, relieve burnout and boredom, and direct professionals toward a more useful and no less rigorous professional practice. Reflection-in-action calls for continually analyzing, evaluating and restructuring responses to new situations, creating new solutions as well as learning from past actions or similar cases, and not being bound by a set of standard technical or organizational solutions. This "art of problem framing" requires an organizational setting that welcomes reflection, invention, and double-loop learning. Learning this approach requires a willingness to reveal uncertainty and accept it as an opportunity for learning in all dealings with clients, customers, and constituents. It also requires an ability to look for and act upon the thoughts and feelings of others, and a willingness to reflect publicly on the practice situation. At the heart of the method is a generative metaphor, a way to think more effectively about work and generate ideas to solve problems that are not accessible to technical, incremental approaches.

It is not easy to change conventional problem-solving approaches. Schön's model gives substance, form, and a name — and thereby legitimacy — to a part of professional practice that some professionals have always known. The increased legitimacy nurtures confidence in professionals, organizations, and the public. Another benefit of the model is that it brings what is usually private mental activity into an academic and professional context where it can be examined, used, and reformulated. Thus, reflection-in-action takes on weight equal to technical rationality as an epistemology of practice.

Many barriers can hinder adoption of this new mode of professional practice — professional, organizational, societal, and psychological. But incorporating reflective practice into the norms of the professions could overcome some of the basic problems of conventional practice. Developing reflection-in-action is difficult and time-consuming, but endangered species restoration, natural resource management, and a sustainable human ecology are surely all worth the effort.

A more civic-minded professionalism will also require practitioners to develop a policy orientation to professional practice. A number of conservation professionals have called for an approach that accounts more fully for problems in context (e.g., Greenwalt 1981, Romm 1984, Thomas 1986, Heinz and Youmans 1985, Carr 1987, Hales 1987, Clark and Kellert 1988). There is widespread recognition from both the profession and the public of the seemingly intransigent nature of the problems that face nature conservation, of their ultimately human rather than biological causes, and of the limitations of the conventional professions that are intended to resolve them. These difficulties seem overwhelming, yet they can be understood more comprehensively and realistically from the vantage point of a policy orientation.

Simply put, a policy orientation means having knowledge or information that is directly useful *in* the policy process, but additionally, and perhaps more important, having knowledge *of* the process itself (Lasswell 1971a). A policy-oriented viewpoint sees the loss of species not as a biological problem (although biological knowledge is critical to solving it) but as a public policy problem. Examples of knowledge used *in* the policy process include an endangered species' status and ecological relationships as well as the consequences and economic and social costs and benefits of various management options. Providing reliable information of this kind requires application of natural resource economics and other social sciences in addition to the wildlife management sciences. The wildlife conservation and management profession is ever striving to improve knowledge used *in* the policy process.

But this kind of systematic, scientific data answers only a small part of the total intelligence needs of public policy making. Knowledge *of* the process is equally important. Civic professionals who are familiar with the functions of decision processes and can analyze their own standpoints in policy processes know how to extend the search for contextual relevance as they solve problems. Insight into policy dynamics then allows participants to understand the overall process by mapping its interactive features comprehensively and realistically. Points of leverage and intervention are often evident from this approach. Questions about the overall problem-solving process might include: Have we explored the problem fully in terms of its history and conditions? Is our search for solutions driven by the problem itself or by other goals of the organizations involved? What kind of outcome do we seek and what means can we use to achieve it? Empirical methods should be used to acquire reliable information on these aspects of the policy process despite ambiguities, uniqueness, uncertainty, and public contention. Professionals who would save endangered species must foster and use this kind of knowledge in addition to knowledge of the conventional wildlife management sciences, and they must learn to think critically in ways that complement strict positivist science.

Civic professionalism is designed to do just that—to integrate and synthesize knowledge for practical problem solving. Lasswell's (1951:3) original description of a policy orientation in professionalism acknowledged a two-part effort to understand how the public policy process works and to improve the reliability of the data that go into the process. The first task, to develop a science of policy formulation and implementation, depends on methods of inquiry from the social sciences and psychology. The second task requires the knowledge, methods, and standards of the other relevant fields to make the information content of the policy process as rigorous as possible. Acquiring and balancing these two kinds of knowledge are not simple tasks for an individual professional, but it seems clear that a policy-oriented professionalism could bring significant improvements in conservation.

Policy orientation is a broad concept, directly connected to an extensive body of social science theory about how individuals behave in a complex and insecure world (Lasswell 1965, Lasswell 1971a, Lasswell and McDougal 1992). Having a policy orientation is not the same thing as being an accomplished planner or administrator (Weimer and Vining 1989), nor does it mean simply using multidisciplinary approaches. Like scientifically trained biologists, planners and administrators are usually scientific positivists, whereas the civic professional uses a post-positivist approach. Developing a policy orientation among its professionals could markedly improve planning and administration as well as the conservation fields.

Professionals in Society

Conventional professionals need to reconceptualize their roles in terms of civic interaction. The reconstruction of professionalism will depend on individuals developing the ability to be more relevant in a complex world. They must be able to address the problems that matter most to people.

CONTRACTS WITH CLIENTS

Professionals are providers of services, based on specialized knowledge, to clients. Although in the case of wildlife management there are no direct consumers like an architect's clients or a physician's patients, the provision of services to the public is still the task of technical experts. Traditionally, the relationship between professional and client has been based on a tacit contract with certain norms and expectations on both sides: the professional agrees to deliver services, and the client agrees to defer and submit to the professional's authority (Schön 1983). The interaction often leads to win/lose games of control by the professional and evasion of control by the client, and these games may take place at individual, organizational, or public policy scales.

But a reflective, civic, or policy-oriented approach requires the practitioner to interact with people in a different way. These terms themselves all indicate a focus on social processes and consequences. Professionals have a more realistic understanding of the workings of social systems and are aware of their own observational standpoints and roles. In this view, professionals do not constitute an expert elite; they serve human dignity. In Schön's terms, professionals must be ready, willing, and able to explore the meaning and limits of their expertise with clients. They must relinquish some claim to authority and some control of the relationship. They must reveal some uncertainties and reflect publicly rather than keep their expertise private and mysterious. Likewise, clients must also enter into the spirit of interchange, give up the security and safety of submitting to the professionals' authority, and cultivate competence and responsibility in a "reflective conversation" between professionals and clients, which can help break the control/evasion pattern.

Reflective conversations are thwarted, however, in bureaucratic settings by the technology, centralization, control system, accountability, evaluation, supervision, rule-governance, order, and isolation characteristic of those organizations — indeed, by the very concept of technical expertise that underlies bureaucracies. It is clear that bureaucracies have profound consequences not only for the people working in them but also for the ability of society to solve its problems. The institutionalization of double-loop learning systems would change the relationship of professionals to the bureaucracy and that of bureaucracies to society.

The model of technical rationality placed the professional in a key role to "mediate between science and society and translate scientific research into social progress" (Schön 1983:338–339). Technical rationalists took the knowledge learned from theoretical, basic science and turned it into applications to benefit society. The public has long held a singular regard for such professionals, who were understood to have specialized knowledge unavailable to most people. In problem solving, technical rationalists imposed their categories and theories on the problem at hand, ignored or explained away whatever did not fit their theories, and applied their stock of techniques appropriate to that problem. Neither the norms of their disciplines, their university training, or the cultures of their organizations obliged them (or even enabled or permitted them) to engage in a dialogue with those they presumably served about common interests, the definition of problems, or the appropriateness of various techniques.

But those skilled in this new kind of professionalism assume a different role: they become agents of a larger, societal deliberation or "cooperative inquiry" about society's problems. Civic professionals can help responsible decision makers by examining how well programs and policies are operating, and they can guide attention to "the effective and formal factors responsible for results" (Lasswell 1971a:76). They can serve as integrators of knowledge and action and as mediators between people who are knowledge specialists and those who are process specialists. They can help focus public debate by demystifying the professions. Although they are specialists in cultivating rationality, they must make explicit the conceptual framework inherent in technical rationality — its biases, the kinds of problems to which it should be limited, and the human values and interests it advances. They can promote more useful problem definitions by insisting that goal clarification and thorough problem analysis precede the search for solutions. Professionals can help create enabling conditions for society's reflective conversation with itself.

PROFESSIONALS IN THE IMPLEMENTATION PROCESS

Real policy is often made during implementation. Most wildlife professionals (especially those employed by government agencies) implement policy, such as the National Forest Management Act, Federal Land Management Act, and Endangered Species Act. As a result, it is important to place special focus on the implementation phase. Enactment of these federal laws is not at the end of the policy process; rather, it is near the beginning. Programs must be established and administered, and many additional decisions made, in order to carry out the stated aims. Sometimes what is intended by policy formulators is significantly different from what is actually done by policy implementers.

Until recently, implementation was not considered a separate policy phase (see Pressman and Wildavsky 1973, Bardach 1977, Radin 1977, Rein and Rabinovitz 1978); thus the large number of professionals who never considered themselves part of the policy process. The classical view, formed between the early 1900s and late 1930s, assumed that "implementation was a technical, non-political activity that proceeded in response to directives from the top" (Nakamura and Smallwood 1980:18), that the direction provided by top-level policy makers was concise and neutral, and that implementers carried out orders automatically. Today, many people still subscribe to this view of their individual working relationship to organizational and policy systems. But numerous studies have found that implementers are key actors in policy processes and that many individual and social factors significantly influence implementation (Pressman and Wildavsky 1973, Van Meter and Van Horn

1975). Eugene Bardach (1977), for instance, analyzed games played by implementers to subvert, frustrate, and impede policies as formulated and enacted. Beryl Radin (1977) described the political intrigue present in some cases. And Martin Rein and Francine Rabinovitz (1978) investigated the sometimes competing set of legal, bureaucratic, and consensus imperatives.

Today, the policy process is seen as a dynamic, reciprocating set of interactions among multiple participants (Nakamura and Smallwood 1980). It is now viewed as having no clear beginnings or end points, and the roles of individuals in these processes are sometimes complex. Yaffee (1982), for instance, found a big difference between the way the ESA was to work in theory and the way it was implemented in reality. In theory, technically sophisticated, neutral, and objective professionals would effectively and efficiently protect species and their critical habitats. In practice, much administrative discretion was exercised, scientific decisions were negotiated, and many forces and pressures both internal and external to the FWS and other agencies shaped implementation. Many of these forces were not scientifically relevant; decisions were made by balancing legal requirements or technical considerations against the need for political consensus. Yaffee (1982:70) found that agency decisions were really based on "a mix of science, art, and politics" and that individuals' attitudes, values, and professional norms often influenced the process significantly. Negotiation often took place because no absolute basis for decisions existed. Political controversy often had a profound influence, as in the case of the snail darter and the Tellico Dam. Negotiation was also clearly visible in interagency consultation, where other resource demands competed with endangered species. Among internal forces that shaped implementation were resource constraints, conflicting organizational goals, norms of biologists and managers, agency hierarchies, agency ideology and culture, scientific and bureaucratic conservatism, and internal advocates. Among the external forces were uneven popularity of issues, constituency groups, conflicting interests, the media, the legislature, and the judiciary. All these factors should be key objects of evaluation to improve performance. More recent discussion and examples of these forces at work in implementing the ESA have been presented by Yaffee (1988, 1994a, 1994b), the General Accounting Office (1988), and Clark et al. (1994).

In short, policy is effectively made by the people who implement it, and despite their misconceptions, self-doubts, or modesty, implementers do play a major role in the policy process. Conservation professionals must understand their roles and grasp both the conceptual and practical tools available to participate most effectively. Otherwise, all they can do is fall back on conventional assumptions, choose sides, and enter the process in narrow partisan ways, armed only with conventional tools. Some professionals may find this parochial style of participation exciting, but it does little to promote comprehensive, sane conservation policies. In the end, species and ecosystems suffer.

A CAUTIONARY NOTE

Realistically, there exist enormous barriers to the widespread adoption of civic professionalism: the primacy of bureaucratic structures, the personal rewards and satisfactions of traditional expert authority, and the apparent sacrifices of sharing authority and power. One deeply rooted difficulty is that only small segments of the overall picture may be visible to individuals who have a predominantly technical frame of understanding. Such a limited view may block discussion about other dimensions. Another barrier lies in the orientation and loyalty to disciplines and organizations and the adoption of their inherent biases. Yet throughout society, there is recognition of the dangers of increasing polarization and rigidification in our political system, and there are urgent pleas for more cooperative inquiry and problem solving. The need in the field of endangered species has been widely recognized, and professionals must now work to create not just nominal partnerships but a new kind of cooperative inquiry.

Kanter and Stein (1979) derived three political lessons that should be included in the knowledge of all professionals. The first is that "perspective is shaped by position" (p. 304). Position in an organization defines what resources, courses of action, and opportunities are open to an individual; it gives a view of what is and is not possible. Because not all positions within an organization (or coalition) share the same environment, differences in perspective between individuals are inevitable. This fact is a central source of tension for both individuals and organizations, as was so well demonstrated in the ferret program. The second lesson is that "power is also shaped by position" (p. 305). Some positions have control over organizational variables that matter to other people, and some have political connections to important power holders or groups of supporters. Thus, position itself gives incumbents advantages in political bargaining to garner resources to accomplish their goals. Expectations develop among other participants about how people will perform in programs based on their roles or positions. The third lesson is that "good guys don't always win" (p. 306). Because all organizations are political systems, individuals who fight fair and demonstrate integrity do not always emerge with the power and advantage in bargaining relations. "This is an unfortunate fact of organizational life" (p. 306) — not a justification for misuse of power or for cynicism. However, those individuals who fight viciously and use power crassly to win in one situation will have increasing difficulties in managing or leading subsequent programs.

It is widely believed that if individual professionals acted with more integrity, program implementation could be significantly improved. But as Richard Betts (1978:82) noted, "integrity untinged by political sensitivity courts professional suicide." He suggested that individuals try to improve situations by asking hard questions of their superiors, acting as skeptics, nagging decision makers into awareness of the full range of uncertainty, making authorities' calculations harder rather than easier, and hoping they pick up on important issues. But most officials will not appreciate these approaches by individual professionals, who may pay a high price for their efforts. Exactly how high the price of integrity can be is recorded by Craighead (1979), Hornocker (1982), and Finley (1983).

Professional Education

Restructuring professionalism toward civic, reflective, and policy-oriented models requires a commitment to learning by practitioners, universities, and workplaces. Donald Michael (1995) distinguished two kinds of learning — one suited to a stable world where learning new ways of doing things will keep practitioners adaptive, and another appropriate to today's world of uncertainty and change, where it is essential for practitioners to learn how to learn, or learn what questions to ask, because the questions will keep changing. This second kind of learning, what I have called double-loop learning, will require fundamental shifts in how the disciplines are organized and what norms they set for effective and justifiable practice. Professional expertise must focus less on fixed bodies of knowledge with rigid standards of "scientific proof" and limited techniques for solving real-world problems. Experts must become more interdisciplinary and more interactive with society. The universities and professional schools have an obligation to teach critical thinking, judgment, reflection, and communication skills (Sullivan 1995). The role of experts must be reconceptualized by both professionals and the public as a partnership.

Formal learning may be accomplished in university and professional schools, on the job in workshops and in-service training programs, and independently by individuals.

UNIVERSITIES AND PROFESSIONAL SCHOOLS

Currently, university and professional schools stress strong training in the heritage, structure, and norms of positivistic science. This permits individuals to hold on to their conventional identities in complex working situations. But since the goal is to prepare students for success on the job, it would seem that curricula need to encompass more than core technical subjects, competency, and skills. They must teach professionalism and its social responsibilities, which should include the ability to clarify the common interest, or represent collective values. They should steer students away from the technical rationalist model of experts outside or above the policy process and all other participants as the source of conflicts and constraints on them. Students should be offered a model of public policy that is sophisticated, realistic, and practical enough to allow them to analyze participants' roles and values (including their own) and to intervene constructively. The ethics they teach of conservation and sustainable use of natural resources should be seen as part of the larger goal of serving human dignity. Natural resource curricula should also develop the skills to see when more information is needed, to articulate problems and alternative solutions clearly, to clarify goals and mobilize support, to craft and carry out adequate programs, and to monitor efforts throughout the program.

Efforts are under way, however, to build curricula to train civic professionals. New professional courses build social and technical capability by focusing on complex problem solving. At Yale University's School of Forestry and Environmental Studies I teach a course entitled "Species and Ecosystem Conservation: Developing and Applying a Policy Orientation." The course educates students about the professional, institutional, and policy setting in which they are likely to work, using the framework of the policy sciences and a wide range of case studies. Other universities are also moving in this direction (e.g., Touval and Dietz 1994, Trombulak 1994). But as Romm (1984:16) noted, the "best an academic program can do, and what it should do best, is to prepare students to learn from experience as rapidly and efficiently as possible, thereby reducing a maturation time that is much longer in policy than in the more technical aspects of resource management."

There are ways to teach professional competence. Apprenticeships, coaching in sports, and conservatories and studios in the arts are all well-established traditions in learning by doing, as are the case methods used in law schools and the internships served by young physicians (Schön 1987). A professional practicum is a specialized educational setting in which natural resource students could work through simulated or real projects without the pressures and risks of real practice. Such a method, which would supplement the regular curriculum of natural and social sciences, would coach them through demonstration, advice, questioning, and criticism. In this way, they would learn to "reason their way" interactively between general knowledge and particular cases (Schön 1987). This is a promising route to improved professional performance in complex situations.

WORKSHOPS

In-service workshops, training programs, and conferences are also targets for upgrading professional performance. Practitioners can insist on workshops and meetings that specifically support and develop successful professional practice. Some agencies are already using this approach to improving problem solving and understanding of conservation processes. The Flora and Fauna Branch of the Victoria Department of Conservation and Natural Resources, in Australia, has used professional development workshops to their advantage (Clark and Begg, Forthcoming). Participants indicated that the new problem-solving framework (again, based on the policy sciences) was highly relevant to their jobs and put their problem-solving efforts in a much more realistic context. For some, it redefined their understanding of the entire policy process and their roles in it, and it permitted them to verbalize their own problem-solving experiences better. Many hoped the new method would be institutionalized in their organization through continued skill development, regular discussions and shaping of ideas, participation by all policy and management staff, and commitment from administrators.

Another kind of workshop could follow Westrum's (1994) suggestion: a national, high-performance training program for endangered species recovery similar to the Navy's Top Gun school for fighter combat skills. Westrum noted two recurring problems in endangered species recovery teams: they lacked consensus on what they ought to be, and they lacked an institutional memory of what works and what doesn't. The proposed training program would provide an institutional memory that would allow the system to perfect and expand the application of solutions that had already proven effective in science, reflective practice, and policy orientation. Such a convocation would also concentrate expertise and experience in a way that might build consensus, clarify goals, and shape a stronger identity for recovery groups. Such training could help professionals develop human relations skills, get comfortable with ambiguity, develop competence in formulating and solving problems, and avoid groupthink.

INDIVIDUAL

Individual pursuit of education can complement more formal university and in-service training. Extensive literature is available on professional development, organizational change, and participation in policy processes. Individual professionals can try new approaches on their own and open dialogues about professional practice with fellow practitioners. It is also helpful to find experienced, successful mentors with whom to discuss daily work issues as well as larger issues such as developing a policy orientation. Individuals can encourage professional societies to have sections and training programs on problem solving.

Learning in all settings — the university, the workshop, and individually — should focus on leadership as well as problem solving. Leadership skills can be developed through teaching and coaching. Mentors can be particularly effective in fostering in young professionals the abilities to envision goals and shared values for a group, explain the group to itself and represent it to outsiders, as well as motivate, manage, and unify the group (Gardner 1990). There would be benefits to society and to professionals for species recovery programs to find, cultivate, and unleash "maestros" — leaders who emphasize high energy and commitment, high standards, and high productivity. Such leaders not only bring "virtuoso talents" and technical expertise to a program, but they are also good at building supportive political coalitions and breeding a culture of excellence within a program (Westrum 1994). Leaders must be able to see and manage the group within the context of the task to be accomplished, the network of involved groups, and society as a whole. This requires both technical and process skills and recognition of the group's responsibility to society.

Civic professionalism focuses a professional's energies outward to meet the challenges posed by the realities of the world. For civic professionalism to come to fruition, an institutional setting is needed that provides a satisfying and worthy professional life while at the same time stimulating a meaningful connection to society. To train civic professionals with knowledge and skill to solve policy problems effectively and to bring about institutional settings that support them, change is needed. Education at multiple levels — university, workshops, and individual — is the key to change.

Conclusions

The process of saving species is much like a competitive market: all individual participants may have an influence, some major and some minor. Their relative contributions are determined not only by their knowledge and skills but also by their power and roles. Having explicit, systematic knowledge of this process, including one's own role in it, is essential in order to compete successfully through modern professional practice. Professionalism, as it has been conventionally promoted, has not focused on this process nor offered concepts to understand it realistically. Professional knowledge is a two-edged sword: it is necessary for problem solving but, defined too narrowly, it can also blind the practitioner and become a problem in itself. Civic professionalism, on the other hand, calls for the mastery of reflective practice and policy orientation and offers the scope, the tools, and the rigor to be relevant in the endangered species recovery process. Reconstructing professionalism to be more civic promises a new phase of successful problem solving.

Conclusions

The destruction of other life forms because of the actions of people is a problem with profound biological, ecological, economic, and ethical dimensions. We must assume that a healthy biosphere is in the common interest of humanity. Appreciation of the fundamental importance and far-sightedness of the Endangered Species Act and other biodiversity protection policies has grown over the last two decades, but that has neither prevented nor appreciably slowed the extinction crisis. Around the globe, the problem of extinction is extreme and growing, with perhaps scores of species disappearing each day. The biologist E. O. Wilson estimates that more than one-fifth of the planet's biodiversity will be pushed to extinction within the next two decades — between four thousand and six thousand species a year in rain forests alone — ten thousand times greater than natural background extinction rates (E. Wilson 1989, 1992).

The ESA is potentially a powerful tool to ameliorate the extinction crisis, and in many ways it has served as a global model. But despite its value both substantively and symbolically, there are problems with it, as both the biological and the political trends in recent years attest. Implementation has fallen short of the promise. Protecting species under the ESA is a long, complex process. Once species are recognized as deserving of protection and are listed, conservation programs must be designed, approved, and then implemented —

usually over years or even decades. Delays in listing and consequent protection of species are doubly regrettable because so many qualifying species are already backlogged (Meese 1989). Almost four thousand species in the United States now wait to be afforded the basic protections of the ESA; several hundred, many of them plants, may already be extinct. Beyond the listing process, there are innumerable steps, activities, and processes that make up ESA implementation. The extinction problem in the U.S. and the world is apparently growing faster than practical policy responses can be generated to stop it.

To illustrate the scope of the difficulties in the conservation process and the limitations of conventional approaches, I have examined one endangered species case in some detail. The black-footed ferret was chosen for several reasons. It is a fascinating and beautiful animal in its own right, and a persistent enigma since it was first recognized by science in 1851. The effort to restore this small, elusive weasel of the plains since the early 1980s has been a high-profile conservation issue and an interesting story. The ferret restoration program has been fraught with problems, which have added to its notoriety in the public eye and in scientific and conservation communities. But this book is not really about ferrets or the people trying to save them. Other cases illustrating the ESA recovery process could have served here as examples instead of the ferret; many tell a similar story and lead to similar conclusions. Despite broad agreement by participants on the ultimate goal, the ferret nearly disappeared under the government program set up to save it, and its future is not yet secure. This account is not meant to malign any person or organization working in ferret conservation, but to illustrate some of the actual difficulties involved in applying the ESA in the field — the only place that really matters.

If we are to improve the policy-making process for conserving biodiversity, we must acknowledge the problems openly, honestly, and realistically, examine them systematically and comprehensively, compare observations, resolve differences, and find workable solutions. The single precept that encompasses the meaning of the ferret story and the significance of the recommendations in the last three chapters is that we must *learn*. Many people would agree that what we *know* about saving species is much greater than what we *do* about saving species. We must capitalize on this existing knowledge and turn it into more efficient, more effective, and more equitable conservation gains. In other words, we must reconstruct the endangered species recovery process.

A new commitment to learning must take place among professionals working in biodiversity conservation and management. The most promising route is for practitioners to cultivate civic professionalism — a reflective, policy-oriented approach to their work — to sharpen their critical thinking skills, and to be more aware of their roles in the process of endangered species recovery.

This offers them the most well-grounded, productive method to solve problems and the most socially responsible way to participate. A policy orientation calls for a particular style of inquiry that compels participants to scrutinize ongoing events in greater depth, to look at the conditions under which problematic situations developed and what their prospects are, to relate problems to people, and to be more sensitive to how problems and proposed solutions will affect various groups of people and institutions. This approach sharpens analytic skills and engages participants in the policy-making process. It makes them, in the words of Brewer and deLeon (1983), more humane, creative, and effective problem solvers. With these skills in inquiry and reflective conversation, practitioners can gain a better sense of the complex dynamics of the species recovery process, practically improve performance, and enjoy better outcomes.

We must also foster learning in our organizations. The ferret case exemplified some of the challenges posed by the profound and pervasive influence of organizations (especially bureaucracies) in our lives as well as the difficulties of group learning. Bureaucratic systems are largely responsible for implementing wildlife conservation policies. Up until implementation, formulated and legally enacted policies are only statements of intention. As Eugene Bardach (1977) pointed out, formulating policy is like drawing up a blueprint for a complex machine, while implementation is actually building the machine and making it run. The structures and cultures of federal and state bureaucracies profoundly influence the ESA implementation process. Of the many actions of government that accumulate to create ESA policy, those that actually shape the outcomes, establish procedures, and set precedents are those of the bureaucracies. Bureaucratic hierarchies and role- and power-oriented cultures often block organizational learning. Yet nongovernmental organizations and businesses have improved their learning capabilities and information-processing skills, and such changes must be encouraged within government. Although bureaucracy is efficient and valuable in handling routine governmental tasks, alternative structures and processes must be ready to spring into action when needed, and these must be supported by the bureaucracy and by the citizenry. The skills required for nonroutine tasks, such as species rescues, are not simply those of the expert scientific technician. They include deliberation, problem solving, decision making, competence, flexibility, and the ability to carry out reflective conversations with oneself, clients, and society.

Finally, we must improve learning as citizens. As citizen participants in the public policy debates over biodiversity, we must accept, first, that restoring endangered species is fundamentally an effort in public policy making. Granted, it requires the science of biology, but at heart it is not a biological task. Science is only one component in what is essentially a social process. We must understand conservation more holistically and engage conceptual and practical tools that are adequate to improve all aspects of the process, including biological aspects of the problem. Second, we must accept the irrationality of the political process. The solutions that emerge from conflicts over inherent differences among people are never the most rational ones but what Harold Lasswell described as the "emotionally satisfactory" ones. Yet rational consensus remains an ideal to pursue (Dryzek 1990). Third, we must learn the knowledge and skills of competent and responsible civic participation, of not surrendering to inadequate government solutions or to narrow experts with all the biases of technical rationality. The American people must help build new relationships with government through which they can share in decision and policy making for better conservation of biodiversity.

The strongest argument for trying these new approaches is a thorough review of the past decades of ESA implementation, including individual cases like the black-footed ferret program. The inescapable conclusion is that the ultimate goal—to pass on a rich biological heritage to future generations—is so important that we have no choice but to engage the best means of achieving that goal and shun all lesser means. We must stop kidding ourselves that conventional positivistic science alone will or can save endangered species, despite the power of this tool as a guiding principle, as a measure of success, as an outcome, or as a primary western cultural value. We must begin to see science as only one contributing part of the much larger set of concepts and practical tools. We must stop enabling a few government bureaucracies to distort, undermine, and overrun society's goals and the social process itself as they serve their own interests. They are not the only vehicle by which to accomplish these goals, and we must begin to envision and invent new ways to protect species and ecosystems. Taking up the problem-solving approach promoted in this book and releasing human creative efforts to tackle the species extinction crisis offer the best chances of meeting these challenges.

Epilogue

Since 1986 there have been many developments in the ferret story and in the policy debate about the Endangered Species Act. The ESA is currently being debated nationally as part of the extended congressional reauthorization process. Powerful forces are lined up both for and against the act. The debate is highly partisan and faces rough going in Congress (Bean 1991b, Eaton 1992, Rancourt 1992, Slack 1992, Jones 1993, Snape 1996, Jost 1996). In 1993 it was reported that the *Congressional Quarterly* listed seventy-two bills that impinged on the ESA in some way (Madson 1993). There are two major targets for changing endangered species conservation: the process itself (which has been the focus of this book) and the resources available to it. Anti-ESA forces see many weaknesses in the current act. For example, the Political Economy Research Center (1991) says that most controversy comes from listing subspecies and other distinct populations as endangered, even if a species overall is healthy. This group considers the act misdirected because it "sets up perverse incentives that actually discourage people from protecting species" (p. 1). In protecting species, the government interferes with the private sector by distorting markets and setting up institutions that make it costly to establish private property rights to natural resources. This group and its allies promote "free market environmentalism" as the way to improve the recovery process. Many variations of this theme are heard (e.g., Mann and Plummer 1992, Winckler 1992, Palmer 1992).

Pro-ESA forces, on the other hand, contend that federal and state policies governing use of plants and animals must catch up to the imperative of sustainability (Reid 1992). At the heart of this complicated debate is the simple question, "How much is a species worth?" (Adler and Hager 1992). This is a question with no easy answer. Some supporters of the act argue that more staff and money are needed by agencies responsible to conserve species (Snodgrass 1991). Shortcomings in the conservation process that must be addressed include the balancing of biological and political issues, inadequacy of funding, and federal/state conflict (Ekey 1992). This national debate has been serious and contentious for years, and it is unclear how it will play itself out.

In the western United States, the Western Governors' Association is one powerful group involved in the reauthorization debate that seeks to amend the act. The governors see that the states are significantly affected by the federal listing of endangered species, that insufficient funding (and tax- and market-based incentives) has prevented effective implementation of the act, and that the states and other stakeholders (landowners and water users) need a much larger role in its implementation (Western Governors' Association 1992, 1995). Demonstrating a strong states'-rights outlook, the Western Governors' Association asserted that the "states possess broad trustee and police powers over fish and wildlife within their borders, including those found on federal lands within their borders" (Western Governors' Association 1992:2). While some governors want the states to assume total responsibility for implementation of the act, others do not. ESA reauthorization brings out vigorous debate even within the states'-rights community.

In Wyoming, the ESA debate is dominated by conservative politics. The Wyoming Heritage Society, for example, has suggested that federal bureaucrats have assumed enormous powers through "protectionist" legislation such as the ESA to deprive citizens of constitutional, economic, and property rights (Casper Star-Tribune 1995b). Ranchers have long complained that the government harbors prairie dogs on federal lands and that these protected colonies serve as reservoirs of pests that invade private property, costing landowners thousands of dollars to control. A Wyoming Farm Bureau representative and rancher charged that the federal government protects prairie dogs because of the possible presence of endangered black-footed ferrets and that the ever-growing reach of the EAS has led to the mismanagement of federal lands (Casper Star-Tribune 1995c). Such perspectives are widespread and seem to be growing in Wyoming and the West.

The issue of federalism versus states' rights around endangered species is receiving considerable media attention (e.g., Kinsley 1995, Dowie 1995, Kosova 1995, Larson 1995, Lacayo 1995) and scholarly attention (Brunner 1994). This multifaceted debate should be tracked closely as part of the continuous effort to map contexts and devise rational, politically practical, and morally justified natural resource management policy.

What has happened in the ferret restoration effort itself since 1986? From its inception in 1985, the captive population of eighteen black-footed ferrets grew — slowly at first, and not without some setbacks. The captive-breeding program was managed under the Species Survival Plan, which is the zoo community's equivalent to a FWS recovery plan. A member of WGF chaired the program. Between 1987 and 1995, 1,541 ferret kits were born in 444 litters. Nine hundred eighty-five kits (64 percent) were weaned. Fifty-eight percent of all females gave birth (Williams 1995, Reading et al. 1996). Much has been learned about ferret ontogeny, the effects of rearing conditions on predatory behavior, post-release survival into the wild, and many other aspects of ferret biology (Vargas 1994).

After no reproduction in 1986, two litters were produced in 1987, thirteen litters in 1988, and twenty-four in 1989. Although all the world's known ferrets were originally housed in the WGF Sybille Canyon facility, by 1988 some of the captive animals were moved to the Conservation and Research Center of the National Zoo at Front Royal, Virginia, and the Henry Doorly Zoo in Omaha. Since then, zoos in Toronto, Phoenix, Louisville, and Colorado Springs have each received a few ferrets, although the Sybille facility continues to hold roughly half of the total population.

Dietary changes were credited with reducing the survival of offspring in 1990. Indeed, captive-breeding success always depends on detailed knowledge of husbandry, disease suppression, reproductive physiology, nutrition, animal behavior, and a host of other factors, many of which must be learned as a program proceeds. In 1991, the captive population attained the FWS recovery plan goal of two hundred breeding ferrets, an achievement that permitted the first reintroduction that year. By 1992, what may be genetic abnormalities were evident in the captive population — webbed feet, misshapen canine teeth, short and kinked tails, and internal bleeding. The possible effects of inbreeding depression remain a concern (Thorne and Russell 1995).

By late 1995, five hundred "surplus" ferrets had been provided by the Species Survival Plan program toward recovery goals: 433 kits and adults were provided for reintroduction in three states, 25 ferrets for the FWS and National Biological Survey for non–Species Survival Plan breeding for reintroduction research, 18 ferrets for nonbreeding canine distemper vaccine research in Wyoming, and 24 ferrets for nonbreeding exhibits at six Species Survival Plan member zoos and five–Species Survival Plan zoos (Thorne and Russell 1995). All other kits were kept in the breeding population.

In early 1996, the FWS assumed management and financial responsibility of the captive-breeding facility at Sybille, which was renamed the National Black-footed Ferret Conservation Center (Thorne and Russell 1995, Reading et al. 1996). Discussion is under way about how to increase the captive-breeding program using private moneys in a new public-private partnership. Captive breeding was initially undertaken to produce animals for reintroduction to the wild. As of mid-1996, reintroductions have taken place every year since 1991.

Because no additional wild ferret populations have been located, restoration of the species will depend on successfully establishing reintroduced populations and on their continued conservation and management both in these reintroduced wild populations and in captivity. The 1987 Recovery Plan called for establishing by 2010 at least 1,500 breeding adults in ten populations in the widest possible distribution, with no fewer than thirty adults in any population. Given the experience to date, this may have been an overly optimistic schedule. A number of studies have examined and described ferret habitat requirements and prescribed the necessary size, location, distribution, and characteristics of potential reintroduction sites.

Several states have sought to reintroduce ferrets. For example, the Montana Department of Fish, Wildlife and Parks, working with the FWS Montana Office, the Bureau of Land Management, and the conservation community, has been active in finding reintroduction sites and developing habitat management plans (Montana Black-Footed Ferret Working Group 1988, North Central Montana Black-Footed Ferret Working Group 1991). By the early 1990s, it was thought that at least two reintroduction sites were also available in Wyoming, and others were possible in Utah, Colorado, South Dakota, Arizona, North Dakota, New Mexico, Mexico, and Canada. Mexico in fact contains the largest potential site in North America. Recent thinking, however, is that suitable sites may be smaller, fewer, and less available than originally believed. Prairie dog colonies, which constitute ferret habitat, continue to be poisoned, shot, and lost at the rate of more than 250,000 acres annually (Roemer and Forres 1996).

As of early 1996, 400 ferrets had been reintroduced to three sites (Reading et al. 1996; numbers are difficult to confirm because of the program's record-keeping methods). Wyoming received 49 ferrets in 1991, 90 in 1992, 48 in 1993, 41 in 1994, and none in 1995. Montana received 40 in 1994 and 37 in 1995. And South Dakota received 36 in 1994 and 59 in 1995. Much has been learned about reintroducing ferrets (National Ecology Research Center 1992, Biggins et al. 1993). Some of the released ferrets were fitted with radio collars, which permitted researchers to determine the fates of the animals after release. Ferrets without telemetry collars could not be tracked. Mortality was high in all the reintroductions; most animals were lost to coyotes and other predators. By 1992 it was shown that ferrets preconditioned in outdoor pens survived significantly better than cage-reared animals (Biggins et al. 1993).

That Wyoming received the first and largest number of reintroduced ferrets reflects the state's dominant role in the program. All 228 of Wyoming's reintroduced ferrets were released in the Shirley Basin/Medicine Bow area of south central Wyoming (WGF 1991a). The site was chosen by WGF with concurrence from the FWS on advice from the Black-Footed Ferret Interstate Coordinating Committee (ICC) set up to advise the FWS on ferret recovery. Meeteetse was not chosen as a release site because its prairie dog population had drastically declined since the early 1980s, when the ferrets were first discovered. The ferrets were reintroduced with an "experimental, nonessential" designation under the ESA as sought by WGF, the FWS, the Bureau of Land Management, and local landowners. The Sierra Club Legal Defense Fund threatened legal challenges because this status did not provide maximum protection to the only known wild population of ferrets, but no law suit was filed.

Reintroductions are planned in 1996 for Montana and South Dakota again and for Arizona. One notable difference among the reintroduction sites is that the Montana and South Dakota sites contain black-tailed prairie dogs, whereas the Wyoming site contains white-tailed prairie dogs. The Arizona site contains Gunnison's prairie dogs, a form of white-tailed prairie dog. Black-tailed prairie dogs live in much higher densities, which may be a factor in better survival rates for ferrets. A large reintroduction site in Mexico, which also contains black-tailed prairie dogs and might support hundreds of wild ferrets, is being assessed for future releases.

Both the captive-breeding and reintroduction efforts remain hopeful, but beginning in 1995 WGF began positioning itself for possible failure in ferret conservation. WGF's magazine, *Wyoming Wildlife,* reported that "with all the positive news, the black-footed ferret's prospects for the future are dim. . . . 'I think the public needs to be prepared,' says . . . one of the leaders in the effort to save the ferret. 'There's an uncomfortable probability that, for one reason or the other, Wyoming's ferret program is *not* going to be successful' " (Madson 1995:31–32). The beleaguered department attributed the program's problems to biology, politics, and funding. But the same issues of states'-rights politics, bureaucratic and scientific conservatism, and resource limitations continue to plague the program.

Has WGF's basic position changed in the last fifteen years? Apparently not, if the statement of WGF's director is an accurate indication. Director John Talbott provided testimony at a U.S. Senate Subcommittee hearing on Endangered Species Act Reform in Casper, Wyoming, on August 16, 1995 (Talbott 1995). Noting that his department had been involved in several contentious endangered species issues, he expressed three concerns about the ESA funding, state responsibilities, and state involvement in administration. He noted that costs had been high for his state and that funding should come primarily from the federal government. He argued that states should have the option to take the lead in implementing some parts of the ESA. Even without the leadership role, states should remain equal partners in administering federal programs, with federal oversight consisting of periodic audits. He reasserted the states' broad trustee and police powers for fish and wildlife management, including those on federal lands. Authority for recovery planning should lie with the states, and these plans "should be construed as having satisfied the NEPA requirements" (p. 5). The basic outlook is abundantly clear — states' rights.

It appears that many of the bureaucratic characteristics and associated problems in ferret conservation I have described remain ten years later. The makeup of the committees and teams in ferret recovery are one indication of continuing bureaucratization. Today, three major committees or teams exist; WGF's Black-footed Ferret Advisory Team (BFAT) was recently disbanded.

Organizational and individual memberships overlap extensively within these committees. The Black-footed Ferret Management Committee (BFMC, sometimes called the BFF Management Group) was established in 1995 by the U.S. Fish and Wildlife Service to assist it in ferret conservation. Twenty-three individuals representing fourteen organizations (including thirteen government agencies) and three "others" make up the committee. The American Zoo and Aquarium Association (AZA), one industry (PCI Technologies, Inc.), the National Wildlife Federation, and the National Fish and Wildlife Foundation (a public-private group for funding wildlife research, closely allied to government agencies) are the only nongovernment entities on the group's 1996 mailing list. The Interstate Coordination Committee (ICC) is made up of eleven state working groups (which in turn consist of state and federal agencies) plus a number of federal organizations and the AZA. The Species Survival Plan (SSP) has seven participating institutions (six zoos and Wyoming's Sybille facility), and other participants include two additional zoos, several state and federal agencies, the ICC, the AZA, and the University of Wyoming. Additionally, the FWS maintains a part-time ferret coordinator position to help implement the 1987 Black-Footed Ferret Recovery Plan and other management initiatives.

A public-private partnership between business and the FWS is forming to aid ferret conservation. The relationship is currently tenuous, and it is not clear how the partnership will work. In the fall of 1995, the business member pulled out of the developing relationship, criticizing working relationships among the partners, but later rejoined. At the time of the withdrawal, the letter of explanation by the private partner noted that "the program is so mired in deception, finger-pointing, petty bickering and bureaucracy that it has become entirely ineffective in implementing actions necessary to recover the species. One can only wonder if these program problems are not a bigger obstacle to recovery than plague or habitat loss. . . . The bottom line is control. With the current participants, we see no way for the two agencies [FWS and WGF] to develop a productive relationship. If you want to move forward, it appears that either the [FW] Service or WGFD must completely and unequivocally step aside" (Aaron Clark, cited in U.S. Fish and Wildlife Service 1995: 18–19).

Wyoming Game and Fish denied these charges and asserted that interagency disagreements provided a beneficial system of checks and balances (Reese 1995). Also in response to the private partner's letter, another BFMC agency member suggested that private partners not be involved in the program until a formal cooperative agreement defined the roles of participants (U.S. Fish and Wildlife Service 1995). The central issues raised in the letter seem not to have been addressed. It appears that after fifteen years, the ferret program remains bureaucratic, government-dominated, heavily power- and role-oriented, and overly concerned with control issues.

The only published review of science in the ferret program has been Reading and Miller (1994; see also Miller et al. 1996). This article stressed the paramount importance of science in species recovery programs and noted that common problems such as program control struggles, incompatible goals, and personnel incompetence can restrict the collection and appropriate use of reliable knowledge. They reported that WGF had been criticized for excluding some participants and for not using science appropriately and fully, and they charged that ferret recovery efforts had suffered because WGF did not incorporate adaptive scientific management.

Reading and Miller cited WGF's altering of reintroduction protocols in 1991 so that only fifteen of forty-nine animals released were radio-collared. This move effectively precluded collection of data on mortality factors and survival rates, and thus hampered the ability to assess the program and the opportunity to improve later reintroductions. Despite the "experimental" designation of the reintroduced population, there has been no experimentation or scientifically rigorous research conducted to compare release techniques. What little research has been done was retroactive and seriously flawed in experimental design. After the releases, field observations of three or four ferrets by WGF personnel were extrapolated, without justification, to prove that at least seven ferrets had survived. Reading and Miller also cited a lack of outside review of WGF's data and the continual citation of unpublished, unreviewed reports that lends a false sense of credibility to the agency's data.

To explain this behavior, Reading and Miller indicated that the agency favored limited, less intrusive research, perhaps in response to a fear that ferret declines were a result of research. They also mentioned that a WGF official had stated that he would ignore ongoing research because the agency had already decided how ferrets would be released, and he refused to compare two reintroduction techniques because the alternative might work better than WGF's. In conclusion, they recommended, among other things, external review by qualified professionals of research proposals, data collection methods, analysis techniques, and implications for future research; assessment of data reliability by all participants; periodic formal program appraisals; incentive systems that reward good science; and incorporation of data reliability into indices of program success.

The overall cost of ferret conservation since 1981 is impossible to calculate given the number of activities and participants involved. Expenditures, apparently, are not shared in a standardized way among participants, making it even harder to determine accurate totals. Some expenditures, however, have been estimated. Between 1982 through 1988, the FWS spent about $2.6 million (Cole 1989). One estimate concluded that it cost the FWS about $235,000 to build the ferret captive-breeding facility in Wyoming and about $150,000 annually to run it (Captive Breeding Specialist Group 1992:38). WGF (1992) estimated that it had spent about $1.8 million between 1987 through 1991. The expenditures of various NGOs and other states, as well as those of other federal agencies, have increased the total sum considerably. This suggests that the ferret program has been relatively well funded compared to other recovery programs. A June 1995 memo prepared for the ICC meeting summarized expenditures in the ferret program: operation of the Sybille captive-breeding facility requires about $250,000 a year (contributed until late 1995 by WGF, including Section 6 funds from the federal government); zoos with breeding facilities have contributed over $800,000 in initial capital investment and $200,000–$300,000 a year in operating costs; National Biological Service research funds total more than $200,000 annually; reintroductions into Wyoming, Montana, and South Dakota have already cost over $5 million, with an expected $1.2 million ($400,000 per site) in support funds needed annually; and several hundred thousand dollars have been spent by state and federal agencies in preparing additional release sites (Anonymous 1995b). This memo indicates that 30 percent of the estimated 1994 total of $2.0–2.2 million dollars came from the FWS, 35 percent from other federal agencies, 17 percent from WGF, 15 percent from the AZA, and the balance from other states.

In recent years, the relative contributions of various participants have changed significantly. In 1994, WGF underwent a major budget cutting process (Oakleaf 1994). This included cutbacks in the black-footed ferret program in field work, surveys of prairie dog populations, time spent caring for ferrets in acclimation cages, and monitoring of released ferrets.

The following year, the department claimed that increased funding from the federal government was needed for the state's continued participation in endangered species programs (Wyoming Game and Fish News 1995a, 1995b). Because of an anticipated shortfall of several million dollars, the agency proposed major restructuring and privatizing of some services to cope with the loss of employees, including stopping ferret reintroductions into the Shirley Basin/Medicine Bow area (Casper Star-Tribune 1995d). Public meetings also revealed some opposition to the use of money from hunting and fishing license sales to fund endangered species programs (Casper Star-Tribune 1995e).

Wyoming earlier was reported to have asked the FWS to take over its ferret captive-breeding program because of these budget cutbacks and because most of the ferrets were being reintroduced into other states (Casper Star-Tribune 1995f). Under the current arrangements with the FWS, Wyoming will retain ownership of the Sybille Canyon facility but allow the FWS to use it, the equipment, and the ferrets for a limited period.

All this has led to an apparent marked change in strategic positions among the state and federal participants in the effort to restore ferrets. This change has not come about because of any basic shift in standpoint or organizational arrangements, but solely because WGF has run out of money, at least temporarily. The commitment and capability described by Lester (1990) as essential to good state implementation of federal policy has proven to be wanting in this case. The ferret story also seems to be in keeping with western history. Patricia Limerick (1987) notes that the West was built on "furs, farmland, timber, minerals, and federal money" (p. 82). Despite the obvious conflict with the myths of independence, self-reliance, and free enterprise, the western states' habit of exploiting federal subsidies has persisted from territorial days to the present.

Despite the persistence of several problems, a number of trends and conditions as of mid-1996 favor the eventual recovery of the ferret. Captive-breeding technology seems to have been worked out, and ferrets are being consistently produced in captivity. Experience with reintroductions and systematic learning are now making it possible to find the best way to establish wild ferret populations. Recent survival rates of reintroduced ferrets in Montana and South Dakota are encouraging. The FWS is assuming a larger role and bringing a national perspective and problem definition to the task. This could result in a better coordinated effort. As part of this growing FWS role, the major captive-breeding facility is in FWS hands. The FWS employs an experienced part-time coordinator and a seasoned field leader. In late 1995 and early 1996, it contracted with the AZA to appraise the recovery effort and recommend ways to improve the process; forthcoming reports should be helpful in this regard. A new recovery plan is in the works. However, a number of issues (such as interstate coordination) must be systematically addressed. Most hearteningly, a growing number of hardworking, committed individuals scattered throughout the participating organizations are laboring to save the species. They are aware of past weaknesses in the program and are working to overcome them, although motivation fluctuates in the face of complex ideological and bureaucratic conditions. Taken together, these trends are promising. Eventual recovery of the ferret seems likely, barring any one of a number of possible catastrophes.

The black-footed ferret restoration effort over the last fifteen years exemplifies the dynamic and complex nature of the endangered species recovery process. There is too much at stake to accept less than our best efforts in conserving the nation's biological wealth.

Literature Cited

The scientific research on black-footed ferrets has been documented widely. Audubon and Bachman (1851) and Coues (1877) were the earliest accounts. Casey et al. (1986) was an extensive bibliography that includes all the early research at Meeteetse; it was updated by Reading and Clark (1990). Hillman and Clark (1980) was a comprehensive species account. Hillman and Linder (1973) reported on the South Dakota studies. Linder and Hillman (1973) edited the proceedings of the ferret and prairie dog workshop in South Dakota, and Anderson and Inkley (1985) edited the proceedings of a later workshop on the Wyoming ferrets. Great Basin Naturalist Memoirs No. 8 (1986) was an overview of the first few years' research on the Meeteetse ferrets. Seal et al. (1989) examined the conservation biology of the species. Clark (1994) provided a twenty-year review of the program. U.S. Fish and Wildlife Service (1987) was the Recovery Plan. Finally, Miller et al. (1996) looked at both the biology of the ferret and the recovery program.

Ackoff, R. 1979. The future of operational research is past. Journal of Operational Research Society 30(2):93–104.

Adler, J., and M. Hager. 1992. How much is a species worth? National Wildlife 30(3):4–15.

Administrative Conference of the United States. 1995. Proposed recommendations: Improving decisionmaking under the Endangered Species Act. Administrative Conference of the United States, Washington.

Allison, G. T. 1971. Essence of decision: Explaining the Cuban missile crisis. Little, Brown, Boston.

Alvarez, K. 1993. Twilight of the panther: Biology, bureaucracy, and failure in an endangered species program. Myakka River Publishing, Sarasota, Fla.

American Society of Mammalogists. 1986. Recovery and restoration of the black-footed ferret (*Mustela nigripes*). Journal of Mammalogy 67:786.

Anderson, S., and D. Inkley, eds. 1985. Proceedings of the Black-Footed Ferret Workshop, September 18–19, 1984, Laramie. Wyoming Game and Fish Department, Cheyenne.

Anonymous. 1995a. Making the ESA work better. Endangered Species Bulletin 20(3): 4–7.

Anonymous. 1995b. Memorandum. Biological and financial information collected relating to black-footed ferret recovery. Draft. Ecological Services, U.S. Fish and Wildlife Service, Pierre, S.D. June 16.

Argyris, C. 1976. Increasing leadership effectiveness. John Wiley, New York.

——. 1982. Reasoning, learning, and action: Individual and organizational. Jossey-Bass, San Francisco.

Argyris, C., and D. A. Schön. 1978. Organizational learning: A theory of action perspective. Addison-Wesley, Reading, Mass.

Ascher, W. 1986. The evolution of the policy sciences: Understanding the rise and avoiding the fall. Journal of Policy Analysis and Management 5:365–373.

Ascher, W., and R. Healy. 1990. Natural resource policymaking in developing countries: Environment, economic growth, and income distribution. Duke University Press, Durham, N.C.

Audubon, J. J., and J. Bachman. 1851. Quadrupeds of North America. V. G. Audubon, New York. 3 vols.

Audubon Magazine. 1985. Ferrets, fleas, false alarms. Audubon, November:163–164.

Backhouse, G. N., and T. W. Clark. 1995. Case studies and policy initiatives in endangered species recovery in Australia: Recommendations. Pp. 110–116 in A. Bennett, G. Backhouse, and T. Clark, eds., People and nature conservation: Perspectives on private land use and endangered species recovery. Transactions of Royal Zoological Society of New South Wales, Australia.

Backhouse, G. N., T. W. Clark, and R. P. Reading. 1994. The Australian eastern barred bandicoot recovery program: Evaluation and reorganization. Pp. 251–271 in T. W. Clark, R. P. Reading, and A. L. Clarke, eds., Endangered species recovery: Finding the lessons, improving the process. Island Press, Washington.

Baden, J., ed. 1980. Earth day revisited. Heritage Foundation, Washington.

Bailey, S. K., and E. K. Mosher. 1968. ESEA: The Office of Education administers a law. Syracuse University Press, Syracuse.

Ballou, J. D., and R. Oakleaf. 1987. Demographic and genetic breeding recommendations for the captive population of black-footed ferrets. Unpublished Draft Report, Captive Breeding Specialist Group, Species Survival Commission, IUCN, Minneapolis.

Bardach, E. 1977. The implementation game. MIT Press, Cambridge, Mass.

Bauman, J. M. 1985. Last ferrets are dying while government fails to act. Deseret News (Salt Lake City), July 19:A9.

——. 1986. Ferrets nearly extinct? It's too late for "I told-you-so." Deseret News (Salt Lake City), January 3:A11.

Bean, M. J. 1983. The evolution of national wildlife law. Praeger, New York.

———. 1991a. Looking back over the first fifteen years. Pp. 37–42 in K. A. Kohm, ed., Balancing on the brink of extinction: The Endangered Species Act and lessons for the future. Island Press, Washington.

Bean, M. J. 1991b. Issues and controversies in the forthcoming reauthorization battle. Endangered Species Update 9(1/2):1–4.

Beatley, T. 1994. Habitat conservation planning: Endangered species and urban growth. University of Texas Press, Austin.

Beedy, E. C. 1995. Ten ways to fix the Endangered Species Act. Endangered Species Update 12(6):12–14.

Belitsky, D. 1984. Letter to the editor. The Wildlifer 201:51.

Bennett, A., G. Backhouse, and T. W. Clark, eds. 1995. People and nature conservation: Perspectives on private land use and endangered species recovery. Transactions of the Royal Zoological Society of New South Wales, Australia.

Betts, R. K. 1978. Analysis, war, and decision: Why intelligence failures are inevitable. World Politics 31:61–89.

Biggins, D. E., and E. T. Thorne. 1994. Management of an endangered species: The black-footed ferret. Pp. 369–374 in G. K. Meffe and C. R. Carroll, Principles of conservation biology. Sinauer Associates, Inc., Sunderland, Mass.

Biggins, D., J. Godbey, and A. Vargas. 1993. Influence of pre-release experience on reintroduced black-footed ferrets (*Mustela nigripes*). U.S. Fish and Wildlife Service, National Ecology Research Center, Fort Collins, Colo.

Bissell, S. J. 1994. Book review: Broadening wildlife policy. Conservation Biology 8:323–324.

Blair, N. 1987. The history of wildlife management in Wyoming. Wyoming Game and Fish Department, Cheyenne.

Bogan, M. A. 1985. Needs and directions for future black-footed ferret research. Pp. 28.1–28.5 in S. Anderson and D. Inkley, eds., Proceedings of Black-Footed Ferret Workshop, September 18–19, 1984, Laramie. Wyoming Game and Fish Department, Cheyenne.

Bracken, P. 1984. The command and control of nuclear forces. Yale University Press, New Haven.

Brayton, D. S. 1983. Ferreting out the whereabouts of a rare and endangered species. Your Public Lands (Bureau of Land Management), Fall:19,22.

Brewer, G. D. 1975. Dealing with complex social problems: The potential of the "decision seminar." Pp. 439–461 in G. D. Brewer and R. D. Brunner, eds., Political development and change: A policy approach. Free Press, New York.

———. 1992. Business and environment: A time for creative and constructive coexistence. The Twenty-fifth Annual William K. McInally Memorial Lecture, March 31, School of Business Administration, University of Michigan, Ann Arbor.

Brewer, G. D., and T. W. Clark. 1994. A policy sciences perspective: Improving implementation. Pp. 391–413 in T. W. Clark, R. P. Reading, and A. L. Clarke, eds., Endangered species recovery: Finding the lessons, improving the process. Island Press, Washington.

Brewer, G. D., and P. deLeon. 1983. The foundations of policy analysis. Dorsey Press, Homewood, Ill.

Brewer, G. D., and J. S. Kakalik. 1979. Handicapped children: Strategies for improving services. McGraw-Hill, New York.

Brewer, G. D., and M. Shubik. 1979. The war game: A critique of military problem solving. Harvard University Press, Cambridge, Mass.

Brinckloe, W. D., and M. T. Coughlin. 1977. Managing organizations. Glencoe Press, Encino, Calif.

Brown, L. D. 1983. Managing conflict at organizational interfaces. Addison-Wesley, Reading, Mass.

Brunner, R. D. 1980. Decentralized energy policies. Public Policy 28:71–91.

———. 1982. The policy sciences as science. Policy Sciences 15:115–135.

———. 1986. Case-wise policy information systems: Redefining poverty. Policy Sciences 19:201–223.

———. 1987. Conceptual tools for policy analysis. Paper presented at the 1987 annual meeting of the American Political Science Association, September 3–6, Chicago.

———. 1991a. Global climate change: Defining the policy problem. Policy Sciences 24: 291–311.

———. 1991b. The policy movement as a policy problem. Policy Sciences 24:65–98.

———. 1992. Performance as promised: Restructuring the U.S. civil space programme. Space Policy 8:116–136.

———. 1994. Myth and American politics. Policy Sciences 27:1–18.

———. 1996. Policy and global change research: A modest proposal. Climate Change 32:121–147.

Brunner, R. D., and W. Ascher. 1992. Science and social responsibility. Policy Sciences 25:295–331.

Burns, T., and G. M. Stalker. 1981. Mechanistic and organic systems. Pp. 278–283 in M. Jelinek et al., Organizations by design: Theory and practice. Business Publications, Inc., Plano, Texas. Excerpted from The management of innovation, Tavistock, London, 1961.

Byars, L. L. 1984. Strategic management: Planning and implementation. Harper and Row, New York.

Callison, C. H. 1953. Man and wildlife in Missouri. Stackpole Press, Harrisburg, Penn.

Campbell, S. 1980. Is reintroduction a realistic goal? Pp. 263–269 in M. E. Soulé and B. A. Wilcox, eds., Conservation biology: An evolutionary-ecological perspective. Sinauer Associates, Sunderland, Mass.

Captive Breeding Specialist Group. 1992. Black-footed ferret recovery plan review. Washington, July 22–24. Apple Valley, Minn.

Carr, A. 1986. Introduction: The black-footed ferret. Great Basin Naturalist Memoirs 8:1–7.

———. 1987. Letter. Conservation Biology 1:80, 86.

Casey, D., J. DuWaldt, and T. W. Clark. 1986. Annotated bibliography of the black-footed ferret. Great Basin Naturalist Memoirs 8:185–208.

Casey, D., T. W. Clark, and J. H. Seebeck. 1990. Conclusions. Pp. 283–288 in T. W. Clark and J. H. Seebeck, eds., Management and conservation of small populations. Chicago Zoological Society, Brookfield, Ill.

Casper Star-Tribune. 1982. Second ferret population possible. March 7:B1.

———. 1986. G&F ferret expert fends off criticism. February 7:B1.

———. 1993. G&F head lauds ferret reintroduction. October 22:D1, 3.

———. 1995a. Officials ponder endangered ferret program. March 29:B3.

———. 1995b. States' rights battle federalism in the West. December 6:A5

———. 1995c. Rancher: Prairie dog problem costly. July 25:B3.

———. 1995d. Reorganization: G&F plans cuts. July 5:A8.

———. 1995e. Feds will assume ferret program costs. December 5:B1.

———. 1995f. G&F wants USFWS to take over ferret breeding project. February 2:B3.

Child, J. 1972. Organizational structure, environment, and performance: The role of strategic choice. Sociology 1:1–22.

Clark, T. W. 1981. The Meeteetse black-footed ferret conservation studies. A Proposal. Unpublished research proposal.

———. 1986. Professional excellence in wildlife and natural resource organizations. Renewable Resources Journal, Summer:8–13.

———. 1989. Conservation biology of the black-footed ferret *Mustela nigripes*. Wildlife Preservation Trust International, Special Scientific Report No. 3.

———. 1992. Practicing natural resource management with a policy orientation. Renewable Resources Journal 16:423–433.

———. 1993. Creating and using knowledge for species and ecosystem conservation: Science, organizations, and policy. Perspectives in Biology and Medicine 36:497–525.

———. 1994. Restoration of the endangered black-footed ferret: A 20-year overview. Pp. 272–297 in M. L. Bowles and C. J. Whelan, eds., Restoration and recovery of endangered species: Conceptual issues, planning and implementation. Cambridge University Press, London.

———. 1996. Learning as a strategy for improving endangered species conservation. Endangered Species Update 13(1/2):5–6,22–24.

———. Forthcoming. Appraising threatened species recovery efforts: Pragmatic recommendations for improvements. Australian Nature Conservation Agency, Canberra. Proceedings of a conference, Sydney, December 1995.

Clark, T. W., and R. J. Begg. Forthcoming. Interdisciplinary problem-solving workshops for flora and fauna branch professionals, Department of Conservation and Natural Resources, Victoria, Australia. Yale School of Forestry and Environmental Studies Bulletin.

Clark, T. W., and J. Cragun. 1994. Organizational and managerial guidelines for endangered species restoration programs and recovery teams. Pp. 9–33 in M. L. Bowles and C. J. Whelan, eds., Restoration and recovery of endangered species: Conceptual issues, planning and implementation. Cambridge University Press, London.

Clark, T. W., and S. R. Kellert. 1988. Toward a policy paradigm of the wildlife sciences. Renewable Resources Journal 6(1):7–16.

Clark, T. W., and A. Harvey. 1988. Implementing endangered species policy: Learning as we go? Endangered Species Update 5(10):35–42.

Clark, T. W., and S. C. Minta. 1994. Greater Yellowstone's future: Prospects for ecosystem science, management, and policy. Homestead Publishing, Moose, Wyo.

Clark, T. W., and R. P. Reading. 1994. A professional perspective: Improving problem solving, communication, and effectiveness. Pp. 351–370 in T. W. Clark, T. W., R. P. Reading, and A. L. Clarke, eds., Endangered species recovery: Finding the lessons, improving the process. Island Press, Washington.

Clark, T. W., and R. Westrum. 1989. High performance teams in wildlife conservation: A species reintroduction and recovery example. Environmental Management 13:663–670.

Clark, T. W., G. N. Backhouse, and R. P. Reading. 1995a. Prototyping in endangered species recovery programmes: The eastern barred bandicoot experience. Pp. 50–62 in A. Bennett, G. Backhouse, and T. Clark, eds., People and nature conservation: Perspectives on private land use and endangered species recovery. Transactions of the Royal Zoological Society of New South Wales, Surrey Beatty, Chipping Norton, N.S.W.

Clark, T. W., R. Crete, and J. Cada. 1989a. Designing and managing successful endangered species programs. Environmental Management 13:159–170.

Clark, T. W., L. R. Forrest, S. C. Forrest, and T. M. Campbell III. 1985a. Cover letter accompanying S. C. Forrest et al., Interim report: 1985 black-footed ferret litter survey at Meeteetse, Wyoming. August 6, Jackson, Wyo.

——. 1985b. Cover letter accompanying S. C. Forrest et al., Final report: Black-footed ferret population status at Meeteetse, Wyoming, July–October, 1985. October 11, Jackson, Wyo.

Clark, T. W., R. P. Reading, and G. N. Backhouse. 1995b. Prototyping for conservation: The endangered eastern barred bandicoot case. Endangered Species Update 12(10/11): 5–7,10.

Clark, T. W., R. P. Reading, and A. L. Clarke. 1994. Endangered species recovery: Finding the lessons, improving the process. Island Press, Washington.

Clarke, J. N., and D. McCool. 1985. Staking out the terrain: Power differentials among natural resource management agencies. State University of New York Press, Albany.

Cody Enterprise. 1985. Ferrets safe from disease. Cody Enterprise, July 18:5-A.

Cohen, A. R. 1971. The human dimensions of administrative reform: Towards more differentiated strategies for change. Development and Change, February:165–181.

Cohn, J. P. 1993. Defenders of biodiversity. Government Executive National Journal, April:18–22.

Cole, B. P. 1989. Recovery planning for endangered and threatened species. Pp. 201–209 in U.S. Seal, E. T. Thorne, M. A. Bogan, and S. H. Anderson, eds., Conservation biology and the black-footed ferret. Yale University Press, New Haven.

Cook, R. E., and P. Dixon. 1991. A review of recovery plans for threatened and endangered plant species. A Report for the World Wildlife Fund, Cornell Plantations, Cornell University, Ithaca, N.Y.

Coues, E. 1877. Fur-bearing animals: A monograph of North American Mustelidae. U. S. Geological Survey of the Territories, Miscellaneous Publication No. 8. GPO, Washington.

Craighead, F. C. 1979. Track of the grizzly. Sierra Club, San Francisco.

Culbert, R., and R. Blair. 1989. Recovery planning and endangered species. Endangered Species Update 6(10):2–8.

Daft, R. L. 1983. Organization theory and design. West Publishing, Saint Paul.

Daily Times (Rawlins, Wyoming). 1986. Ferrets' future hangs by a slender thread. April 18.

Dana, S. T., and S. K. Fairfax. 1980. Forest and range policy: Its development in the United States. 2d ed. McGraw-Hill, New York.

Defenders of Wildlife. 1995. Saving America's wildlife: Renewing the Endangered Species Act. Defenders of Wildlife, Washington.

deLeon, P. 1988. Advice and consent: The development of the policy sciences. Russell Sage Foundation, New York.

Dery, D. D. 1984. Problem definition in policy analysis. University Press of Kansas, Lawrence.

Dingell, J. D. 1991. The power and potential of the act. Pp. 25–30 in K. A. Kohm, ed., Balancing on the brink of extinction: The Endangered Species Act and lessons for the future. Island Press, Washington.

Diver, C. S. 1983. The optimal precision of administrative rules. Yale Law Journal 93:65–109.

Dowie, M. 1995. With liberty and firepower for all. Outback 20 (November):60–67.

Dryzek, J. S. 1990. Discursive democracy: Politics, policy, and political science. Cambridge University Press, New York.

Eaton, P. P. 1992. ESA amendments: The good, the bad, and the unnecessary. Endangered Species Update 9(5/6):9–10.

Ecological Society of America. 1995. Strengthening the use of science in achieving the goals of the Endangered Species Act: An assessment by the Ecological Society of America. Pre-publication copy. Ecological Society of America, Washington.

Edgerly, L. 1983. A history of Wyoming game management and numbers. Wyoming Heritage Foundation, Cody.

Eisner, T., J. Lubchenco, E. O. Wilson, D. S. Wilcove, and M. J. Bean. 1995. Building a scientifically sound policy for protecting endangered species. Science 268:1231–1232.

Ekey, B. 1992. The Endangered Species Act: A strong law for conservation foiled by politics. Greater Yellowstone Report 9(1):1,8–10.

Ernst, J. P. 1991. Federalism and the act. Pp. 98–113 in K. A. Kohm, ed., Balancing on the brink of extinction: The Endangered Species Act and lessons for the future. Island Press, Washington.

Etheredge, L. S. 1985. Can governments learn? Pergamon Press, New York.

Etheredge, L. S., and J. Short. 1983. Thinking about government learning. Journal of Management Studies 20:41–58.

Etzioni, A. 1961. A comparative analysis of complex organizations. Free Press, Glencoe, Ill.

——. 1964. Modern organizations. Prentice-Hall, Englewood Cliffs, N.J.

Fesler, J. W. 1980. Public administration: Theory and practice. Prentice-Hall, Englewood Cliffs, New Jersey.

Finley, R. E., Jr. 1983. Letter to the editor. The Wildlifer 199:34.

Fischhoff, B., S. Watson, and P. Hope. 1984. Defining risk. Policy Sciences 17:123–140.

Follett, M. P. 1970. Dynamic administration: The papers in Mary Parker Follett, H. C. Metcalf, and L. Urwick, eds. Harper and Row, New York.

Forrest, S. C. 1986. Letter to U. S. Seal, Captive Breeding Specialist Group, March 1. Jackson, Wyo.

———. 1987. Letter to Max Schroeder, U. S. Fish and Wildlife Service, September 12. Jackson, Wyo.

Forrest, S. C., D. E. Biggins, L. Richardson, T. W. Clark, T. M. Campbell III, and K. A. Fagerstone. 1988. Black-footed ferret (*Mustela nigripes*) population attributes, Meeteetse, Wyoming, 1981–1985. Journal of Mammalogy 69:261–273.

Forrest, S. C., T. W. Clark, L. R. Forrest, and T. M. Campbell III. 1985a. Interim report: 1985 black-footed ferret litter survey at Meeteetse, Wyoming. Jackson, Wyo.

———. Final report: Black-footed ferret population status at Meeteetse, Wyoming. July–October 1987. Jackson, Wyo.

Fri, R. W. 1995. Using science soundly: The Yucca Mountain standard. Resources for the Future 120:15–18.

Galbraith, J. R. 1977. Organization design. Addison-Wesley, New York.

Gardner, J. W. 1990. On leadership. Free Press, New York.

General Accounting Office. 1988. Endangered species: Management improvements could enhance recovery program. GAO/RCED-89-5. GPO, Washington.

———. 1992. Endangered Species Act: Types and number of implementing actions. GAO/RCED-92-131 BR. GPO, Washington.

Giblin, E. 1978. Professional organizations need professional management. Organizational Dynamics, Winter:41–57.

Gilbert, B. 1984. In God's countries. University of Nebraska Press, Lincoln.

Great Basin Naturalist Memoir No. 8. 1986. The black-footed ferret. Great Basin Naturalist, Provo, Utah.

Greater Yellowstone Coalition. 1990. GYC's first 1990 program plan progress report. Greater Yellowstone Coalition, Bozeman, Mont.

Greenwalt, L. A. 1981. Political realities and wildlife: Do politicians listen to biologists? Unpublished paper.

Gruber, J. E. 1987. Controlling bureaucracies: Dilemmas in democratic governance. University of California Press, Berkeley and Los Angeles.

Hales, D. F. 1987. Letter. Conservation Biology 1:81,86.

Hampton, B. 1986. G&F mishandled recovery of ferret. Casper Star-Tribune, April 3: A15.

Hancock, R. K. 1980. The social life of the model corporation: Changing resources and form. Journal of Applied Behavioral Sciences 3:279–298.

Harré, R. 1972. The philosophies of science: An introductory survey. Oxford University Press, New York.

Harrison, R. 1972. Understanding your organization's character. Harvard Business Review, May-June:119–120.

Harrison, R. 1975. Diagnosing organizational ideology. Pp. 169–176 in J. W. Pfeiffer and J. E. Jones, eds., Annual handbook for group facilitators. University Associates, La Jolla, Calif.

Harvey, A. H. 1987. Interagency conflict and coordination in wildlife management: A case study. M.S. thesis, University of Michigan, Ann Arbor.

Heinz, D., and C. Youmans. 1985. Conservation in the political arena. Forest Planning, May:12–15.

Hillman, C. N., and T. W. Clark. 1980. *Mustela nigripes*. Mammalian Species 126.

Hillman, C. N., and R. L. Linder. 1973. The black-footed ferret. Pp. 10–20 in R. L. Linder and C. N. Hillman, eds., Proceedings of the Black-Footed Ferret and Prairie Dog Workshop, September 4–6. South Dakota State University, Brookings.

Hoben, A. 1980. Agricultural decision making in foreign assistance: An anthropological analysis. Academic Press, New York.

Holden, C. 1990. Ecology hero in Interior Department. Science 250:620–621.

Hornocker, M. 1982. Letter to the editor. The Wildlifer, November/December:51–52.

Houck, O. A. 1993. The Endangered Species Act and its implementation by the U.S. Departments of Interior and Commerce. University of Colorado Law Review 64:277–370.

Howard, T. 1985. Wyoming expert doubts ferret-decline report. Billings Gazette, August 13.

Hrebiniak, L. G. 1978. Complex organizations. West Publishing, New York.

Jackson, H. 1994. Scott: Wyoming must file lawsuits, defy feds while waiting out Clinton. Casper Star-Tribune, July 3:A1.

Jackson, J. A. 1986. Biopolitics, management of federal lands, and the conservation of the red-cockaded woodpecker. American Birds 40:1162–1168.

Janis, I. L. 1972. Victims of groupthink: A psychological study of foreign-policy decisions and fiascoes. Houghton, Mifflin, Boston.

Jaques, E. 1980. Essential developments in bureaucracy in the 1980s. Journal of Applied Behavioral Sciences 16:439–447.

Jelinek, M., J. A. Litterer, and R. E. Miles, eds. 1981. Organizations by design: Theory and practice. Business Publications, Plano, Texas.

Jones, S. R. 1993. Reauthorization of the Endangered Species Act in the 103rd Congress: The battle begins in earnest. Endangered Species Update 10(9/10):1–4.

Jonkel, C. 1984. Status of two American bears. IUCN Species Survival Commission, Newsletter 4:9–13.

Jost, K. 1996. Protecting endangered species. CQ Researcher 6:339–356.

Kanter, R. M. 1983. The change masters: Innovation for productivity in the American corporation. Simon and Schuster, New York.

Kanter, R. M., and B. A. Stein, eds. 1979. Life in organizations: Workplaces as people experience them. Basic Books, New York.

Katz, D., and R. L. Kahn. 1978. The social psychology of organizations. 2d ed. John Wiley, New York.

Keiter, R. B., and P. T. Holscher. 1990. Wolf recovery under the Endangered Species Act: A study in contemporary federalism. Public Land Law Review 11:19–52.

Kellert, S. R. 1996. The value of life: Biological diversity and human society. Island Press, Washington.

Kinsley, M. 1995. The case against the states. Time Magazine 146 (January 26):78.

Korten, D. C. 1980. Community organization and rural development: A learning process approach. Public Administration Review, September/October:480–511.

Kosova, W. 1995. It came from the outback. Outback 20 (November):70–73.

Krumm, B. 1986. Wyoming was urged to handle ferrets better. Billings Gazette, March 13:2-D.

Lacayo, R. 1995. This land is whose land? Time Magazine 146 (October 23):68–71.

Langenau, E. E. 1982. Bureaucracy and wildlife: A historical overview. International Journal Studies of Animal Problems 3:140–157.

Langston, A. 1982. Black-footed ferret management programing. Press Release. February 19. Wyoming Game and Fish Department, Cheyenne.

———. 1983. Ferret research continues during winter. Press Release. December 16. Wyoming Game and Fish Department, Cheyenne.

Larson, E. 1995. Unrest in the West. Time Magazine 146 (October 23):52–56, 63–64, 66.

Lasswell, H. D. 1930. Psychopathology and politics. University of Chicago Press, Chicago.

———. 1936. Politics: Who gets what, when, how. McGraw-Hill, New York.

———. 1951. The policy orientation. Pp. 3–15 in D. Lerner and H. D. Lasswell, eds., The policy sciences. Stanford University Press, Stanford, Calif.

———. 1955. Current studies of the decision process: Automation versus creativity. Western Political Quarterly 8:381–399.

———. 1956. The decision process: Seven categories of functional analysis. Bureau of Government Research, College Park, Md.

———. 1960. Techniques of decision seminars. Midwest Journal of Political Science 4:213–236.

———. 1963. The future of political science. Prentice-Hall, New York.

———. 1965 [1935]. World politics and personal insecurity. McGraw-Hill, New York.

———. 1970. The emerging conception of the policy sciences. Policy Sciences 1:3–14.

———. 1971a. A pre-view of the policy sciences. American Elsevier, New York.

———. 1971b. Transferability of Vicos strategy (chapter 7) and The significance of Vicos for the emerging policy sciences (chapter 8). Pp. 167–177 and pp. 178–193 in H. R. Dobyns, P. L. Doughty, and H. D. Lasswell, eds., Peasants, power, and applied social change: Vicos as a model. Sage, Beverly Hills.

Lasswell, H. D., and A. Kaplan. 1950. Power and society: A framework for political inquiry. Yale University Press, New Haven.

Lasswell, H. D., and M. S. McDougal. 1992. Jurisprudence for a free society: Studies in law, science and policy. 2 vols. New Haven Press, New Haven.

Latour, B. 1987. Science in action: How to follow scientists and engineers through society. Harvard University Press, Cambridge.

Lawrence, P. R., and J. W. Lorsch. 1967. Developing organizations: Diagnosis and action. Addison-Wesley, Reading, Mass.

Leeuw, F. L., R. C. Rist, and R. C. Sonnichsen. 1994. Can governments learn? Comparative perspectives on evaluation and organizational learning. Transaction Publishers, New Brunswick, N.J.

Lester, J. P. 1990. A new federalism: Environmental policy in the states. Pp. 59–79 in N. J. Vig and M. E. Kraft, eds., Environmental policy in the 1990s: Toward a new agenda. CQ Press, Washington.

Light, S. S., and J. R. Wodraska. 1990. Forging a new state-federal alliance in water management. Natural Resources Journal 30:479–484.

Limerick, P. N. 1987. The legacy of conquest: The unbroken past of the American West. Norton, New York.

Lindblom, C. E. 1980. The policy-making process. Prentice-Hall, Englewood Cliffs, N.J.

Linder, R. L., and C. N. Hillman, eds. 1973. Proceedings of the Black-Footed Ferret and Prairie Dog Workshop, Rapid City, S.D., September 16–17. South Dakota State University, Brookings.

Lippmann, W. 1922. Public opinion. Free Press, New York.

Littrell, W. B. 1980. Editor's introduction: Bureaucracy in the eighties. Journal of Applied Behavioral Sciences 16:263–277.

Litwak, E., and L. F. Hylton. 1962. Interorganizational analysis: A hypothesis on coordinating agencies. Administrative Science Quarterly 6:395–420.

Lorsch, J. W. 1977. Organizational designs: A situational perspective. Organizational dynamics, Autumn:2–14.

Lowry, K., and R. A. Carpenter. 1984. Holistic nature and fragmented bureaucracies: A study of government organization for natural systems management. Report of a seminar on Alternative Organizations for Managing Natural Systems, June-August 1983, East-West Environment and Policy Institute of the East-West Center. The East-West Center, Honolulu.

McCann, J. E., and D. L. Ferry. 1979. An approach for assessing and managing inter-unit interdependence. Academy of Management Review 4:113–119.

Madson, C. 1993. The Act. Wyoming Wildlife. January:5–9.

———. 1995. Ferret future? Wyoming Wildlife. February:31–35

Maguire, L. A. 1991. Risk analysis for conservation biologists. Conservation Biology 5:123–125.

Maguire, L. A., and T. W. Clark. 1985. A decision analysis of management options concerning plague in the Meeteetse black-footed ferret habitat. Unpublished report to U.S. Fish and Wildlife Service, Region 6, Denver.

Majone, G. 1989. Evidence, argument, and persuasion in the policy process. Yale University Press, New Haven.

Mann, C. C., and M. L. Plummer. 1992. The butterfly problem. The Atlantic 269(1):47–70.

March, J. G. 1978. Bounded rationality, ambiguity, and the engineering of choice. Bell Journal of Economics 9:587–608.

Marston, B. 1986. Ferret colony edges closer to extinction. High Country News, January 20:13.

May, R. 1986. The cautionary tale of the black-footed ferret. Nature 320:13–14.

Meese, G. M. 1989. Saving endangered species: Implementing the Endangered Species Act. Pp. 47–62 in G. Mackintosh, ed., In defense of wildlife: Preserving communities and corridors. Defenders of Wildlife, Washington.

Michael, D. N. 1995. Barriers and bridges to learning in a turbulent human ecology. Pp. 461–488 in L. H. Gunderson, C. S. Holling, and S. S. Light, eds., Barriers and bridges to the renewal of ecosystems and institutions. Columbia University Press, New York.

Miles, R. E., C. C. Snow, and J. Pfeffer. 1974. Organization-environment: Concepts and issues. Industrial Relations 13:244–264.

Miller, B. J. 1992. History of black-footed ferret captive propagation. Seminar manuscript. University of Rhode Island, Providence.

Miller, B. J., R. P. Reading, and S. Forrest. 1996. Prairie night: Black-footed ferrets and the recovery of endangered species. Smithsonian Institution Press, Washington.

Miller, B. J., R. Reading, C. Conway, J. A. Jackson, M. Hutchins, N. Snyder, S. Forrest, J. Frazier, and S. Derrickson. 1994. Improving endangered species programs: Avoiding organizational pitfalls, tapping the resources, and adding accountability. Environmental Management 18:637–645.

Montana Black-Footed Ferret Working Group. 1988. Montana prairie dog management guidelines. Montana Bureau of Land Management, Billings.

Morgan, G. 1986. Images of organization. Sage, Beverly Hills.

Morris, B. 1986a. Letter to Tim Clark, July 9. Cheyenne.

———. 1986b. Letter to Tim Clark, July 22. Cheyenne.

Murphy, D. D. 1991. Invertebrate conservation. Pp. 181–198 in K. A. Kohm, ed., Balancing on the brink of extinction: The Endangered Species Act and lessons for the future. Island Press, Washington.

Nadler, D. A., and M. L. Tushman. 1980. A model for diagnosing organizational behavior. Organizational Dynamics, Autumn:35–51.

Nakamura, R. T., and F. Smallwood. 1980. The politics of policy implementation. St. Martin's, New York.

National Ecology Research Center. 1992. Reintroduction of the black-footed ferret *Mustela nigripes*. Progress Report. U.S. Fish and Wildlife Service, Fort Collins, Colo., June 1.

National Research Council. 1995. Science and the Endangered Species Act. National Academy Press, Washington.

———. Committee on the Application of Ecological Theory to Environmental Problems. Commission on Life Sciences. 1986. Ecological knowledge and environmental problem-solving: Concepts and case studies. National Academy Press, Washington.

Neal, D. 1995. Bill Morris' G&F legacy: Wildlife trust, saving ferrets. Casper Star-Tribune, April 20:E4.

New York Academy of Sciences. 1995. Science and endangered species preservation: Rethinking the environmental policy process. Special Science Policy Report, August.

Nice, J. 1982. Endangered species: A Wyoming town becomes ferret capital. Audubon Magazine 84(4):106–109.

———. 1983. Long road to recovery. National Wildlife Magazine 21(3):16–19.

North Central Montana Black-Footed Ferret Working Group. 1991. A cooperative black-footed ferret reintroduction and management plan for the northcentral Montana complex. September, Draft.

Northern Wyoming (Worland) Daily News. 1982. Ferret research team formed. March 18:5.

Noss, R. F. 1991. From endangered species to biodiversity. Pp. 227–246 in K. A. Kohm, ed., Balancing on the brink of extinction: The Endangered Species Act and lessons for the future. Island Press, Washington.

Oakleaf, R. 1994. Cuts hit ferret program. Drumming Post 7(4):1–2.

Oakleaf, R., and E. T. Thorne. 1992. Reintroduction of black-footed ferrets (*Mustela nigripes*) in Wyoming, 1991. Submitted to IUCN/SSC Re-Introduction Specialist Group May Newsletter.

O'Connell, M. 1992. Response to "Six biological reasons why the Endangered Species Act doesn't work and what to do about it." Conservation Biology 6(1):140–143.

O'Laughlin, J., and P. S. Cook. 1995. Endangered Species Act at the crossroads: New directions from Idaho case studies. University of Idaho, Moscow. Idaho Forest, Wildlife and Range Policy Analysis Group Report No. 13.

Ontiveroz, M. 1985. State says ferret scare unnecessary. Cody (Wyo.) Enterprise, August 14.

Palmer, T. 1992. The case for human beings. The Atlantic 269(1):83–88.

Parker, P. 1989. Forward. Pp. ix–x in T. W. Clark, Conservation biology of the black-footed ferret *Mustela nigripes*. Wildlife Preservation Trust, Special Scientific Report No. 3.

Perrow, C. A. 1961. The analysis of goals in complex organizations. American Social Review 26:854–866.

———. 1970. Organizational analysis: A sociological view. Brooks/Cole, Belmont, Calif.

———. 1979. Complex organizations: A critical essay. 2d ed. Scott Foresman, Glenview, Ill.

Peters, T. J., and R. H. Waterman, Jr. 1982. In search of excellence: Lessons from America's best-run companies. Harper & Row, New York.

Peterson, I. 1985. Six endangered ferrets are under strict guard. New York Times, December 15:30.

Pfeffer, J. 1978. Organizational design. AHM Publications, Arlington Heights, Ill.

Poffenberger, M. 1990. Facilitating change in forestry bureaucracies. Pp. 95–118 in M. Poffenberger, ed., Keepers of the forest: Land management alternatives in southeast Asia. Kumarian Press, West Hartford, Conn.

Political Economy Research Center. 1991. The Endangered Species Act: Time for change. PERC Reports, Bozeman, Mont. 9(3):1–2.

Porter, M. E. 1980. Competitive strategy: Techniques for analyzing industries and competitors. Free Press, New York.

Prendergast, A. 1986. The last of the breed? Frontier, August:34–40,52–53.

Presidential Commission on the Space Shuttle Challenger Accident. 1986. Report of the Presidential Commission on the Space Shuttle Challenger Accident. 5 vols. GPO, Washington.

Pressman, J. L., and A. Wildavsky. 1973. Implementation: How great expectations in Washington are dashed in Oakland; Or, why it's amazing that federal programs work at all. University of California Press, Berkeley and Los Angeles.

Quade, E. S. 1975. Initiating the analytical process. Pp. 67–82 in E. S. Quade, ed., Analysis for public decisions. American Elsevier, New York.

Radin, B. A. 1977. Implementation, change, and the federal bureaucracy. Teachers College Press, Columbia University, New York.

Rancourt, L. M. 1992. Saving the Endangered Species Act. National Parks 66(3–4):28–33.

Randall, D. 1983. Born-again ferrets. Defenders 58(5):2–6.

———. 1986. Survival crisis at Meeteetse. Defenders 61(1):4–10.

Reading, R. P. 1991. Experimental black-footed ferret reintroduction program in Wyoming and its implications for Montana. Report prepared for Montana BLM and Montana Black-footed Ferret Working Group, Billings, November 27.

———. 1992. Letter to World Conservation Union's Re-Introduction Specialist Group. April 15.

Reading, R. P., and T. W. Clark. 1990. An annotated bibliography of the black-footed ferret 1986–1990. Montana BLM Wildlife Technical Bulletin No. 3.

Reading, R. P., and B. J. Miller. 1994. The black-footed ferret recovery program: Unmasking professional and organizational weaknesses. Pp. 73–199 in T. W. Clark, R. P. Reading, and A. L. Clarke, eds., Endangered species recovery: Finding the lessons, improving the process. Island Press, Washington.

Reading, R. P., T. W. Clark, A. Vargas, L. R. Hanebury, B. J. Miller, and D. Biggins. 1996. Recent directions in black-footed ferret (*Mustela nigripes*) recovery. Endangered Species Update 13(10/11):1–7.

Reed, N. P., and D. Drabelle. 1984. The United States Fish and Wildlife Service. Westview Press, Boulder.

Reese, A. 1995. Letter to Aaron Clark. Wyoming Game and Fish Department, Cheyenne. October 19.

Reffalt, W. 1991. The endangered species lists: Chronicles of extinction? Pp. 77–85 in K. A. Kohm, ed., Balancing on the brink of extinction: The Endangered Species Act and lessons for the future. Island Press, Washington.

Reid, W. V. 1992. The United States needs a national biodiversity policy. World Resources Institute, Issues and Ideas, February:1–12.

Rein, M., and F. Rabinovitz. 1978. Implementation: A theoretical perspective. Pp. 307–335 in W. D. Burham and M. W. Weinberg, eds., American politics and public policy. MIT Press, Cambridge, Mass.

Richardson, L., T. W. Clark, S. C. Forrest, and T. M. Campbell III. 1986. Black-footed ferret recovery: A discussion of some options and considerations. Great Basin Naturalist Memoirs 8:169–184.

Roemer, D. M., and S. C. Forrest. 1996. Prairie dog poisoning in northern Great Plains: An analysis of programs and policies. Environmental Management 20:349–359.

Rohlf, D. J. 1992. Response to O'Connell. Conservation Biology 6(1):144–145.

Romesburg, H. C. 1981. Wildlife science: Gaining reliable knowledge. Journal of Wildlife Management 45:293–313.

———. 1991. On improving the natural resources and environmental sciences. Journal of Wildlife Management 55:744–756.

Romm, J. 1984. Policy education for professional resource managers. Renewable Resources Journal 2:15–17.

Roy, R. H. 1980. The cultures of management. Johns Hopkins University Press, Baltimore.

Sabatier, P. 1978. The acquisition and utilization of technical information by administrative agencies. Administrative Science Quarterly 23:396–417.

Salancik, G. R., and J. Pfeffer. 1977. Who gets power and how they hold on to it: A strategic-contingency model of power. Organizational Dynamics, Winter:2–21.

Schein, V. E., and L. E. Greiner. 1977. Can organization development be fine tuned to bureaucracies? Organizational Dynamics, Winter:48–61

Schlesinger, J. R. 1968. Systems analysis and the policy process. Journal of Law and Economics 11:281–298.

Schön, D. A. 1971. Beyond the stable state. Norton, New York.

——. 1983. The reflective practitioner: How professionals think in action. Basic Books, New York.

——. 1987. Educating the reflective practitioner: Toward a new design for teaching and learning in the professions. Jossey-Bass, San Francisco.

Schön, D. A., and M. Rein. 1994. Frame reflection: Toward the resolution of intractable policy problems. Basic Books, New York.

Schroeder, M. 1987. The black-footed ferret. Pp. 447–455 in A. Gross, ed., Audubon Wildlife Report 1987. National Audubon Society, New York.

Seal, U. S., E. T. Thorne, M. A. Bogan, and S. H. Anderson, eds. 1989. Conservation biology and the black-footed ferret. Yale University Press, New Haven.

Senge, P. M. 1990. The fifth discipline: The art and practice of the learning organization. Doubleday Currency, New York.

Sierra Club Legal Defense Fund. 1991. Letter to G. Buterbaugh, Regional Director, Region 6, U.S. Fish and Wildlife Service, Denver. October 15.

Simon, H. A. 1957. Models of man. Wiley, New York.

——. 1969. The sciences of the artificial. MIT Press, Cambridge, Mass.

——. 1985. Human nature in politics: The dialogue of psychology with political science. American Political Science Review 79:293–304.

Skinner, S. 1985. Black-footed ferrets "plagued" by columnists. Wyoming Wildlife 49(11):36–38.

Slack, G. 1992. Natural law: Congress reconsiders the Endangered Species Act. Pacific Discovery, Spring:22–30.

Smith, D. A. 1977. State view of endangered species management. Proceedings of the Western Association of Game and Fish Commissioners 1977:287–290.

Snape, W. J., III, ed. 1996. Biodiversity and the law. Island Press, Washington.

Snodgrass, R. D. 1991. The Endangered Species Act under fire: An opportunity to strengthen the law. Public Lands 8(3):1–3.

Snyder, N. F. R., and H. A. Snyder. 1989. Biology and conservation of the California condor. Current Ornithology 6:175–267.

Soulé, M. E. 1986. Conservation biology and the "real world." Pp. 1–12 in M. E. Soulé, ed., Conservation biology: The science of scarcity and diversity. Sinauer Associates, Sunderland, Mass.

Stahr, E. J., and C. H. Callison. 1978. The role of private organizations. Pp. 498–511 in H. D. Brodaw, ed., Wildlife and America. GPO, Washington.

Stanley Price, M. R. 1989. Animal re-introductions: The Arabian oryx in Oman. Cambridge University Press, New York.

Stein, B. A., and R. M. Kanter. 1980. Building the parallel organization: Creating mechanisms for permanent quality of life. Journal of Applied Behavioral Sciences 16:371–388.

Stein, M. 1975. Stimulating creativity. Vol. 2: Group procedures. Academic Press, New York.

Steiss, A. W., and G. A. Daneke. 1980. Performance administration: Improved responsiveness and effectiveness in public service. Lexington Books, Lexington, Mass.

Stone, D. A. 1988. Policy paradox and political reason. Scott Foresman, Glenview, Ill.

Strickland, D. 1983. Ferret update. Wyoming Wildlife 47(3):4–6.

Sullivan, W. M. 1995. Work and integrity. HarperCollins, New York.

Talbott, J. 1995. Testimony submitted to the Senate Subcommittee for Endangered Species Act reform, August 16, Casper.

Tear, T. H., J. M. Scott, P. H. Hayward, and B. Griffith. 1995. Recovery plans and the Endangered Species Act: Are criticisms supported by data? Conservation Biology 9:182–195.

Thomas, J. W. 1986. Effectiveness: Hallmark of the natural resource management profession. Transactions of the 51st North American Wildlife and Natural Resources Conference:27–38.

Thomas, K. 1976. Conflict and conflict management. Pp. 889–935 in M. D. Dunnette, ed., Handbook of industrial and organizational psychology. Rand McNally, Chicago.

———. 1977. Toward multi-dimensional values in teaching: The example of conflict behavior. Academy of Management Review 2:484–490.

Thompson, J. D. 1967. Organizations in action: Social science bases of administrative theory. McGraw-Hill, New York.

Thompson, J. D., and R. W. Hawkes. 1962. Disaster, community organization, and administrative process. Pp. 268–303 in G. W. Baker and D. W. Chapman, eds., Man and society in disaster. Basic Books, New York.

Thorne, E. T. 1984. Doctoring the black-footed ferret. Wyoming Wildlife, March:11–19.

———. 1987. Captive propagation of the black-footed ferret in Wyoming. Pp. 419–424 in American Association of Zoological Parks and Aquariums Regional Conference Proceedings. AAZPA Publications, Syracuse, N.Y.

Thorne, E. T., and B. Oakleaf. 1991. Species rescue for captive breeding: Black-footed ferret as an example. Symposium Zoological Society London 62:241–261.

Thorne, E. T., and W. C. Russell. 1995. Annual report of conservation and science black-footed ferret (*Mustela nigripes*). Wyoming Department of Fish and Game, Laramie.

Thorne, E. T., and E. S. Williams. 1988. Disease and endangered species: The black-footed ferret as a recent example. Conservation Biology 2:66–74.

Thuermer, A. 1985. State to trap ferrets, Clark urged move last year. Jackson Hole (Wyoming) News, September 3:27.

Tichy, N. M. 1983. Managing strategic change: Technical, political, and cultural dynamics. John Wiley, New York.

Tober, J. A. 1989. Wildlife and the public interest: Nonprofit organizations and federal wildlife policy. Praeger, New York.

Tobin, R. 1990. The expendable future: U. S. politics and the protection of biological diversity. Duke University Press, Durham, N.C.

Touval, J. I., and J. M. Dietz. 1994. The problem of teaching conservation problem solving. Conservation Biology 8:902–904.

Tribe, L. H. 1973. Policy science: Analysis or ideology? Philosophy and Public Affairs 2:66–110.

Trombulak, S. C. 1994. Undergraduate education and the next generation of conservation biologists. Conservation Biology 8:589–591.

Tushman, M. L., and D. A. Nadler. 1978. Information processing as an integrating concept in organization design. Academy of Management Review 3:613–624.

U. S. Congress. 1983. The Endangered Species Act as amended by Public Law 97–304. 15–9420, GPO, Washington.

U. S. Fish and Wildlife Service. 1983. Only known ferret population receives careful attention. Endangered Species Technical Bulletin 8:5–8.

———. 1987. Black-footed ferret recovery plan. Denver.

———. 1993. Grizzly bear recovery plan. Missoula, Montana.

———. 1995. Memorandum to Black-footed Ferret Management Committee Participants. From Wilbur Ladd, Jr., Assistant Regional Director, U.S. Fish and Wildlife Service, North Dakota/South Dakota. November 29.

Van Meter, D. S., and C. E. Van Horn. 1975. The policy implementation process: A conceptual framework. Administration and Society 6:445–488.

Vargas, A. 1994. Ontogeny of the endangered black-footed ferret (*Mustela nigripes*) and effects of rearing conditions on predatory behavior and post-release survival. Ph.D. diss., University of Wyoming, Laramie.

Wambaugh, J. 1984. Lines and shadows. William Morrow, New York.

Warwick, D. P. 1975. A theory of public bureaucracy: Politics, personality and organization in the State Department. Harvard University Press, Cambridge.

Weber, M. 1947. The theory of social and economic organizations. Translated by A. M. Henderson and T. Parsons. Free Press, New York.

Weimer, D. L., and A. R. Vining. 1989. Policy analysis: Concepts and practice. Prentice-Hall, Englewood Cliffs, N.J.

Weinberg, D. 1986. Decline and fall of the black-footed ferret. Natural History Magazine 95:62–69.

Weinberg, G. M. 1986. Becoming a technical leader. Dorset, New York.

Weiss, J. A. 1989. The powers of problem-definition: The case of government paperwork. Policy Sciences 22:97–121.

Wertz, S. 1984. How fare Meeteetse's ferrets? Wyoming Magazine, December:26–27, 30–31.

Western Governors' Association. 1992. Reauthorization of the Endangered Species Act. Resolution 92–017, December 4. Las Vegas.

———. 1995. Essential elements of amendments to the Endangered Species Act, April 21. Denver.

Westrum, R. 1986. Management strategies and information failure. NATO Advanced Research Workshop on Failure Analysis of Information Systems, August, Bad Winsheim, Germany.

———. 1988. Organizational and inter-organizational thought. World Bank Conference on Safety and Risk Management, October, New York.

———. 1991. Technologies and society: The shaping of people and things. Wadsworth, Belmont, Calif.

———. 1992. Cultures with requisite imagination. NATO Verification and Validation Conference, Portugal.

———. 1994. An organizational perspective: Designing recovery teams from the inside out. Pp. 327–349 in T. W. Clark, R. P. Reading, and A. L. Clarke, eds., Endangered species recovery: Finding the lessons, improving the process. Island Press, Washington.

Westrum, R., and K. Samaha. 1984. Complex organizations: Growth, struggle, and change. Prentice-Hall, Englewood Cliffs, N.J.

White, P. 1985a. Federal officials praise G&F for ferret efforts. Casper Star-Tribune, November 18:A1,A16.

———. 1985b. Disease threatens rare ferret colony, says G&F. Casper Star-Tribune, October 24:A1,A12.

———. 1985c. Critic says ferret-breeding program was needed in '84. Casper Star-Tribune, November 28:A1,B1.

———. 1985d. Biologists try again to catch ferrets. Casper Star-Tribune, October 26:A1, A14.

———. 1986. Black-footed ferrets get expert breeding assistance. Casper Star-Tribune, February 26:B1.

Wildavsky, A. 1979. Speaking truth to power: The art and craft of policy analysis. Little, Brown, Boston.

Wildlife Conservation International. 1986. Saving the Sybille six. WCI News, Winter:5.

Willard, A. R., and C. H. Norchi. 1993. The decision seminar as an instrument of power and enlightenment. Political Psychology 14:575–606.

Williams, B. 1995. Summary data of black-footed ferret captive breeding. Unpublished. University of Wyoming, Laramie.

Williams, E. S., E. T. Thorne, D. R. Kwiatkowski, S. L. Anders, and K. Lutz. 1991. Reproductive biology and management of captive black-footed ferrets (*Mustela nigripes*). Zoo Biology 10:383–398.

Williams, N. M., G. Sjoberg, and A. F. Sjoberg. 1980. The bureaucratic personality: An alternate view. Journal of Applied Behavioral Sciences 16(3):89–405.

Williams, T. 1986. The final ferret fiasco. Audubon 88(3):111–119.

Wilson, E. O. 1989. Threats to biodiversity. Scientific American 261:108–116.

———. 1992. The diversity of life. Harvard University Press, Cambridge.

Wilson, J. Q., ed. 1980. The politics of regulation. Basic Books, New York.

Wilson, J. Q. 1989. Bureaucracy: What government agencies do and why they do it. Basic Books, New York.

Winckler, S. 1992. Stopgap measures. The Atlantic 269(1):74–81.

Wolman, H. 1981. The determinants of program success and failure. Journal of Public Policy 1:433–464.

Worrel, A. C. 1970. Principles of forest policy. McGraw-Hill, New York.

Wyoming Game and Fish Department. 1983. Ferret research continues during winter. Press release, December 16. Cheyenne.

———. 1985. Ferret breeding program. Wyoming Wildlife 49(1):34.

———. 1987. Letter to Deputy Regional Director, U.S. Fish and Wildlife Service, August 21. Cheyenne.

———. 1991a. A cooperative management plan for black-footed ferrets, Shirley Basin/ Medicine Bow, Wyoming. August. Cheyenne.

———. 1991b. The land ethic. Wyoming Wildlife 55(9):2.

———. 1992. 5 year T&E expenditures. Letter, March 13, 1992. Cheyenne.

———. 1994. Black-footed ferret work continues. Drumming Post 7(4):3.

Wyoming Game and Fish News. 1995a. Lack of federal funding may limit state's T&E work. August 24. Cheyenne.

——. 1995b. G&F funding decreases—wildlife programs jeopardized. October 5. Cheyenne.

Yaffee, S. L. 1982. Prohibitive policy: Implementing the federal Endangered Species Act. MIT Press, Cambridge.

——. 1988. Protecting endangered species through interagency consultation. Endangered Species Update 5:14–19.

——. 1994a. The northern spotted owl: An indicator of the importance of sociopolitical context. Pp. 47–71 in T. W. Clark, R. P. Reading, and A. L. Clarke, eds., Endangered species recovery: Finding the lessons, improving the process. Island Press, Washington.

——. 1994b. The wisdom of the spotted owl: Policy lessons for a new century. Island Press, Washington.

Zimmerman, D. R. 1986. Protecting the black-footed ferret. New York Newsday, January 21, Part 3:1,6–7.

Index

Salancik, G. R., 71
Schein, V. E., 74
Schön, D. A., 123–124, 196, 209, 211–212, 215
Schroeder, M., 114
Science: and conservation, 1; and endangered species recovery, 164, 167–168, 226–227; and ferret recovery program, 234–235; perspectives of, 14–15; positivistic science, 147, 209–211, 219, 227; and professionalism, 209, 211; scientific conservatism, 7, 146–148, 154
Seal, U.S., 110
Senge, P. M., 133
Shirley Basin/Medicine Bow, 92, 232, 236
Short, J., 123
Sierra Club Legal Defense Fund, 5, 156, 232
Skinner, S., 129
Smallwood, F., 67
Snyder, H. A., 154
Snyder, N. F. R., 154
Society for Conservation Biology, 95
Soulé, M. E., 146–147
South Dakota, 23, 26–27, 47, 103, 106, 231–232, 235, 237
Species Survival Plan (SSP), 230–231, 233
Sport hunting, 31, 32, 39, 141
SSP. *See* Species Survival Plan (SSP)
Stanley Price, M. R., 188
State governments: and Endangered Species Act, 3–4, 6, 34; and endangered species recovery, 170; federal/state relations, 6, 10, 38, 90, 107, 119–120, 141, 209; Fish and Wildlife Service's cooperation with, 28; rodent control programs of, 22; and sport hunting, 141; wildlife management role of, 9, 141–142, 158
State Lands Board (Wyoming), 29, 63, 104, 105
States' rights, 9, 34–35, 38, 141–142, 154, 157, 229–230, 232–233

Stein, B. A., 203, 218
Steiss, A. W., 137
Sullivan, W. M., 211
Sybille Canyon Wildlife Research Unit, 5, 54, 55, 230–231, 235–236
Sylvatic plague, 25, 44–46, 117

Talbott, John, 233
Teams. *See* Advisory teams; Field teams; High-performance teams
Tear, T. H., 164
Texas, 10, 22
Thompson, J. D., 77
Thorne, E. T., 47, 53, 93, 142, 147–148
Tober, J. A., 119, 169
Tobin, R., 8
Turner, J., 10

Uncertainty: and bureaucracies, 66, 83, 130; and goals, 86; and high-performance teams, 198; and information, 190; and ISU/Biota research team, 120; and organizational learning, 128; and organizational structure, 190, 191; and parallel organizations, 203; and problem definition, 138–139, 154, 159; and professionals, 83, 215, 219; and prototypes, 182; and reciprocity, 67; and resources, 139; and science, 147, 209
University of Wyoming: and Black-Footed Ferret Advisory Team, 63, 104, 105; and captive breeding, 108; Cooperative Research Unit, 29, 33, 76, 91, 115, 157; co-optation of, 68; resources of, 151; and Species Survival Plan, 233; and Wyoming Game and Fish Department, 70

Values, 123, 176–177, 184, 188, 191–193, 210, 220

Warwick, D. P., 71–72, 200, 202, 206–207
Washington State University, 26